Pelican Books
In the Fist of the Revolutio

Jose Yglesias was born in Tampa, Florida, in 1919.
He worked for some years in a pharmaceutical company
before resigning to devote his time to writing. He
published a novel, *Ybor City*, in 1963, and his book
The Goodbye Land was widely praised in the United
States on publication in 1967. Writing in the *New York
Review of Books*, Gerald Brenan said, 'Mr Yglesias is a
writer of considerable subtlety and perceptiveness with
a strong sense of narrative form.'

Jose Yglesias

In the Fist of the Revolution

Penguin Books

Penguin Books Ltd, Harmondsworth, Middlesex, England
Penguin Books Australia Ltd, Ringwood, Victoria, Australia

First published in the U.S.A. 1968
Published in Great Britain by Allen Lane The Penguin Press 1968
Published in Pelican Books 1970
Copyright © Jose Yglesias, 1968

Made and printed in Great Britain by
Hazell Watson & Viney Ltd,
Aylesbury, Bucks
Set in Linotype Plantin

This book is sold subject to the condition that it shall not, by way of
trade or otherwise, be lent, re-sold, hired out, or otherwise circulated
without the publisher's prior consent in any form of binding or cover
other than that in which it is published and without a similar condition
including this condition being imposed on the subsequent purchaser

For Tamar, Richard, Andrea,
Lewis and Rafael:
a little community of the heart

Contents

'Cuba can only be held responsible for one thing: for having made a revolution and being willing to carry it to its ultimate consequences.'

FIDEL CASTRO, *13 March 1967*

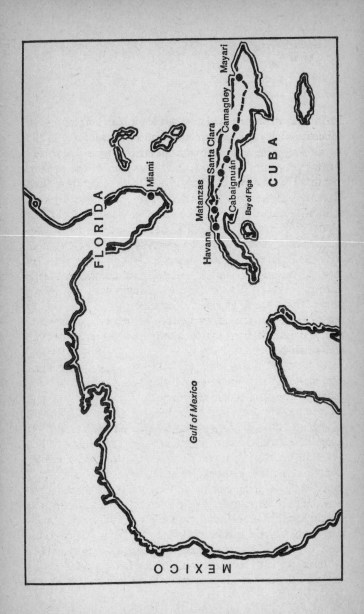

1. The First Day

In Havana the functionaries of the Press Department of the Ministry of Foreign Affairs shook their heads when I told them I was going to take a bus to Mayarí, the town in northern Oriente province where I had decided to live for two or three months. They didn't know how long it takes to get there from Havana, but they knew it would be an uncomfortably long ride. Why didn't I take the plane to Santiago de Cuba, the capital of Oriente, on the Caribbean coast, talk to the provincial heads of the Party there, and then proceed north to Mayarí, just inland on the Atlantic, properly escorted – or, they added when they saw this didn't please me, with introductions to the Mayarí Party people? I didn't take any of this advice. On a Monday early in February 1967, I boarded the one o'clock afternoon bus on which I had reserved a seat Sunday, and learned from the conductor that it was a fourteen-and-a-half-hour ride to Mayarí.

All the seats were taken and there were many more passengers than places on the buses going east. The conductor tried to make adjustments, shifting to other buses passengers who were not going far. The lady next to me – who at fifty-four considered herself ancient – consented to shift, since she was going no further than Matanzas, only two hours away. 'Yes, yes, I do not mind,' she said. 'The Revolution looks after me.' Despite this initial planning, there was to be much activity at every stop, for going east the buses all take the central highway, built in the twenties by the dictator Machado, and pass the principal cities of Cuba: people got off and on at Matanzas, Santa Clara, Camagüey, Holguín, and at any spot on the road they chose. There were never, however, any empty seats.

Before we left Havana it was clear that only ten of us were going all the way to Mayarí; everyone seemed to be a worker or a *campesino* (the Cuban word for farmer or country worker), and explanatory conversations broke out as the bus took off. A fat lady going to Mayarí was making the long return trip within three days of her original departure for Havana; she had received a telegram from her Havana daughter-in-law reading, 'Send money, Antonio in bed,' which in Spanish, *en la cama*, means 'Antonio sick'; whereas it should have read *en la caña*, which means 'in the cane-field', working in the sugar-cane harvest.

In February the harvest was well under way; it had always begun with the new year but this year there had been 'a little harvest' before Christmas, in the attempt to reach a new high of seven million tons, since the goal is ten million in 1970. 'You can imagine,' the fat lady said in her sweet, lilting Oriente accent, 'I ran with all my weight and little money to take care of him!'

We stopped for dinner in Cabaiguán, halfway across the island, at a simple restaurant where the good items kept being struck off the menu. My seat companion and I had *pito con huevos y papas*, eggs and home-fries scrambled together, white rice, the Cuban crackers most prefer to bread, and several glasses of cold water, since there was no other refreshment left; for dessert, mango marmalade with the crackers. My seat companion hoped to catch a bus for Bayamo (in southern Oriente) at Holguín, where our bus would get off the central highway and continue along the north coast for two hours to Mayarí. If he didn't find a bus going south, he was going to hire a taxi, for he was newly married, worked in the Ciénega de Zapata, near the Bay of Pigs, away from his wife, and the next day was St Valentine's, here called *El Día de los Enamorados*, The Day of Those in Love. 'I want to surprise her,' he said.

When we got back on the bus, he paid me a compliment. 'You are not like the foreigners who are quiet and still,' he said, and made a motion with both hands, like a hen creating a stir. 'You are more like us.'

It was then I explained, as I was to do often, that my

mother's parents were born in Cuba and it was from them I
learned Spanish. 'That explains it,' said the fat lady. 'And I
suppose you like Cuban coffee and are wishing we could have
some now, to help settle the dinner?'

An Army sergeant who had helped lady travellers with their
bags throughout the trip came back to the bus with a large cake
he had bought at the restaurant, and offered a piece to everyone on the bus. No one refused and no one acted as if it were
an unusual gesture, but it made everyone long all the more for
un buchito, a swallow, of coffee. Once plentiful, coffee was
now strictly rationed, so that people lined up at the appointed
hours when the coffee stands were 'straining coffee', a phrase
that derives from the fact that Cubans at home make their
espresso with a cloth strainer. At the next town, a lady stood on
the sidewalk toward the back of the bus, out of the way; she
was the driver's wife, and she had brought a thermos with her
to serve coffee to her husband and the conductor. The Army
sergeant walked over and stood by them, until they offered him
a swallow, and he came back into the bus smacking his lips.
Everyone laughed.

After that, for a period of three hours before we reached
Holguín, the largest city in northern Oriente, the places the
bus stopped at had not only run out of refreshments but did
not even have cold water for us. People dozed in the quiet,
dark bus, an old General Motors one which had been recon-
ditioned after the Revolution but was again showing signs of
wear. A short exchange took place after a woman was let off near
her home. The fat lady explained that the woman had been
to Santa Clara to see her son in the U M A P.

'U.M.A.P.' are the initials for work-prison camps called
Military Units for Aid to Production; they were begun in
1965, presumably to rehabilitate young men of military service
age whose ways made them unsuitable for integration in the
regular Army; in Havana, intellectuals were particularly dis-
turbed about the U M A P, because it had become a catchall for
delinquents denounced by their neighbours, and Fidel was

reported to have criticized the camps in the fall of 1966 as concentration camps. In November a group of important artists
and theatre people were tapped for the U M A P, solely for being homosexuals, and the Artists and Writers Union held an
emergency meeting to defend their colleagues. They were
successful, the roundup was called off, and I was told Fidel
and President Dorticós and Raul took turns visiting the individual artists and apologizing to them.

'She said that her son had been temporarily out of a job and
that is why they took him,' said the fat lady.

A man laughed and then a couple of people giggled.

'They say there is a group of them at Central Guatemala
cutting cane,' said the fat lady.

'It is good for them to work,' a man said, and everyone went
to sleep again.

Those of us going on to Mayarí did not get out at Holguín,
but slept, and in a while a few people joined us and went to
sleep too, as soon as the bus started. In 1960 I had made the
trip by jeep during the day from Holguín to Nicaro, fifteen
minutes beyond Mayarí, and so I knew that the dense dark
ocean on either side of the road was the sea-green cane-
fields that once belonged to the United Fruit Company. I woke
up in Cueto, a half hour from Mayarí and beyond which
there is no railroad in north-eastern Oriente, and then again
when the fat lady said, '*There* is the hospital.'

It was a three-storey modern structure, and there were lights
at the ground-floor, emergency entrance. At the hospital the
street lights, sparse and dim, began, and there appeared to be
open fields all around, but in two blocks, past a little bridge,
the bus suddenly threatened a narrow, frail town street. The
street quickly came to a dead end, and the bus turned into the
main street of Mayarí, dark and deserted and totally un-
familiar. I had ridden down this street in 1960 but I could not
recognize it in the dark.

The conductor took out my big heavy bag and my typewriter from the belly of the bus, and told me that down the

street was a hotel: I would recognize it because the downstairs was lit. I dragged my things past wooden one- and two-
storey structures like the Hollywood fronts for a Western
town. At one spot there was an empty lot, a black chasm beyond which there seemed to be nothing but countryside,
strange and unexpected on the main street of a large town like
Mayarí. Then again the wooden buildings, until a dim light
showed me the lobby of the hotel: a wooden floor, high ceiling, old paint, at one side a coffee and cigarette counter, and
to the back, down a couple of steps, a bare dining-room. In one
corner, wooden stairs led up the second and only other floor,
where I imagined the rooms were.

There were none vacant, the night-watchman said, and I
would have to ask the cashier when he came at six thirty
whether there would be any for the next day. 'Have you been
to the Bitirí?' he asked, and I said no. 'It is the new motel,' he
explained. 'The Indian name for a natural bridge which is in
the mountains some place.'

He cranked the phone until he woke the town operator, and
talked to the Bitirí. They had a room, and he walked me to the
door and pointed to the street across the way which came to a
dead end at the corner. 'You can walk there,' he said. 'You
keep walking on that street and you cannot miss it. About five
blocks and you will see the fence and the back entrance.'

The bag and typewriter were heavy, the sidewalks and gutter uneven and cracked, and there was a ditch along one side
of the street. The occasional bare bulb of a street light scarcely
peeked through the foliage of the trees, and I had to put my
things down often and rest. Once, a man suddenly materialized on a porch, and said, 'It must be near four, right?' And
he, too, informed me that I could not miss the Bitirí. A block
later, a rat suddenly decided to make a dash for the other side
of the street and almost knocked into me.

In the dark all I could see of the Bitirí was that it was made
of shallacked pine logs, with red tile roofs and walks of glazed
tile; the rooms faced each other along two sides of an isosceles

triangle, its base a landscaped lawn. There was another area below the triangle where there loomed a tall roof; in the morning I discovered this was the top to an open-air dining-room, and beyond it was a swimming-pool and bar. There was a counter where you expected one of the rooms to be, and a young man came out from behind it and greeted me.

He smiled and it made his light eyes look eager, and he picked up my heavy bag, not like a motel employee whose duty it is to do this for the guests, but as a friend who wants to help. 'You must be tired from carrying this,' he said, and headed for the rooms on the other side of the flower beds, directly across from the reception desk where he had been sitting. I was going to be in room number 1.

'You came in on the Havana bus?' he said. 'All the way from Havana?'

The room was small, the single bed took up almost all of it, but it had a private bath; there was a writing surface built into the wall, a night table, a clothes wardrobe and a chair. Outside was a covered walk along the fronts of the rooms, with a high-backed chair for each room. He was proud of it all and watched me look around. He was not waiting for a tip, and stayed not only to suggest where to put my things but also to tell me that he was the night-watchman and would leave a message for the regular people that I wanted the room for a long stay. In the light of the room, I could see that he was thin, his face creased, his light eyes green. He spoke in a thin sweet voice, in the high pitch that is typical of the Orientales.

'You live in Havana then?' he said, and I told him no, that I came from New York.

He was inexpressibly pleased. 'You are an American!' His eyes opened and his face creased deeply as he held his smile and stared at me. He was too shy to ask the question most Cubans had immediately asked, so I volunteered my reply: 'I sympathize with your revolution and I have come to see how it is.'

He did not stay because he thought I was tired, whereas I was wide awake and excited, but a moment later, when I went outside to smoke a last cigarette and try the high chair on the porch-walk, he came back. His name was Armín Vasquez and he was twenty-eight; he had been injured in a jeep accident in Los Pinares de Mayarí, a *mesa* nearby, and until he mended he was not allowed to work at anything more strenuous than this night job at the Bitirí. It made him restive, the job, for he wanted to be doing something more useful.

When he was eighteen he had joined the clandestine movement in Mayarí. At first all his activity consisted of selling bonds to collect money for the Rebels or being the look-out while others placed bombs. But he had other adventures too. Once he was sent to Camagüey to deliver bullets and some explosives, and he carried them in a package with his baseball suit and his player's identification card, for he was on the Mayarí team and this made a good cover. On the way back, with nothing incriminating on him, he was called out of the bus at Victoria de las Tunas, just before Holguín, by a sergeant and three guards.

'Send that fellow out, he has the face of a Rebel,' the sergeant said from the sidewalk. Armín said, 'Me?' And they said yes.

'So I got up', Armín told me, 'and behind me came everyone in the bus. That saved my life, those good people. The sergeant said, "You are a Rebel, I think, and we are going to take you with us and find out." I told them I had been to Camagüey to play ball, but the sergeant said, "You can start the bus and all of you can go now – we are going to give this Rebel what he deserves." But the people said, "If that young man stays, we are going to stay too," and the sergeant looked me up and down and I looked calm. Then he said, "All right, go."

'And do you know, I got picked up as soon as I got off the bus in Mayarí itself, by a little Negro policeman. He asked me what family I was from in Mayarí and I said Vasquez. He said, "Oh, then you are a cousin of that young fellow whose tongue was cut off and his testicles, the one the Rebels killed." So I said, "Yes, he was killed by the Rebels and that is why I hate them." We were both lying, for it was the Batista Guards who castrated him and tore out his tongue and then hanged him from a pole and he was only nineteen. But do you know, the policeman said I must get someone to identify me, so I called a friend passing by and he said, "Oh yes, he is a Vasquez and he is a good boy." And do you know, they followed me as I walked home anyway. I took off my shoes to make no noise when I ran and I got ahead of their car and pushed open the door fast at home and got in. I looked through a peephole and watched for them and they stopped in front of our home a long time. Oh my poor mother and father, what a time we gave them, for my younger brother was already up in the *monte* with the Rebels.

'One time, from the top of the schoolhouse, I threw a grenade at a jeep with five men, and do you know, it bounced on the canvas top of the jeep and on to the street and it never exploded! Oh God, how I had to run that night! I had not thought much about revolution and those things, it was my younger brother, Argelio, who inspired me to get into the clandestine movement and I wanted to go to the monte, but Argelio said not yet.

'Once I was collecting a gun and bullets from a house here to send them to the monte and I was standing in front of the house with the pistol and ammunition in my hands and did not know that a jeep with three of them was parked behind me. I do not know – I could not tell you – how I saw them but I was frozen to the spot. I called to the woman in the doorway, to dissimulate, "Lady, will you please spare me a glass of water?" but she got scared and ran inside the house and did not come back. If they called me or if I turned, they would see the gun and the most I could accomplish would be to kill one and be killed, for they had a machine gun. Then one of the Guards coughed and they took off – what luck!

'Finally in 1958 my brother came into town disguised in the yellow uniform of the Guards – I used to stand in the middle of the street on the look-out, for sometimes he sent a message that he was coming – and he said I could come to the monte any time because the clandestine activity was not so important now. I had to get a gun, for that was the rule, you got a gun one way or the other and then you went to the monte. I was on the look-out for one when at a coffee stand near the ball park close by here, at eight in the morning, I saw ten Guards. Nine left and one stayed, because he liked to drink even early in the morning. I borrowed a butcher knife, placed it at his ribs and disarmed him. I ran to the meadow that is here on the other side of the town to get to the mountains. The Guard had set up such a holler that they shot after me from the town and I kept jumping in the *maya* bushes, and do you know, I never got scratched, not by the bullets nor the sharp points of the *maya*, which is like a pineapple. But they sent out an *avioneta*, one of the little planes they had, and there was no place to hide in that long meadow, so I walked along a lane like a campesino as calmly as I could. I hid the rifle under my shirt and I tore off the 26 of July armband I had put on, for the plane could fly very low and see it. It was behind me and above me making that loud noise and I looked up with my eyes but I never twisted around or seemed to be looking. It was then I was really frightened – my back got ice cold. The pilot turned the plane on a slant to look at me and then I heard a loud noise which made me think I was done for, but it was just the plane climbing fast and away. So I walked to Seboruco where there was a Rebel post, for the Guards did not dare go there except in whole companies with armoured cars and bazookas. They sent for my brother and we had a wonderful reunion.

'Our last combat was at Guanina when the whole company of four hundred men in Mayarí tried to escape to Central Guatemala, the old Preston sugar mill, to get a boat. I was not on the hill over the road, but when the trumpet sounded we came down from the other hills and surrounded them. We lost twelve men. Before that I used to come into Mayarí at night from the monte to shoot at street lights and disrupt generally, and I would only carry a short arm because with a rifle you could be recognized from far away. Once I passed a house where there were five people on the porch and I heard the man say, "See that fellow, he is a Rebel!" I took out my gun and shot four times in the air, and you should have seen them all trying to get into the house at once through one doorway! The people of the town were with us, they supported us, but that was an indiscretion which could harm us and I had to teach them a lesson.

'After Guanina, on 30 December, Mayarí was liberated, but the town was in a fright because the radio kept saying that five bombers were on the way to bomb us. People running into the tunnels they had built under the floorboards of the houses to escape the shooting that had been going on nights for the last two years. My father built his in the yard, because it stands to reason that if the house is bombed and it burns, you would suffocate in such a tunnel. It was terrible in Mayarí under the dictatorship – a married man would go out with his wife and in his presence the Guards would *piropear* her, call out amorous things to her. Is it not better to have a bit of a hard time but to be free?

'The things those Guards did, and all for the whim of it, because of the fun of it. My cousin who was only nineteen and had not done anything. Of course, he was in the clandestine movement, but they could not have proved it. It was just that they were to kill three persons that night and it was my cousin's luck to fall into their hands. They had a list and they would check off the names – they were Guards from here and so they knew who belonged to what name. There is an alley near here that is known as the Alley of Death because one day at dawn six Batista Guards were found there dead. They had killed a campesino, an old man, coming into town followed by a boy – they shot him down as he came down the street and the bullet went through him and killed the boy too. Just for fun they did it.

'In the monte we were like brothers. We stood guard and when the word came – three men to do this or that – we would go and do it or something else. When the Revolution triumphed and I came back home, it was terrible, I missed the monte so. I had always been very much by myself before I joined the clandestine movement and now I wished I were back living in the monte with my comrades and the campesinos. Why, today when I go to the country, the campesinos cannot do enough for me because of the old days. They call me in, everyone wants me to eat with them, they make me gifts of chickens – oh!'

The phone at the Bitirí desk rang and Armín left to answer it. As I went outside, I heard him say there were no rooms. I opened the clothes wardrobe to hang up the clothes I had taken off, and found no hangers; in the bathroom, no water came when I turned on the faucets.

At nine in the morning the sun made the room so bright I could sleep no longer: I had not closed the wooden jalousies at the windows and there was no other way to keep out the light. There was still no water, and I took a carafe from the night table and threw some on my face.

Outside, the Bitirí was a pleasant surprise: a melange of INIT (Institute of Tourism) architecture combining the pine logs of Cuban Indians, the tiles of the Spanish, and the lightness and openness of modern tropical style. Across from room number 1 where I stood were the lawns and flower beds; to my left the rooms on either side of the grounds proceeded to the apex of the triangle; and to my right was the circular driveway, the dining-room with the vaulted ceiling, light and airy in the sunlight, and beyond it the handball and basketball court, an empty swimming-pool, a high fence but not high enough to blot out the tops of huge mango trees on the other side. The sky was blue, the sun bright. I was glad I had chosen Mayarí.

At the desk, directly across, were a young woman and a man. They looked at me with open curiosity, and I went over and introduced myself. I said that I planned to stay for a while and the girl said she wanted me to fill out their form. The man was the manager of the motel, and I said that the night man had mistakenly put me in a room without water; also, that my wardrobe had no hangers.

The manager said he was glad that I had reminded him about the hangers because they had been on order since the Bitirí opened and had not yet arrived, but today he would get some, if only wire ones. 'About water,' he said. 'That is our problem – there is no water in Mayarí.' I was so stunned that it embarrassed me to ask the ordinary questions of how one was supposed to make do. Seeing my look, he added that some time that day supply trucks would fill the cistern and I would be able to take a shower. 'In the afternoon, before dinner,' he said – Cubans cannot sit down to dinner anywhere without a bath and a clean starched shirt.

The unbroken porch-walk in front of the rooms continued on that side to the back of the dining-room, where the kitchen quarters were, and I opened the door in the high fence to retrace my steps of the night, for there was no breakfast to be had at the Bitirí at this late hour of the morning. The scene on the other side of the fence had lost the mystery the night had lent it, and lacked the charm and cleanliness of the motel.

Close up, across the dusty, uneven street, was a derelict of a house, made of unpainted old boards, an outhouse in the yard; clumps of banana trees, some corn rows, bushes, scattered fruit trees, all planted without order, dribbled away into open country away from the town; a pig was tied to a pole, two or three chickens picked about in the grass, and a dirty child stopped and stared at me. But next to it, toward the town, was a stucco house. Along the street there were one or two more like that one; they looked as if they were built during the last ten years. Most, however, were old wooden houses, close to each other, all of the same type one sees in small

Cuban towns: the porch right up to the sidewalk and all of it on the same level, so that as you walk by you can look into the bare living-rooms, the kitchen beyond, and if the back door is open, into the back yard. The street level of the floors and the tall ceilings are the only vestiges of colonial proportions and elegance; the wood and lack of paint, however, made them look like barns.

This street, which was to become so familiar to me that in time it took an effort to see that it was ugly, ran for four blocks before it ended at the main street, and traffic on it was one-way, leading out of town. The side streets off it were unpaved, though gravel had been ground into the clay, and the first one, which ran beside the tall fence of the Bitirí, had a huge open ditch along one side, so that when I arrived at it I had to step out into the street to continue into town. Farther along were filling-stations, grocery stores, a lawyer's office, the court building, a bar and one or two drink stands, the office of Micons (the Ministry of Construction) – all of them interspersed among those wooden houses, sometimes indistinguishable from them.

The darkness had been kind to that street: there seemed to be not a single new coat of paint on any house, and where any paint had survived the years it had lost its colour, so that over all the effect was of greyness. The trees that had cast such awesome shadows were small, the sidewalks even more broken than one could tell at night, and there were puddles at street corners that I had miraculously missed in the dark. Each time a car or truck went by, it raised a cloud of dust that made it almost necessary to close one's eyes and stop breathing. From a metal plaque on one of the corner houses I learned that the street was named Antonio Maceo, a grandiose name, the legendary Negro general of the War of Independence, the Hero of Bronze.

But the darkness had also robbed the street of its life. People were everywhere: women washing down the living-rooms and porches as if they were tile and not tired wood, men repairing cars and old tyres, a girl attendant in curlers and slacks dispensing gasoline at the filling-station, little children on the sidewalks, men at the corners and the bar and the juice stands chatting, women in a bunch at the grocery, the vegetable stand and the butcher's. Down the narrow street went campesinos on motor bikes, jeeps, new construction trucks, cars so old they seemed to be running on nerve, donkey carts dragging fifty-gallon drums from which women filled cans with water. Radios were turned on loud, the high-pitched, lilting sound of Oriente speech was everywhere, and if you greeted anyone, he paused, nodded, said 'Buenas' or 'Qué tal?' or 'Bueno y qué?', ready to talk.

The only place with a yard was the Catholic church where the street came to an end, and the yard was unkempt. On the main street, Leyte Vidal, the architecture did not change, except that here most structures were stores, the buildings flush with each other, and some, only some, were two storeys high like the hotel, making Leyte Vidal a closed-in street even in daylight. I turned left and in one block came to a new building under construction, which I had not noticed in the dark, brick and stucco and almost completed: a sign on the sidewalk said *Mayari Pizzeria*. The government's attempt to vary the Cuban's diet – particularly to find a partial substitute for scarce rice – had reached even remote Oriente.

The pizzeria's dining-room was out in the open and next to it one or two buildings had been torn down, for there was still debris on the ground, and all this allowed for a break in the street, on the side I faced as I approached from Maceo. Last night it had been a dark chasm; today it was a window on the south-east: a view of such extraordinary charm that it was a surprise everyone on the main street had not gathered to contemplate it. The edge of the rubble strewn lot stood high over a valley, the land dropping steeply to a river which ran parallel to the street and then edged away from the town through the meadow in the foreground. On its banks, horses and cows grazed, and on the other side of the river were farmhouses with guano palm leaf roofs. The valley rose gradually into hills, green with cane-fields, then jaggedly into a mountain range, among whose blues and purples a patch of red-orange had spread. Here and there were royal palms, graceful, stately, austere, walking across the landscape. Above, the bright blue tropical sky.

Going north-west on the main street, past where the bus had stopped, I still recognized nothing from the day in 1960 when I had passed through here. There were shops, coffee stands, barbershops, offices, a movie theatre that looked new, two more breaks the size of tiny houses with slightly different views of the valley; and then the main street emptied into a triangular plaza with a little park in the centre filled with cement benches and a few shade trees. Facing it was a cafe called El Parque Cafeteria, on whose second floor were fur-nished rooms, and catty-corner at the base of the triangle – at last! – was La Casa Gold. I knew then that if I continued along the main street for two blocks it too ended and on the right a road crossed the river over the wooden planks of a low, makeshift bridge. I looked closer, and the bridge seemed sturdier and stood higher over the river than the one we'd taken in 1960; but there was no traffic on the road and that made me doubt it could be the one to Nicaro.

Back on the plaza, across from El Parque, I noticed a build-ing which I decided must have been a social club, that now, a sign announced, was the *Regional de Cultura*, the regional headquarters for cultural activities. As I approached it, two young men came out and stood at the top of the steps. I decided this was a good place to start learning about the offi-cial life, and introduced myself. But they were on the way to another town, and invited me to come back another time. Any time. During the *zafra*, as the sugar-cane harvest and milling is called, their work was concentrated in the main on getting groups to go out to the *albergues* – which means inns, but now in Cuba almost exclusively refers to the barracks, tents, barns or sheds where the cane cutters stay. Any day around six thirty, I could join a group going out to the cane-fields for the evening to entertain.

It was ten o'clock and they were straining coffee at El Parque Cafeteria, and the young men took me there for a demitasse. We stood at the long counter until each of us got our swallow of espresso. They wanted to know if I wouldn't have trouble with my government when they found out I'd been to Cuba; if I could publish the truth about Cuba; if the authorities wouldn't, in any case, discourage the sale of the book. 'You must come and visit us, there are so many things I want to ask you,' one said, and the other wanted to know if I were staying at the Bitirí. 'How do you like it?' he asked proudly. I said I liked it and did not mention the lack of water. 'Well, Fidel did not like it,' he said just as proudly, for Castro's irascibleness charms the Cubans. 'Because of its location – too noisy, and they have a nightclub show on weekends.'

On the plaza, across from El Parque, the town's taxis were lined up, all old models of American cars. I noticed a 1955 Plymouth model that I had bought the year it came out and sold five years later for $250 much the worse for wear; this taxi was in perfect condition. When the others left, I decided to look up the local Party. The Ministry in Havana had persuaded me that they could be helpful, and pointed out that, after all, if I was doing a study of the life of a town I could not leave out the Party. I asked a taxi driver where the Party was, and he did not look upon me as a customer; he told me how I could walk there.

It was on a side street off a busy street parallel to Leyte Vidal, a two-storey stucco building that seemed to have once been two apartments. Across from it was the Ministry of the Interior (which is in charge of the police and also security), lodged in two stucco houses no doubt acquired from middle-class exiles; across the driveway between the houses was hung a neon sign in the form of an arch announcing somewhat gaily that this was the Ministry of the Interior. There was a guard there but none at the Party headquarters, where I wandered in and told a secretary my mission. She suggested I go out again and take an outside stairway to the second floor and ask for Franklin Rodriguez. 'Franklin?' I asked, and she nodded unselfconsciously.

A girl sweeping out one of the rooms upstairs went looking for him, and he came out in a moment, a tall serious man of about thirty. He was the Organizing Secretary of the Party for the Region – I learned from him that Mayarí was the headquarters for the region (sub-division of a province) of Mayarí-Sagua-Moa – and he listened with interest to what I was doing in Mayarí. I gave him the name of the Party man in Santiago to whom the Ministry in Havana had referred me, and he smiled and nodded and said he would check with him. 'Not that you cannot go about as you please,' he added, and I remembered the Ministry's advice that I would have no trouble with authorities travelling through Cuba but more likely with ordinary citizens, all of whom were on the alert for C.I.A. activity.

I told him that I wanted the Party's help with various things: getting lodging and introductions in Central Guatemala and Nicaro, and introductions to local official bodies, such as the city administration, the Federation of Cuban Women, the police, the Committees for the Defence of the Revolution; I also wanted to spend a full day with him – an ordinary day, not an unusual one – to see what a Party functionary's day was like. He looked shy, then said he would have to discuss that with his *compañeros*. When I said I wanted to sit in on a meeting of the regional Party committee, he said no kindly but firmly .

He said that during the zafra it might be difficult to find lodging for me at Central Guatemala, but there would probably be no trouble at Nicaro. He recommended that I remain at the Bitirí during my stay since it had the kind of living conditions writers need for writing. It was expensive at the Bitirí, he said, but there were people who still had money or high salaries, and at places like that compañeros should not be lax and allow the water to run out. The lack of water in Mayarí was an inheritance of capitalism; they were building an aqueduct – had I not noticed the broken-up streets? – but it would be a couple of years before it could be complete. 'There is so much to do and not enough hands,' he said. In the old days *macheteros*, cane-cutters, earned as little as 50 cents a day, $100 a season, if the landlords were kind enough to give one a job, for there was enormous unemployment and it was take it or leave it. He said the head of COR (the Party's Committee for Revolutionary Orientation; the propaganda arm) would be in touch with me in a day or so; he was out of town but he would be the man to work with me.

Back at the Bitirí, there was still no water and the chambermaids had removed the sheets from the bedrooms and placed them on the chairs outside. There was still water in the carafe and I worked out a system, which was to stand me in good stead, for shaving with two glassfuls. At the bar they had broken out the *suaves*, mild cigarettes, and I was able to get two packs; I inhaled with pleasure, and figured this was the way a Cuban housewife felt when she got to a vegetable-stand at the right moment, for although you can get strong cigarettes, the kind Cubans prefer, at any time, the mild are hard to come by.

The sixteen tables in the airy dining-room were all taken and one of the waitresses suggested I might sit with another man who was alone at a table. The way she looked at me, I saw she knew I was the American guest. My lunch companion was a middle-aged man from Central Frank Pais (formerly the Central Tánamo that belonged to the Cuban industrialist and banker Julio Lobo), and he was in Mayarí for a meeting of the managers of clothing stores of the region to discuss distribution problems. He had been working at the Central in different stores since he was a little boy, but this year since the beginning of the zafra he had been cutting cane; he preferred it to dealing with the public at the store.

These distribution meetings, he said, were unnecessary, because thus far distribution had not got any better, despite all the discussions. He had stocks of large sizes of everything, and when he ordered the sizes most in demand, he still got the large sizes. 'Thank God for the Jamaicans,' he said. 'They have big feet. People have taken to buying size 40 pants and cutting them down, but shoes are another matter.' There was a man at the Central with a 50 waist; they had got him a pair of pants that fit him around the middle but none which would go around the lower belly.

He lived a few kilometres outside Sagua (which he said was almost entirely burned down during the insurrection) and had a bit of land which he cultivated. He said many people had left and many were waiting; mostly office people from the Central. 'You could call them middle-class,' he said. 'The ones with a lot of money and property left a long time ago.' Since he had had a steady job before the Revolution, I asked him if he had suffered. 'No, I have always lived in the countryside,' he said. 'My parents too.' All this with a signal lack of enthusiasm, in a kind of monotone. He seemed one of those whom the Revolution neither excited nor alienated. He said there were many more volunteer sugar-cane hands this year; last year the mill would work one day and close down another for lack of cane to feed it. Not this year, it was going to be a big harvest. 'A good thing,' he said diffidently. He never asked if I was a foreigner; he took me for a Cuban or didn't care.

During lunch it began to get cloudy, but I walked back to the main street, when I finished, to get a haircut, and people I had nodded to in the morning now greeted me first. Of the several barbershops I had seen in the morning, I picked a one-man operation, a neat place next to the Planification Office, where men worked at large drawing-boards, and across from the small INIT office and the Playa Girón, an eating-place with a winding counter like Chock Full O'Nuts. The barber, a mulatto, was named Clemente Columbie. Clients ahead of me were a black boy and a light-skinned Negro; we all got excellent haircuts, each according to the texture of his hair. It was difficult to be aware of colour because no one else seemed to be.

Columbie and the light-skinned Negro, Flores, both in their late fifties were old friends; Flores had started as a musician but had ended up a tailor. They talked about schools, and after a casual tribute to the Revolution's efforts in this field, the tailor said, 'The schooling today is more practical but easier.'

'Oh yes, that cannot be denied.'

'I know because I see it with my grandchildren.'

'Humberto Rosales made you work. He must have taught until his eighties.'

'I had language, history, geography, arithmetic, morality and civics.'

They disagreed about whether the old Mayarí school went through fifth or sixth grade.

Outside it began to rain, and it reminded both about Hurricane Flora in 1963. They told me Mayarí was inundated for four days, the first time in its history, and it took two months to clean up the mud. In the upper part of the town, toward the Bitirí, where it looks higher but is not, the houses were completely under water. 'Across the street,' said Columbie, pointing to the side of Leyte Vidal that overlooks the valley, 'houses were swept away – it was like an ocean down there.'

'Soon they are going to knock the rest of those wrecks down,' said the tailor, 'and there will be a *malecón*, an open walk along that whole side of Leyte Vidal. It will be nice, don't you think?'

When my turn came, the tailor hung around because of the rain and the *norteamericano*. They were discussing an article on the Sugar-Cane Workers Union in the current issue of *Bohemia*, a weekly magazine, and Columbie put it on my lap. The article referred to a strike in the thirties against the United Fruit Company, and they laughed at the fact that one man listed as a militant had at the start been on the strike committee but had in a short time, as everyone in Mayarí knew, broken the strike. 'They must have taken the list from the records and not talked to anyone here,' said Columbie with a chuckle.

It had been a violent strike; the tailor said the campesinos had to take refuge in Mayarí because they would have been killed if they had remained in the countryside; most stayed at the Methodist church – 'The Methodists were good that way,' said Columbie – and the townspeople helped by bringing them food. The tailor recalled that a police sergeant, recruiting strike-breakers, had offered him a job at the Central, and he had replied that he had a job – 'when the truth was I was dying of hunger'. The police did not have to force anyone to break the strike, because there were so many hungry people in the area who would take the place of the striking campesinos, and later, when the strike was lost, Jesús Menendez had to come back to the area to reorganize the union, for the repression and fear were so terrible. Jesús Menendez was a prominent Communist who was assassinated later in Manzanillo, and the tailor and Columbie disagreed as to whether it was the Batista régime or the Grau San Martín government that had assassinated him.

Columbie insisted that it was the Grau government that did it. Under the 1940 constitution the Communists had been in government, but when Grau won the elections under the new constitution, there was a question whether he would be allowed to take office. 'Grau's chief of staff went Up North,' said Columbie, 'and they told him that the Communists had to be stopped. Otherwise the United States would bring his government down.' He turned to me to explain: 'You understand, that Jesús Menendez was loved does not mean that the sugar-cane workers were Communists. Look at us barbers, we are Liberals, *Auténticos*, of all political opinions, but our union leaders were Communists and when it came to union matters, we were as one in supporting them.'

To comb my hair Columbie sprayed it with a sweet-smelling liquid, and asked me if I wanted some grease. I said no automatically, and he said he'd asked just to ask, for he knew that I would not want it, since I was getting bald. The tailor and he agreed that I should use iodized water to keep what I have. They were surprised I did not know about that. The formula is one small bottle of iodine to a gallon of water, plus the juice of ten to fifteen limes. 'You are right not to touch grease, but you must use iodized water, for you do not want to lose your hair,' Columbie said, as seriously as when he discussed politics, and the tailor nodded.

They directed me to the post office, where I wanted to mail a letter and cable my new address to New York. At the telegraph window most people were sending St Valentine's greetings; the young man ahead of me dispatched six. On the counter was a glue pot, and those buying stamps held up the line by spreading glue on each stamp. The glue on the stamps was perfectly fine, but people looked at me curiously when I licked mine.

On my way back to Leyte Vidal, I first realized that no matter how old the building, or unpainted, every public place had its new, shiny sign; only the Communist Party headquarters had none. Jeeps, trucks or cars that belonged to an organization whether worn or new, usually had a hand-painted sign on the door next to the driver's seat identifying it. And there were hand-painted posters everywhere hailing the VII People's harvest, the *Plan Tomate* in Los Pinares de Mayarí, or Heroic Vietnam. At the plaza was one which read: *Long Live the Activism of Technical Pedagogy*. Another: *We salute the Trade Union Leaders Who Have Gone to the Canefields for Two Years*.

The library at the beginning of the plaza also had its sign, aimed at children:

> *A la escuela iré*
> *y Pionero seré*
> *y al plan de la calle asistiré.*

(To school I shall go
and a Pioneer be
and take part in the street plan.)

Inside, on a desk that faced the street, was a sign which said:
We are in the cane-fields while one is still standing. I asked the
librarians about a book published in 1961 which, among other
documents of the Revolution, contained Raul Castro's diary
of the early days of the second front in the mountains nearby.
They didn't have it: Hurricane Flora had wiped out their
whole collection, and almost everything they had now had been
published after 1963. I said I thought it had also been serial-
ized in *Verde Olivo*, the Army magazine, and the librarian
said they had old copies of that; they would be happy to bring
them out whenever I chose. My questions answered, one of
them, a plump Negro woman, said, 'Tell me, will you not have
trouble with your government when you return ... ?' The other
said eagerly, 'Yes, it occurred to me too!'

At the Bitirí the girl at the desk told me my key was in the
room, and I had only to look across to see the door open.
'There is also water now,' she said. 'The truck came.' (In the
future, I was always to leave my key in the room, the door
unlocked, and they were to yell across the grounds, 'Jose, time
for your shower – the water is on!') At my room, the chambermaid, in a lemon-yellow dress with a tiny cap the same colour
pinned to the side of her head, the uniform of all the girls who
worked there, had just finished mopping the tiled floor. She
was young, slight and very shy, though she smiled slyly while
looking beyond me or away. I sat outside and waited for the
floor to dry; she told me her name was Angela, she was nineteen, had a year-old son, and was separated from her husband.
'What happened?' I asked. She shrugged and smiled and went
away as if I had made a pass at her.

She had placed jasmines, from one of the beds outside, in a
glass on the night table, and their perfume filled the room.
There was water in the bathroom but no hot water. The

dining-room in the evening was not filled as at lunch, and I
ate by myself. But at the bar later I talked to Aldo Gonzalez,
a young man of twenty-one who was exchanging notes on
girls with the young, chocolate-coloured bartender; Aldo was
white, though Cubans like to say, '*Los que no somos del Congo
somos de Carabalí*' – Those of us who are not from the Congo
are of the Carabalí tribe. He was waiting for one of the girls
who would be through at ten. 'One must try,' he said, 'or you
get out of training.'

He came from the countryside and now worked in Mayarí
at the office of the 'refreshments' distribution centre. Because
I was American, he told me that it was Mister Jacoby, an
American farmer near home, who taught him how to drive a
jeep; it was also Mister Jacoby who got him accepted at a
Methodist agricultural school. All Americans had left, but he
knew that some had sympathized with the Revolution; one
was a Rebel and had got wounded in one arm; he didn't remember his name and it was a while since he had heard it
mentioned. After the Revolution, Aldo spent four years in
Havana studying on scholarship, then at a Navy school to become an officer; but he failed some courses, and he became
discouraged and returned to Mayarí. He worked at the Bitirí
for a month, until recently, but then they decided that only
men thirty-five and over could work there – 'So they would
not fool around with the girls.'

The bartender interrupted to say, 'You are making a mistake to take this one out – it is the little one who gives.'

Aldo shook his head. 'You cannot do anything with the little
one. But this one rolls around as soon as she has two drinks.
She will give.' He looked at his watch; it was ten. He started
off and then turned back and shook hands. 'You have to try,'
he said.

I walked to Leyte Vidal again, and across from the piz-
zeria under construction there was music from the Prague
Club. I didn't go in because the rum *añejo* I had drunk at the
Bitirí had not gone down well: all the good rum now went

to export. Instead, I stopped in at the counter cafeteria across
from my barber's, for a guava cold drink. The girl who served
me asked loud enough for everyone to hear, 'You are not from
Mayarí, are you?' I said no. 'From Nicaro, then?' I said I
was from New York, a Yankee.

She laughed, then gathered herself together and said,
'Listen, you tell Johnson that a bomb should explode and blow
him up!'

Everyone laughed.

'That Vietnam war is a crime,' she said, and waited for my
opinion. I said it was bad.

'You are going to have trouble when you go back,' she said.
I told her I did not expect to, because I had permission to
come. 'Then they will not let you write things sympathetic
to Cuba,' she said. 'For in that country they live by the lie!'
She did not say 'your country' because that would have been
discourteous.

Walking back along Leyte Vidal, a man I passed turned to
me and smiled. 'You are not from Mayarí, are you?' he said.
I said I was an American and he said, 'Imagine!' His name
was Jose Martinez – he stopped to shake hands when he said
it and then added, 'A new friend' – and he was an elementary
school teacher. We walked for three blocks together, and he
told me he was one of five brothers, one studying to be a doctor, another in Poland to be an engineer, and the rest all working.

'You are a writer,' he said, 'so what do you think of Jose
Martí?' Jose Martí, the leader of the War of Independence,
was also a great poet and essayist.

He was on his way home from a discussion group on
teaching techniques. 'We have a lot of problems. For example,
the question we are asking ourselves is whether in building a
new society we are not giving the children too free a rein.' The
younger children, that is: the older scholarship students
knew the schooling they were getting was a blessing of the
Revolution. He shook hands again, and watched me skirt

a puddle. 'Welcome to Cuba,' he said when I turned to wave.

In my room I found a skinny Negro woman who apologized for not having filled my carafe with cold water sooner. She spoke with a real campesino lilt, and she would look at me after every word as if she were asking a question. 'You are the new guest,' she said, and waited a moment. 'Is it true you are American?'

'Yes,' I said, 'But not one of the bad ones, not one who came to invade.'

'Oh, there are good everywhere, and there is an air about you,' she said, and kept looking at me. Then she nodded. 'We are all good and also bad. But we *are* all good. I think so, yes, we are all good.'

She looked at me a little more, squinting her eyes. 'So you come from Up North. And there nothing is rationed!'

It had been a long day, and I lay back on the bed and tried to write my notes lying on my back. I turned on the radio on the night table and had to fiddle with two stations fighting for the same kilocycle. The one I settled on turned out to be a Spanish-language station from Miami. A woman in an exacerbated tone was saying that there was no better proof of Castro Communism's attempt to destroy the Cuban family than the absence of children for five days a week at school. I took it that she meant the live-in schools, and turned her off. Three months later, when I read my notes on my first day in Mayarí, I discovered that the things I saw and the talk I heard that day were like an old-fashioned overture: everything was touched upon and yet to be developed.

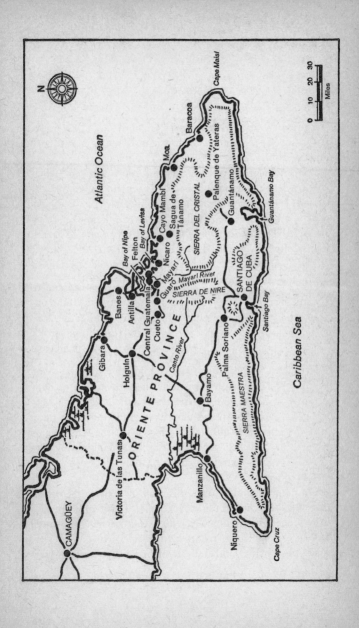

A Delayed Foreword

The presence of an American in Cuba during 1967 needs to be explained; it is not, for my countrymen, in the natural order of things, as is the base at Guantánamo. (For Cubans both phenomena inspire much discussion, some of which I have tried to report in this book.) I went to Cuba, let it then be said, to comply with an assignment from Pantheon Books to write a book for their 'village' series, auspiciously begun by Jan Myrdal's *Report from a Chinese Village* and followed up successfully by Studs Terkel's *Division Street: America*.* One of their editors, Sara Blackburn, proposed the project at lunch and I accepted immediately, knocking over an untouched martini in my haste.

Pantheon had no strictures or demands about the kind of book they would like – not as to form or approach or even as to what constitutes a village – and they expected I would want to roam a bit in Cuba before I settled on a place of my liking. Before the new martini arrived, I told Mrs Blackburn that I would go to Mayarí, a town near the Atlantic on the northeastern coast that I had driven through in December 1960 on the way to Nicaro, and where two hours later, on the way back, I spent some time under arrest while the Army sergeant from Nicaro checked our credentials with Holguín by phone. It had been an extraordinarily pleasant experience, and I wanted to see the area again.

This sentimental motive was not, of course, the reason I gave Mrs Blackburn for my choice. I thought up several serious ones. First, it was a village in Oriente, the province further east in Cuba, known as the cradle of Cuban revolutions; but not in southern Oriente near the Sierra Maestra,

* Published in Great Britain by Allen Lane The Penguin Press, 1968.

for that would be begging the question about the people's revolutionary morale, since it was from the Sierra Maestra that Castro began the uprising. Second, Mayarí was in the heart of the sugar country, still Cuba's main asset. Third, the nearness to Nicaro, where the United States government had set up a mining and nickel-processing operation during the Second World War, promised local knowledge of and contact with Americans, an element that makes Mayarí's story more typical of the Cuban historical experience. Fourth, there had been fighting in the area during the Revolution, for it was in the nearby mountains, the Sierra del Cristal and Sierra de Nipe, that Raul Castro had started a second front during 1958.

I knew that the nearby cane-fields had belonged to the United Fruit Company but not that its largest sugar-mill, Central Guatemala, was as close to Mayarí, in the opposite direction, as Nicaro. Nor that some twenty minutes to the south-east was Birán, where Fidel and Raul Castro were born and raised. Their father was a prosperous landowner, but he was an immigrant Galician without social pretensions, and in any case, their home was in too remote an area for the boys to have companions of their own class: there is consequently much of the northern Oriente campesino in Fidel and Raul Castro.

In late 1965, then, I made applications for a visa from the Cubans and for validation of my passport by the State Department. The latter did not act with alacrity – Leonard Boudin, the civil rights attorney, had to jog them a bit – but the Cubans responded much more slowly: they took thirteen months. I wrote friends in Cuba to intercede for me, phoned the Czech Embassy in Washington innumerable times, and even made a trip to Prague to speak to the Cuban Embassy there. When I had given up, the first week in 1967, a year for which one of my resolutions was *not* to think of my visa application, I heard from the Cubans that it was approved. I could pick it up in Mexico City.

Three days before I was to leave I found out that I needed a licence from my government in order to spend money for food and lodging in Cuba. Without it I could be prosecuted under the Trading with the Enemy Act. The Treasury Department was wonderfully cooperative about this, however, and I left on time. In Mexico City, friendly clerks at the airport lost their smiles when I announced my through ticket to Madrid had to be rewritten for a stop in Havana, and private taxi drivers were unhappy about taking me to the Cuban Consulate – what kind of a gringo was I?

I took no tape recorder and no sociological disciplines with me, only a typewriter, four notebooks and three ballpoint pens. This book owes no acknowledgements or thanks to any-one not already mentioned. Not even to my typist or my wife. The former is I and the latter saw me off grudgingly and enviously: she would have liked it to have been as in 1960, when the simple desire to go to Cuba was sufficient warrant for any American. Me too: an end to forewords!

2. Town Without Soup

Of most Cuban towns it used to be said that it was a town without soup – *pueblo sin sopa* – but today Mayarí even has an apocryphal story to account for the origin of the epithet. A campesino with only a dime in his pocket spent three hours in Mayarí between buses, and he spent them in the few eating-places trying to buy a meal, only to find at each place when he tried to settle for just a bowl of soup, for which his dime should have been enough, that there was none. He made his bus eventually, and as it pulled away, he looked back at the trail of dust the bus left along the Leyte Vidal and waved: 'Good-bye, Mayarí, town without soup!' Mayarí citizens love to tell the story, and over the years have added other epithets to it, so that now there is a kind of non-rhyming jingle, entitled *Mayarí*, that adds up to a dirty dozen about the town:

> *Pueblo sin sopa,*
> *río sin pescado,*
> *mujeres putas*
> *y niños malcriados.*
> *Cocal sin cocos,*
> *Guayabo sin guayaba,*
> *Naranjal sin naranja,*
> *Guerrita sin guerra,*
> *y Linea sin ferrocarril.*
> *Narciso Prieto no es prieto,*
> *y Noel Noés si es!*

> (Town without soup,
> river without fish,
> whoring women

> and spoiled kids.
> Coconut Grove without coconuts
> Guava Grove without guavas,
> Orange Grove without oranges,
> Little War without fighting,
> and Railroad Line without trains.
> Narciso Prieto is not dark,
> and Noel Noés *is* one!)

Cocal (Coconut Grove), Naranjal (Orange Grove), etc. are the names of sections or neighbourhoods in Mayarí, of which there are about a dozen, all with names of their own: Narciso Prieto, whose last name means dark, is a townsman; Noel Noés also, and since his last name, Noés, means He-Is-Not and he is also an old bachelor, the assertion that he *is* – meaning a homosexual – was inevitable.

'This is a gossipy, mean town,' said Dr Celia Chacón, a girl doing her second year of rural medicine at the Mayarí hospital; particularly conscious of small-town talk because she and another young doctor at the hospital were trying to pair off without causing comment. We were sitting around at the Bitirí one Sunday afternoon, the only time doctors seem to have off, and the others there, also from the hospital staff, compared it with the towns in the same region where they had done their first year of rural medicine. None had a good word for Mayarí: the people were gossipy, unfriendly, hardheaded, self-seeking.

'Well, I have had enough of the countryside,' said the dentist's wife. 'We have three more months of rural medicine and then, thank God, it is back to Havana for us!'

Dr Raul Padrón, the director of the hospital, also in his second year of rural medicine, did not like this comment; he was a twenty-nine-year-old Negro from Havana, and devoted to the Revolution, and did not think anyone should complain about being in the countryside. 'It is not that it is provincial, we expected that,' he said. 'For Cayo Mambí is near here, it is a tiny town, and the year I spent there is the happiest I have known. I would serve as many years there as the Revolution would ask!'

Dr Padrón thought that over and then added, 'I would serve as many in Mayarí, too, if the Revolution required it.'

'Oh doctor!' the dentist's wife moaned.

When the dentist's wife was gone, Dr Padrón continued to criticize Mayarí, more freely since he wasn't giving her ammunition. 'Mayarí people are provincial without having the wonderful, open, healthy qualities of country people.' Havanans are always using the word healthy to characterize the morality – not morals – of country people. 'Look at that trouble you had with the police when you first arrived – it was due to the nosiness and lack of culture of people here,' he said to me.

On my second day in Mayarí, I had gone to the library again to read Raul Castro's diary of the second front, and the plump Negro librarian took me into the back room and brought out a pile of old copies of the magazine where it had appeared. Before she allowed me to settle down to them, she sat at another table and asked in an intimate tone, as if showing impatience with the polite, formal ways in which we had dealt with each other until then, 'And so, who are you? What *are* you doing here?' I was astonished, for I had already explained the previous day, and she seemed to be saying there was something fishy about my story.

I made the mistake of not matching her tone; instead, I brought out my wallet and took out the press card that the Ministry in Havana had given me for purposes of identification; I also repeated my story about the kind of book I hoped to write. Not to be outdone, she explained again and again that at the library they too had their procedures: a monthly report of the services the library had rendered, a report which, she was certain I would understand, must include a listing of foreign visitors. All very friendly, but in a half hour, she led into the empty back room a soldier and two civilians.

She said that he – meaning the soldier – had come asking

for me, and I confused them by jumping up and shaking hands and thanking him, because I took him for a young soldier I had heard about who had been involved in the nationalization of the United Fruit Company and whom I wanted to interview. But in a moment it became quite clear that the soldier was a member of Orden Pública (the police); one civilian looked official, the other simply curious and he therefore soon left. The librarian remained to enjoy the spectacle of the questioning and possible arrest of the American.

The soldier looked nervous, deadly serious, embarrassed, and wanted to know who I was and what I was doing there; the remaining civilian, who had sat down at the table with us, smiled slyly all the while. Questions which other Cubans asked me with wonder and delight – such as, why did I speak Spanish so well that I sounded like a Cuban – sounded like accusations. When they were done, I asked them questions and wrote down the soldier's name in a notebook, something I was not accustomed to doing but which I did because I thought it would discomfit him. Then I turned to the civilian, who had been writing down some of the information I gave him, and said, 'I see from this compañero's uniform why he would question me, but what is your position? Do you belong to the Ministry of the Interior? To the Committees for the Defence of the Revolution?' He looked from side to side, smiling all the while, so that he seemed to be denying that he was. 'Then you are simply a vigilant Cuban?' He nodded, delighted with the out I had given him, and left the room with the librarian.

Alone, the soldier, whose name was Emilio Blet, was more at ease – he even told me everyone called him El Chino – and explained why he had to come and question me when he was told of my presence in the library. 'After all, you come from a country some of whose people are our enemies.' He assured me that once he got clearance, for some aspects of his job were confidential, he would be happy to talk to me; he would introduce me to people who were much more interesting than he. Then he asked me for his name. I dissembled; I said I had written it down but could still remember it, and repeated it for him. He nodded, embarrassed again, and pointed to the note-book; I asked if he wanted me to write it down for him and give him a copy of it. He swallowed and said he would like me to tear out his name from the notebook and give it to him. I did it, and he shook my hand several times before he left and spoke with a flow of emotion. I liked him, and when we said good-bye many weeks later, he recalled our first encounter – 'Oh what a state I was in when I went to find out who this suspicious character was!' he said. By then, too, the civilian, who was a plainclothesman, had gotten over his embarrass-ment at running into me at the police station whenever I passed. The librarian's motives were no doubt compounded of revolutionary vigilance, but I was willing to concede to Dr Padrón that nosiness also played its part.

That Sunday afternoon conversation with the doctors took place two months after I arrived in Mayarí, and I was al-ready used to such talk, not just from outsiders but from Mayarí people too. During my first two weeks, I had spent a great deal of time with Dr Morales, an important surgeon from Havana, who was voluntarily spending fifteen days in Mayarí as a consultant at the hospital, because the govern-ment would no longer allow doctors to go to the countryside during the harvest to cut cane and he wanted to help; and it was he, restless, speculative, witty, who had the most damning question about Mayarí: 'Tell me, what is Mayarí's reason for being? Think about it – it has no industry, no sugar mill, no railroad, no nothing!'

I pointed out that it had commerce; the people of surround-ing areas came to Mayarí to do their shopping. We were on Leyte Vidal, and the irony of my statement was not lost on either of us: the shops had almost nothing to sell and were closed more often than not. It reminded Morales of a joke: two counter-revolutionaries condemned to hell are given the choice of a capitalist or a socialist hell, and the one who chooses the socialist hell explains, 'No knives, no forks, no nails to torture you, no gasoline for the fire ...' As soon as I laughed, Morales got very serious and called me down for it; such stories were now frowned on and Morales was a good Party member. 'Diplomatic gatherings used to deteriorate into superficial joking of that sort,' he said; then, asked, 'But what reason is there for Mayarí?' and laughed, his old self again.

There were no histories of the area, no reference room at the library to look for answers to the question; there were only the old inhabitants, and one of them came out of Columbie's barbershop and stopped us. He was Felix Estol, Columbie's brother-in-law, and he was not under the impression, as were many during the two weeks when I walked around with Dr Morales, that I was the new pediatrician from Havana. 'I have heard that you speak like one of us and that you are an American,' he said, with the impertinence that is allowed the old. 'Let me hear you talk.'

I asked him if he had lived in Mayarí when he was a boy and if it were true that the Mayarí River was navigable then. He was sixty-seven and had been born in Mayarí – 'In the days when all there was was this street we are standing on. It was known as the town with one street.' He spoke with great elegance, and we stood for an hour on the street while he unfolded his tale.

'The river came closer to the town in those days,' Felix began. 'Some people do not realize it but rivers are like living beings and they change their course. Right where the pizzeria is, the river rose higher than it is now, and it was there that the piers were. The ships – of course not big ones – came up to the piers and followed the river as it is now until it came to the Bay of Nipe at the point just below the little peninsula of Central Preston. There one took a ferry across the bay to Antilla, which then as now was the big port.

'Not until the twenties – we have been speaking more of the old days since Hurricane Flora in 1963 and Inez only last year – was the lane to Cueto, where the railroad is, widened. It was simply widened, not paved in any way, and so when it rained it was impassable, and people, as late as the twenties, took the boats from here to Antilla to travel almost anywhere. But I was speaking of when I was a boy, for already in the twenties Mayarí had attained a certain cultural level; and it was at the beginning of the century, when I was only eight, that I used to travel all the way to Antilla every week with my father, for I was such a hell-raiser that my mother, who could not deal with me, asked my father to take me with him for the six days of each week that he spent working in Antilla.

'It was in those days that the United Fruit Company began to build the sugar mill and to buy up the land around here and plant cane. It was never all cane, you know; there was a lot of tobacco, it even had a certain fame, and now after the triumph of the Revolution some are planting it again. They have even started a little cigar factory. But what Mayarí was really famous for was its cedars and *caobas* and pines. They had been there since time began, and two blocks from here, where the court building is, right there they began, east, west and south, so that the little donkey lane to Cueto was a path among those enormous trees. Up into Los Pinares the trees went.

'Do you know how much all that fine wood was worth? I estimate at least ten to twenty million pesos! La United sold them all to Las Bahamas, and they were cut down and rolled into the river after a railroad-tie nail was driven into the head of each log. In spring the river would rise and the logs floated all the way to the Bay of Nipe. It is a mystery to me – one of those things that nevertheless has its scientific explanation – why those big nails made it possible for those heavy logs to float, but that is what they did!

'Those trees were marvels, and with some it took a few men holding outstretched hands to surround them. Once at an *arroyo* by the Guayabo – you know the little Guayabo River on the way to Los Pinares? – whose water is still pure and delicious, right near there I saw a caoba cut down, so large I thought it would take ten men to embrace it. Old man, I asked my father, why did they cut it down when this little arroyo does not get sufficient water in spring to float it? And my old man explained that they could quarter it and if it still did not move, they could slice it again. Do you know what I think such a tree would be worth now? I would say ten to twelve thousand pesos!

'Those were the days when people were run off their own lands – though they had papers dating back to colonial days to show it was theirs – because corrupt officials would sell the land to La United. They began their measurements of huge tracts with just a millimetre off at the start, but when the line was extended to a distance that little millimetre widened out to become whole towns and farms. You may ask yourself what a pass we had come to that eventually we had to beg La United for a tiny bit of land to have a cemetery! It was these things that made me have a certain view of life.

'I have always had ideas that have put me in the left wing, not Communist, you know, but left wing. I am what you could call a tame left-winger, for I have always known that what makes men is economic and political interests and passions of the heart, and that it is no use intervening in these factors. What do men seek but to dominate others and impose their wills? And I have known that it is futile to come between men and these aspirations. I have always wanted peace and reasonable fraternity between men, an end to those interests which create injustices. This was but a foolishness of mine, for it could not be.

'Yet listen to how, being a tame leftist, I came to a laughable pass. I had been an *alzado*, a rebel, here in 1918, another foolishness, for there was no difference between the group in power and the group out of power; but some of us took to the monte in rebellion, not knowing that these were two bourgeois parties, whose differences were simply the different personal ambitions of the leaders. I did not know this then, I learned it later with the Revolution – the Revolution has taught Cubans many things. Cubans have never liked to work, for example, because we have always seen that to get ahead or to gain this or that you do not work, you do it through friends, never through sustained study or work but always by the proper cultivation of friendships and politicking.

'It was not difficult to see this because men, by and large, speak what is on their souls. Sometimes they repeat what they have heard or what they think you want to hear, but in the main, men say what is on their hearts. And so it was, listening to men, that I thought, All this will never end: it will always be these interests which will rule men. That is what it was like with my first experience of revolution and with the Machadato in the twenties and again in 1933 and then with Grau and Batista. Why should I hope?

'The Revolution triumphed here, and during the first months I said to myself, It is the same thing: so-and-so wanted to be mayor, and the judges were still the same ones who had been selling themselves, and all the same people were scurrying around to maintain their positions or change to another, for there *were* a lot of vacancies. And the time passed and before I noticed it very intransigent things happened. The Revolution said to La United, You have to go, I say you have to go and you will go, man. And so it happened. La United went – incredible!

'And Cubans who do not like to work go off in droves to cut cane for nothing, fifty per cent real volunteers full of enthusiasm and fifty per cent – well, they go, carried along by the others and catching some of their enthusiasm for the while. For it is wonderful how the government does this. It does not grab anyone and say, Here, you have to cut cane. Oh no, for no one is forced any more. They go instead to a work centre and say, It is our hope and need that three or four here will go cut cane. They say this to someone who is responsible, and they are the ones who by psychology and their own enthusiasm find three or four and even more to go.

'So it was that three years ago I suddenly came to this laughable pass that all the things I had learned in a lifetime were superseded. There is a real revolution, and those woods will never again be cut down and shipped away to make money for someone else. Of course they are not there, you cannot replace that fine wood in a short time – it was the work of centuries – but they are planting everywhere and scientifically, and the pines and the fruit trees grow faster and bear sooner. See those houses behind you, old and crooked like me, they are going to be cut down and there will be a malecón to walk on and look at the view!'

'I know what you are going to say,' I said to Dr Morales when we had left Felix Estol. 'You are going to say that Mayarí has a reason for coming into being, but none for existing under socialism, right?'

'Right,' he said.

One of the mornings when Dr Morales was lecturing to the staffs of the Mayarí hospital and of near-by hospitals and clinics, I walked into the Administración Regional to ask them the question. The Regional Administration governs – it is often referred to as the *poder regional* (the regional power) – this northern stretch of Oriente on the Atlantic, and Mayarí is one of its fourteen municipalities. Its offices are on Carlos Manuel de Céspedes Street, the second most important street in Mayarí and parallel to Leyte Vidal, on the corner of Maximo Gomez, a block away from the pizzeria under construction. Céspedes was the leader of the Revolution of 1868, and Gomez a general in that revolt, as well as in the Ten Years War ending in 1878 and in the successful one of 1898; Leyte Vidal was a landowner of the Mayarí area who joined the revolt of 1868. The weight of these names lies lightly on that corner: sidewalks are broken; the rows of luxuriant trees have to be trimmed almost to shrubbery height to keep them from the low-hanging electrical wires; there is a wooden candy-stand directly across one entrance to the Administración Regional's offices; the local bus takes up almost the entire width of the street when it goes by; and the Administración's offices are in a one-storey stucco building against which people lean to chat or into which they wander with no sense of awe.

The first time I walked in I took the entrance on Maximo Gomez because there were counters here behind which were scattered desks that gave it the formal air of a reception office (on Céspedes the entrance was into a small office and it seemed more private), but I was to learn that you could walk in and out of any entrance without being stopped. Only if you hesitated would anyone question you, and then it was simply to help. If you knew your way, you could walk undisturbed to a back corner office where the President of the Region could sometimes be found. There was an old desk there behind which he sat, another for his secretary, a battered couch and a couple of wooden chairs. There was a toilet and wash-basin in a closet-size room which could only be reached through the President's office, and no one ever hesitated to use it with no more leave than a greeting to whoever was in the room.

Behind the desk was a window on to a back yard common to three buildings, and to the right another window which gave on to an alley between the Administración's offices and the Federation of Cuban Women's place; along the alley people walked and sometimes addressed people in the offices on either side of it. When the old phone on the desk rang, the President answered it as soon as he had a chance; it would have to ring a long time before anyone picked it up for him. There was no incoming or outgoing basket on the desk, no piles of papers, no letters to sign, no clue that whoever sat behind it could not be interrupted for information, help or just a pleasant chat. The President, Alfredo Beccles, was a tall Negro, as relaxed and casual as his office but with a dignity that the Administración headquarters never achieved.

There were two small rooms leading out of the President's offices to Céspedes Street, and the Secretary of the Region, Antonio Salomon, came in from one of them when I introduced myself. I was to find out that one was seldom without the other and that they spent more time travelling around their

region than in the office. Everyone knew them although few
knew their formal titles; Salomon, being of Lebanese descent,
was called El Moro, and Beccles, who is of Jamaican descent,
was called Soní, which is the way Cubans pronounce the
nickname Sonny.

El Moro came from Cueto and Soní from Cayo Mambí,
and this may have been the reason they enjoyed my question so
much. They simply leaned back and laughed, and El Moro
looked at Soní and said, 'Yes, what reason *does* Mayarí have
for being!'

Soní explained that Mayarí was now the head of the region,
a natural because of its position in relation to all the towns. In
the town proper there were some 8,000 people and in the
municipality, which includes all the outlying areas, some
18,000. But of course, towns could now be planned with more
logic than Mayarí. The little village of Levisa near by on the
approach to Nicaro had a planned future: it was to be the
town for the workers in the mines, the nickel plants and
the iron mills which were in the designing stage. It should not
matter then which way the wind blew, for the fine, pervasive
dust from the chimneys would not reach the homes of the
workers.

Soní knew Nicaro well, and the first steady job he got was
there; until then he had worked in the cane-fields, seasonal
work during the harvest, and the rest of the time scrounging
around like most men of the region. But at twenty-four, in
1952, he got his first steady job, as gardener for the Niedermeyers at the fine kind of home that the United States
government supplied for the managers and technicians of the
different companies represented in the operations at Nicaro. Mr
Niedermeyer was the representative of the National Lead
Company, and so he had one of the large homes along the side
of the cape that was away from the nickel plant and its belching smoke-stacks. For several years Soní, who had not been
able to attend school beyond the second grade, worked as a
gardener.

While El Moro went out to discuss a problem that had arisen about the emergency aqueduct for the hospital and the Bitirí, Soní talked about his past in a sweet English which was a mixture of Jamaican and Southern, for the Niedermeyers were from Texas. 'We established relationships of mutual respect,' he said. 'They knew after a while that if they said anything to me about another worker, that I would only listen, that I would not say anything about them. Also, they got to trust me. They said to me – I do not know if this is true – that in Mexico and in other Latin American countries where they had lived, that every day they had to lock up everything and count the silver. Alfredo, they said to me, why is it you Cubans are not like that?'

I was to see Soní very often while I was in Mayarí, and the only time that I heard the name Alfredo used by anyone was in the conversations that he reported having had with the Niedermeyers; I never pointed it out to him, but it seemed to me this was one intimacy he would not allow them. All that had happened long ago but Soní still wondered about it, and he asked me again if they had been truthful when they told him that servants in other countries could not be trusted. When I told him that might well be, he shook his head, it seemed so strange to him.

'I suppose they trusted me then,' he continued, 'because once they went back to Laredo on leave for four months and they left me alone in the house. Their children were so close to me, I was like family to them. They were building the swimming-pool in that section then and little Johnny used to say, "Mommie, I can't wait for the pool to be finished so I can go swimming with Alfredo." Yet I knew Alfredo would never swim in that pool. There was one Italo-American there – is that how you say it? – who said to me right out, "Alfredo, I don't want to see you near this pool because if you accidentally fall in it you will stain it."

'I don't know if I am expressing myself right, if you understand what I mean by that. You see, in Cuba when we say

Negro it is a friendly thing. If I say, Hello *negra*, how are you? – it is the sweetest term of endearment I could use.

'Once I made a sailboat for little Johnny, a toy one he could float, and he was so proud of it he took it to school. They had a school at Nicaro for the American children, and little Johnny came back and told me, for he told me everything and this bothered him, that the teacher had shown it to the class and said that Negroes were very good at that kind of thing, because they weren't capable of learning and education. "Is that a fact, Alfredo?" – that's what little Johnny asked me.

'Well, the Niedermeyers were very nice to me, they really liked me, I do believe. But I always knew that after all I was just a Negro to them. Do you know what I mean? When they left for good, they wanted to take me with them, and when I said no, Mr Niedermeyer got me a job in the factory. That was nice, because I certainly didn't want to be a gardener any more. Still, I always knew what I was and in my family from childhood I had always been rebellious.'

Soní began to hear talk of rebellion after the 1953 assault on the Moncada in Santiago, but it was not until 1957, when someone at the factory handed him a copy of the statement by the students who tried to assassinate Batista, that he made contact with the 26 of July Movement. 'What do you think of it?' the man asked him. Soní read it and said he liked it. 'Well, let us talk, then,' the man said, and they talked. Soon Soní found that all sorts of people he didn't know began to greet him, others stopped to chat. When the fighting in the Sierra Maestra began in earnest, Soní thought more and more of going to the monte. The Movement approved, and he went back to Cayo Mambí and persuaded a group of friends to collect guns and rifles and take to the monte with him. That was early in 1958, before Raul opened the second front in northern Oriente, and Soní didn't remember many discussions of politics, though he imagined that socialism and issues like that were discussed at higher levels.

'I was out to see Batista brought down,' Soní said. 'There

are compañeros who say that even in the fighting or early in
the Revolution they had a notion, a knowledge of some sort of
what was coming, but for me I can tell you I didn't know any
such thing. I wanted what Fidel wanted. If you had asked me
then, I would have said, I want whatever Fidel wants, and
there's still a bit of that in my thinking. Why not? What do
you think of Fidel? Isn't he a man out of the ordinary?

'After the Revolution I still did not discuss the issue of communism. If someone came to me and talked about it, I would
say, I don't know anything about that – I am for what Fidel
wants. Then, of course, began the revolutionary process, and
Fidel explained this so well that by the time Playa Girón
[the Bay of Pigs invasion] came, I was ready to understand
and accept socialism. But I do not know if I can explain this or
even if there is real truth in it – in the monte the life we led
was of such complete equality it was like communism. If
someone came with a package of food, as sometimes happened,
before it got to Soní, Soní knew that it was to be opened and
equally divided, and if one man was out on a mission his share
was put aside and when he returned it would be there.
Though most of the time we were hungry and that little share
waiting for some compañero we could have well used.'

Nor was it that if four packages of cigarettes arrived, Soní
put one in his pocket and distributed the other three among
his compañeros. No, every pack was divided up and if it came
to two cigarettes each, Soní got two cigarettes and no more.
'There was a feeling among the compañeros there in the
monte that I shall never forget. And if I have to go elsewhere
to fight like that I shall do it gladly. Not because I like killing,
it has nothing to do with killing.'

'Yes, yes,' said El Moro. He had come back into the room
and heard this last, and he nodded to Soní. How true, he
seemed to say, it had all been foreshadowed.

When I asked them what they did now, they became very
businesslike. The Administración, whether on a regional or a
municipal level, deals in services which they explained are

divided into two responsible areas: distribution to the public
and construction of communal services. The Ministry of Construction (Micons) is responsible for major projects, and the
Administración lends Micons help with problems it meets in
their area. But the Administración also engages in minor
construction in the region, sometimes with technical advice
from Micons – parks, emergency housing, maintenance of
shops that they administer. And Micons never carries through
any plans in their area without the Administración having
a say.

Until three years ago, all activity was subject to national
control; that is, the Havana ministries governed and adminis-
tered vertically, so that at the local level everything had to be
referred back to the capital. It was paralysing. The separation
of responsibilities made for bureaucratic delays, for a division
of labour that separated rather than united the community,
and kept the people from becoming directly involved in
planning. With decentralization have come more democratic
practices. At one time the construction of the aqueduct would
have been solely the responsibility of Micons, whereas now the
municipality and the region were involved in carrying it
through. El Moro, as a matter of fact, was responsible with
Sarmiento, a young man I was yet to meet who was the head of
the municipality and the equivalent of the mayor of Mayarí,
for an emergency aqueduct to supply water to the hospital, the
Bitirí and a block of apartment buildings called La Reforma
Urbana: a project of local initiative which was to be the subject of much grumbling and joking during my three months in
Mayarí.

With decentralization came the idea of the *asambleas* – the
assemblies – as base and checkpoint for all organized activities.
For the Administración Regional this meant the calling of
meetings in every municipality twice a year, at which the entire population could attend to hear, discuss and suggest bud-
gets and work plans. The first assembly in Mayarí took place
in 1965, the second in the summer of 1965; the next would

be the summer of 1967. The one which was to have taken place the month before I spoke to Soní was changed to a meeting of the 278 delegates from all the microdistricts of the region: with the sugar harvest under way, it was decided that it would be unwise to lose a day, particularly in a region so dense with sugar cane.

The 1966 summer assembly was held on a Sunday morning at the baseball field some two blocks from the Bitirí, and about one thousand people attended. Soní was very disappointed with the turn-out but was heartened by the fact that smaller communities in the region had turn-outs of three and four thousand because they held their assemblies at night. Mayarí's next assembly would be at night. Did people get up and speak? I asked. Oh yes, said Soní. The biggest criticism was the municipality's failure to install some street lights that were in the work plan. I laughed, it seemed so unimportant, but El Moro said it was an important matter and the street lights were put in immediately.

In between assemblies, the supervision of the work plan and the implementation of criticism are carried on by the different commissions into which the 278 delegates of the region are divided. At first, these were specific works commissions responsible for, say, parks or roads, but the Administración has learned the lesson of decentralization and has now made them zonal or district commissions, responsible for all the types of services in their district. 'It was like Fidel's example of the tree that falls across the road,' said El Moro. 'No one cleared it away because it was no particular commission's responsibility.'

Soní went over to a file and selected, from a pile, the report that was given at the summer assembly at Nicaro. 'You want to pick another?' he asked me, and I shook my head. He then began to read it aloud to show me what one was like, and as soon as he read an item announcing that some work plan had not been met, he looked up at me and smiled, to show he had been honest. As he read, his voice got a formal tone and his phrasing became measured, and I could see that the year he had spent at the Party school in 1965 had included a course in public speaking. Later I was not to be so sure, for I found at local meetings that ordinary participants could get up and speak in the same way, finding also a vocabulary for such occasions that was a radical departure from conversational speech.

There was no reference in the report to international or national politics, no rhetorical flourishes; it was a dry, detailed listing of the work planned, that accomplished and the new goals. A speech which was all mundane details, and I interrupted to say it must be difficult to hold an audience with that. Soní smiled understandingly, but El Moro said, 'Oh no, this is what interests people.' Soní nodded, and said that it was a new experience for Cubans to have their leaders account to them for things that were happening in their own town. Before, they simply heard about appropriations for roads, schools, hospitals that never materialized.

Perhaps the only personal and ideological part of the report was the introductory remarks: *el responsable*, as Cubans today call the leader of any organization whether his title is president, mayor, administrator or manager, said that the most important failing they had encountered in the previous six months was their own lack of experience in administration. This was another sign of the need for decentralization, for developing leadership at the local level and involving the masses in the needs of the community. At the end of the report, in the section dealing with new goals, he listed education of the delegates and the setting up of a specialized school.

The report then listed the work accomplished: hours of voluntary work done by citizens of Nicaro, breaking it down by projects, such as new quarters for bachelors working at the plant, the children's playground, the new roof on the school, repairs, necessitated by Hurricane Inez, the town park; the funerals paid for by the municipality for families without means; the equipment lent to other communities; the houses built; the progress of parks and sports fields, and the paving of streets and clearing of unhealthy areas; the metres of garbage collected; the number and variety of trees planted; the clothing and food distributed free to families who had suffered from the hurricane. In each case, the exact percentage of the work plan realized was cited, and wherever the plan was not met, an explanation was given and a new time-table set. In most cases, the failure to meet the plan was due to equipment not being delivered on time.

Anticipating criticism, the report listed twenty-four items that the Administración in Nicaro set themselves as new goals. Besides educating the leaders to become better administrators, they hoped to get 2,000 volunteers to cut cane during the coming harvest; clear large areas of weeds and undergrowth and plant 10,000 trees and 10,000 garden plants; clear a minimum of 6,500 metres of trash from the streets; cooperate with three mass organizations to ensure cleanliness and neat appearance of homes; speed up distribution of rationed goods; repair the pool at Nicaro; improve transportation within Nicaro and to outlying communities; cooperate with Public Health on hygienic conditions, which meant in the main discouraging families from raising pigs around their houses or at least getting them to tie up the pigs so they could not roam at will. Besides this, they were going to coordinate cultural activities with the Regional de Cultura, to entice more groups, I suspected, to Nicaro.

One of their goals particularly interested me: to prevent 'clandestine homes'. I looked from Soní to El Moro: 'Clandestine homes? Have you got counter-revolutionaries hiding out in Nicaro?'

I had an idea what was meant by clandestine homes, but I put the question the way I did because in Cuba being provocative is a way of being witty. With officials I always pretended to be looking for counter-revolutionaries or to interpret local opinions as anti-revolutionary; not Soní, but most responded by explaining every problem as the result of the blockade. Most often they were playing closer to the truth than I was, but one joke a volunteer cane-cutter told me while we were stacking cane one Sunday morning pleased me and everyone I repeated it to: a funeral orator kept referring to the dead man as a victim of imperialism until someone protested, 'Compañero, he was run over by a car!' 'Yes,' answered the orator, 'a Ford!'

'Clandestine houses,' said Soní, 'are houses people build without permission wherever they find a place they like.'

'And once they move into them, you cannot get them out,' added El Moro. 'They are a real problem.'

Our conversation had been interrupted many times during my first short visit to the Administración – men from a cooperative who wanted help in finding wood for a project they had undertaken voluntarily, someone looking for a ride to Los Pinares, four cane-cutters who just dropped in to tell how they were doing, a soldier who needed black paint and was willing to exchange some extra white they didn't need – but this time Soní was reminded he was due at Party headquarters for a meeting, and El Moro was eager to be off in the Administración jeep to see how the emergency aqueduct was doing.

I told El Moro I hoped this emergency aqueduct meant that I'd soon be able to bathe at the Bitirí whenever I wanted and not have to hang around in the afternoon for the municipal truck to come by with water for the cistern. 'In seven days we shall have it completed,' he said. 'You can count them. We decided that we can do it ourselves. No waiting for Micons to give us an engineer – we shall pump the water out of the Guayabo directly and lay new pipes up to the main leading to the hospital, the Bitirí and the Reforma Urbana. It occurred to us the other day, for otherwise we would have to wait for the new aqueduct to be completed, and with the shortage of hands that is going to take a long time.'

El Moro was to regret that speech, but at that moment it made both of us very happy. And when I next ran into him and Soní, five days later on a Sunday afternoon, I forgot to ask him about it because I had just discovered for myself the

largest group of clandestine homes in Mayarí. I had taken a
walk up to Loma Rebelde – Rebel Hill – to look at the view
of the town, the river and the valley climbing into the mountains, an idea I'd got from Jaime Hernandez, an old man
who owned a juice stand on Maceo, the street I always took
from the Bitirí to Leyte Vidal.

Hernandez lived in an old wooden house which, like many
others, had had a stucco front plastered on it, so that it looked
grander than it was. On the stucco front, he had painted signs,
on one side, urging people to eat Cuban fruits; on the other,
lauding science and industry; both primitively illustrated. He
had turned the front of the house into two rooms with a low
dividing wall six feet high which still allowed you to look from
one to the other; one room was a refreshment stand, the other
the family living-room. Depending on what was available, he
sold fresh fruit juices for ten cents a glass.

On the wall behind the counter was a large painting entitled 'Imaginary Landscape: The Roads of Life'; at its centre
was a farmhouse with a wide road near by, a lane leading to
the farmhouse, and a winding river. The window of the farmhouse was cut out, for at one time Hernandez used to light it
up at night and he hung a tiny bulb in the window. It was the
work of a primitive, and Hernandez had painted it; he was
fifty-seven and had begun painting three years ago. 'A lady
came by and admired it one day,' he said, 'and told me I
should call it The Roads of Life because it showed the many
ways people could travel.' Since then, Hernandez had hung a
toy airplane from the ceiling at the level of the blue sky and
white cumulus clouds.

On a side wall was a smaller painting of the Bay of Havana,
copied from a photograph in the weekly *Bohemia*, and under-
neath it a little handwritten sign which said, *Art, like the
thoughts of men, should be looked at from the point of view of
the soul that painted it*. But the painting that interested me the
most was a large unfinished mural in the living-room, where
Hernandez took me to see it. It was a landscape with Mayarí

in the foreground, and in the background the meadow and mountains one saw from the breaks in the houses on Leyte Vidal. Hernandez had gone up to Loma Rebelde, a lovely hill one could see from any spot in Mayarí, and drawn it in pencil first. It contained every house and street, and Hernandez worried that if building continued he would never finish it. 'All my life I hoped I would get a scholarship to study painting, and now my son is in Havana on scholarship, but he is interested in sculpting!'

The sun was hot that Sunday morning; the paths leading to Loma Rebelde were not an easy climb and soon became a forty-five-degree angle. I passed an old woman and commented, in the way Cubans in the country have of addressing each other though unacquainted, 'It is a hot day.' The woman sighed and answered, '*Ave Maria purisima!*' and went on into town. On the way towards the top, I kept pausing and looking back to check on the accuracy of Hernandez's mural, and children detached themselves from the houses and followed me because of my camera.

The houses here were flimsy and dreadfully ugly, put together with old worn wood, pieces of tin, wooden crates – all of it unpainted. What trees there were had been there long ago, and since Loma Rebelde had once been pasture land that belonged to two local landowners, there were very few, so that the loose sows lay somnolent in the thin strips of shade around the ramshackle houses, the piglets running and snuffling about. There was no order to the houses, some close together, others widely separated; some faced the dirt road squarely, others at an angle, and none seemed to have a garden nor fences to denote where the pebbly grounds of one began and the other's ended. The outhouses stood apart in the bare grounds, and it was hard to tell which went with what house. But when one looked away, the view was glorious.

Coming down, one of the women standing outside the houses said to me, 'You have made the children happy taking their picture.' She was tanned, her hair had blondish glints, and she held a light-skinned Negro baby in her arms; it made her laugh when I replied, the other women came forward, and the children gave up their play to listen. I took a photograph of them, and they laughed even more.

The woman who spoke first was named Adelaida, and she told me most of them had moved to Loma Rebelde after Hurricane Flora. 'Nature has turned bad the last few years, that is the problem,' she said. 'Otherwise Mayarí would be very beautiful. It is not only that the wooden houses are old but that Flora inundated them with mud. And then Inez last year – oh what it would be like if not for them!'

Everyone had told them that up on the hill there would be no way to get water. 'But the Administración comes up all the way – the trucks get up this road – two or three times a week and they fill the drums for thirty cents. So you see, we do all right.'

'That is important, especially for you women,' I said, meaning they needed it for housework.

'Oh, that is the truth, we women cannot do without it for an hour!' said Adelaida. 'Otherwise they think we have got codfish in the house!' They doubled with laughter at that, the children too. And Margarita, who was thirty-one, said, 'Stop flirting, Adelaida, just because the men are away cutting cane.'

Adelaida laughed at that; she was forty-one and considered herself old. And she had five children, but she considered that few. 'All the families around here are large – there is nothing else to do. I am a little backward, but Margarita married at fourteen and now has five too.'

A third volunteered, 'I am married fourteen years and I have six!'

Two of Adelaida's children were on scholarships – *becados* – one at the school for the fishing fleet at Playa Girón, and I told her I had visited it and liked it. Margarita said to her, 'You ought to go on a visit, Adelaida.'

'Oh, there are the other children to take care of, it is a long trip and it costs forty dollars. But some day ... Now I want the three others to get becados. At the Secundaria [junior high school] they take them from seven to six in the afternoon and they get a fine lunch, milk and meat and all. They are like semi-live-in students. You know what a relief that is to a mother? And our men ... in the old days if your man was not at home, you worried that he was beaten up or dead. Now if they are not home at midnight or even three in the morning, you have no worry. So let them have their forty-one shots of rum, they make it home somehow. Or if they get drunk, they pick them up and let them sleep it off or give them a cold shower. But they never give them a beating – they do not even touch them or jail them.'

'Look at me, I have already made four dollars today,' said Margarita. 'I got up at six, took care of the children and washed the clothes and made four dollars. When could I have made that before? Not even four cents!'

Adelaida pointed to a clothes-line across the road. 'Look, there are the clothes drying already!' And they all laughed, as if they'd put one over on fate.

It was then I saw the large cement cistern behind one house, the sturdiest structure on Loma Rebelde. 'We sold our motor bike,' said Adelaida, 'and built it.'

'So you have water all the time?' I said.

'And my neighbours too, for there are times the Municipal truck does not get up here.' Her neighbours looked at her and nodded and looked at me and nodded again. We were silent a moment, and then Adelaida shifted the baby to her other arm. 'Of course, there are some problems still here – you know, the Municipal helped with tin and some cement when we started making our houses – but there are no problems the Revolution cannot resolve. Yes, there are no barriers we cannot overcome.'

I went down Loma Rebelde on the other side, past the new grammar school, through the neighbourhood called El Naranjal, where in truth there are no orange trees, and crossed the little bridge over a tiny arroyo. At the beginning of Céspedes

Street, Soní stopped his jeep alongside me, and El Moro, who
sat next to him, asked if I had found any counter-revolutionaries. I told him I had found the clandestine houses up on
Loma Rebelde but that the inhabitants had all turned out to
be strong revolutionaries. El Moro grimaced. 'You know the
trouble they give us?' he said. 'Our trucks are old and hard to
keep in repair and they have to go up that hill with water.'

I got in the jeep with them and Soní drove slowly, pointing
out the old houses in Mayarí, the ones they hoped to tear
down to build a new bus station on the site – 'All these things
we want to get rid of, that's why we don't like to see houses
like that on Loma Rebelde.' He kept on driving past Leyte
Vidal until the paving stopped and the road was uneven
gravel; this was El Cocal, the neighbourhood without coco-
nuts, and Soní and El Moro had come to check on a neighbourhood project to build a fence along the road.

For several blocks along the road the fence until recently
had been a thick, tall hedge of mayas, the prickly bush that
looked like pineapple, but the neighbourhood, like much of
Mayarí, had long been plagued with rats and they discovered
the rats were nesting in the maya hedge. The Committees for
the Defence of the Revolution of those blocks voted to clear
out the mayas and asked the Administración for posts and
wire to replace them.

'See how they have cleaned out the whole area,' said El
Moro. 'Every bit of it with volunteer labour – they cleared
thirty-five truckloads of mayas! – and now they are going to
plant trees when the fence is finished.'

Soní had slowed down in order to greet the men who were
stringing wire from post to post, and one came over and told
him that they needed more wire. 'Sarmiento told me,' Soní
said, 'and we got some from Micons. It should be here soon – I
thought it already was, I was checking on it.'

'It better come soon,' the man said. 'We want to finish this
Sunday.'

When we drove away, Soní said, 'You may think we do

things in a very disorganized way here, and we do need to organize better. But it's also good to just go ahead and do things even when they are not in the work plan, expecially if the masses want them. See, on that corner there, the neighbourhood is going to build a place for a general store because there is none near them. We just give them the material and some construction man to design it.'

We passed a little truck carrying more wire out to El Cocal and that made Soní feel good. I said to him, 'You like the job, don't you?'

'Oh yes,' he said; he smiled and looked away and kept smiling: Soní liked a question that allowed him to say what, as he would put it, was on his soul. When he talked again, it was understood between us that he had taken up the thread of our last talk, when he had talked of the experience in the monte that was like communism.

'Well, now we have responsibilities, and we must do what is needed. I like my work very much, but a man must not fall in love with his job. I do not know if you see what I mean. A man who falls in love with his job thinks only he can do it well, when we and the Party are now making substitutes for everyone and everything. A man in love with his job begins to do it badly, because he begins to think that whatever he did was the best that could be done. Do you know what I mean? – I don't know if I express myself well.'

3. The Practice of Medicine

Dr Morales, the surgeon from Havana, arrived at the Bitirí
the evening of my first day there, and I met him at lunch the
next day, after he had reported to the hospital that morning.
He wore his militia uniform – army fatigue pants with huge
patch pockets, a blue denim shirt, heavy Soviet army boots
which the Cubans call rockcrushers – and sat alone at a table,
a dour expression on his face making him look rather forbid-
ding. The moment I addressed a casual remark to him,
however, he flashed a brilliant smile. He was tall, slim, even-
featured, with a wide moustache and large black eyes framed
by long, curled, feminine lashes: the Hollywood Latin Lover
of the thirties. But Morales was a Communist, serious and
lighthearted by turns, the changes sometimes taking place so
rapidly that they constituted a kind of wit of his own. The
militia uniform was his seriousness, and after that first morning he did not wear it again to the hospital. Some weeks
later, Dr Padrón, the director of the hospital, who admired
Morales greatly, said, 'You should have seen how we looked at
him. No one said anything, but the Martyrs of Mayarí Hospital is not the trenches. I like to keep a neat hospital – ladies in
white coats, men in white jackets, all starched and proper.'

Morales was thirty-six, one of the last class to get their
medical degrees before Batista closed down the University of
Havana, and he had married a girl of his class, or in any case,
a girl who expected to lead a certain kind of social life. Before
– *antes*, Morales always said (and smiled) when he meant the
days before Batista fell – a doctor was automatically bound
for the upper middle class. But Morales and his two brothers,
sons of a small landowner from Las Villas province, began as
sympathizers for the 26 of July Movement, led by Castro and
named after the date, in 1953, when they attacked the military

barracks in Santiago, and have remained with the Revolution.
Yet many friends and relatives left and some are waiting to
leave, and Morales' wife would too if he showed the slightest
inclination. He forgets this sometimes, however, as he did two
years ago when he came home and announced elatedly that he
had been voted Exemplary Worker at an *asamblea* at the hospital.

'Dear God, dear God,' his wife moaned. 'The only misfor-
tune that had yet to befall us – they will now make you a member of the Party!'

Morales said to me, 'It is strange – isn't it? – the process of
the Revolution.' *El proceso de la Revolución* is a phrase con-
stantly on people's lips, one which usually makes them pause,
for it makes it possible for them to stand off and look at what
has happened to them in a few years. 'In 1958, I told a fellow
student in the Movement that I expected our Movement would
establish a decent constitutional government and he said to me,
Is that all you think this enormous effort will accomplish? It
was then I got my first suspicion of the process set in motion.
Who would have thought that it would take us to socialism and
me to the Party!'

Since the government would no longer allow doctors to go
to the country to cut cane full time for the Playa Girón fortnight (this year they expected, when the anniversary of the Bay
of Pigs victory came round, that volunteers would go for forty-
five days), Morales had volunteered to help in rural medicine;
most of the doctors at his Havana hospital had also and
Morales was taking the first turn at it. After this initial visit
to the hospital, he was afraid it was going to be tedious; he
had scheduled operations for two days hence with the young
surgeon there, discussed the two lectures he would give the
staff during the only time they would have available while he
was in Mayarí, and now there was nothing more to do. In
Havana his days were filled with his work as assistant director of the hospital, surgery, outpatient consultations, teaching,
Party meetings. 'I did not come for a vacation,' he said. 'I

think I shall go to Public Health and offer my services – a courtesy call is in order, in any case. Then there is the Party, I should drop in on them . . .'

I took him to these places; he loved the idea of my being his guide. 'No, no, do not buy a straw hat!' he said, when he saw me looking at some on a street corner. 'You already have a camera – with a straw hat too it would be *like before!*' He brought me bits of information about Public Health's problems, got me rides with them up to Los Pinares, where a horticultural project had been started, discussed the medical and sanitation problems they could expect in this virgin mesa when several hundred students and twelve thousand women were settled there. 'Already, they are very sad at Public Health – rats have shown up and there are cases of flu, things totally unknown at Los Pinares.' He shook his head gravely, then suddenly reached over and slapped my knee. 'We are taking the first doctor up there tomorrow – I got you a ride – and you know what his speciality is? Gynaecology!' And he burst into laughter.

Talking about Castro's February speech to the steelworkers who in three weeks, working many hours without a stop on a volunteer basis, constructed heavy ploughs, graders and bull-dozing equipment for the spring clearing and planting, Morales said, 'The concept of cost accounting is disappearing with socialism.' I told him that with Libermanism in the Soviet Union it seemed just the contrary; from the way he listened he appeared not to have heard about it. 'That is very interesting,' he said, when I told him about the Czechs' concentration, which I had noted during my visit to Prague a couple of months earlier, on making enterprises pay their own way; it bothered him that another socialist country could be so different, but he repeated, 'That is very interesting, very interesting.'

His eyes lit up. 'You know what I finally say to all those relatives and friends who leave to your country? After we have discussed this and that and come to no agreement, I finally say, Are you not interested in this fascinating process? How can you leave and not stay to watch these extraordinary developments?'

Everything interested him. The horticultural project in Los Pinares, the coffee plantations up in the mountains, my own project. And while waiting for the water to be turned on to take a shower, he'd be busy observing or talking to the chambermaids, Angela and Margarita. 'Either eight hours is too long a shift,' he said to them, 'or there is not enough work here for the two of you.' They laughed; so did he; but in a while he had managed to have a discussion with them about their work that made them feel important and valuable.

He would pursue an observation of mine and come back a few hours later with more information. I had said the girls in Mayarí – or at least at the Bitirí, for this was during my first week there – seemed all to have married and had children and divorced by twenty, and he was taken enough with it to report back immediately on one, then another, until he decided, yes, there was definitely a pattern. 'It is a combination of innocence and sensuality – this heat!' and he laughed. 'But they are good girls and their moral sense is remarkable. Yet take Angela, she has a six-month-old boy, is divorced, she says, but she was telling me that she had not come down this month yet – that is their expression for their periods – and she has already given herself two abortions. Obviously, her husband cannot be the responsible party. These country girls seem more relaxed about sex, I guess that is what it is. But when it comes to their children you will see how responsible they are, how devoted.'

The third day after we met, he came by my room in the morning and took me off to the hospital with him. 'We have to do something about your One Hundred Eleven,' he said. One Hundred Eleven was the name given the flu going the rounds in Mayarí because 'it began with one, stayed with one, and finished one' – in Spanish the pun worked better. My head was big with it, my chest clogged, and I trudged with Morales up

the street – which soon became a road – that the bus from Holguín came down. There was a lumber yard beyond the Bitirí
(where they decided, seeing me with Morales, that I was a
pediatrician and spread the news), then a tiny bridge where the
Mayarí River was a thin stream; to the left of the road the
houses and the hospital were all stucco and new, built since
the Revolution; to the right, all ramshackle and old, 'the inheritance of capitalism,' said Morales. On the edge of the road
were the ditches opened for the new aqueduct and pipes laid
alongside.

The Martyrs of Mayarí Hospital – built after the Revolution; there was none before – was a three-storey building in the
shape of an H, one long side set back about ten yards from
the road, the other, towards the back, facing open fields and
the town cemetery. Morales and I caught the tail end of a
funeral procession as it turned into the side road beyond the
hospital that leads to the cemetery; like all I was to see,
the procession consisted of an open car with the coffin and
flowers, and relatives and friends on foot. From balconies
on the second and third floors, patients in pyjamas
watched.

I said to Morales, 'That is no place for a cemetery – it must
depress the patients to see the funerals.'

'It depresses the doctors even more!' he replied, and burst
into laughter.

We didn't enter the hospital through the tall glass doors of
the lobby – they are always kept closed or the relatives of hospital patients would camp there waiting for news – but
through the outpatient clinic entrance. The reception room
there was one large one with benches, a desk for the woman
who assigned people their turns, and posters on the walls giving the health statistics of the region. The benches were taken,
groups stood about talking, and in the hallway beyond, on
either side of which were the consultation rooms, people sat
waiting and also stood, so that it was like a crowded New York
subway; we had to pick our way through it past curious and

friendly townspeople and campesinos to the doors at the end
that led into the lobby of the hospital.

There it was quiet and orderly, and Morales introduced Dr
Padrón, who had already finished his *paso del salón clínico*,
the morning visit to each bed on the clinical floor. He was a
thin, black young man, formal and unruffled, equable and
pleasant, a Havana man like Morales but with apparently none
of his easy *camaraderie* or slanginess. He was on his way to his
office, but as soon as he stopped to talk to us he was besieged
by several people. It was only a month and a half since he had
come to Mayarí, but he seemed fully in command: telling me
that aerosol penicillin inhalation would help me immediately;
informing Morales of the final arrangements for his lectures;
instructing the administrator about a corner of the grounds
that needed to be cleared; asking whether the Municipal had
called about the emergency aqueduct; promising a photo of
himself, for his military I.D. card, to a young Army man, an
encounter he put to more practical use by adroitly making the
soldier decide on a schedule for physicals for recruits. All these
things he did calmly in turn, until detaching himself from the
administrator, he led me down another corridor to the emergency room. There he left me in the hands of a nurse.

My head cleared, but I spent the morning looking up people
and talking, so that the good effects of the inhalation were gone
by one in the afternoon. I was having lunch at the Bitirí, and
one of the girls, who had just got over the flu, recommended
tetracycline for mine: my first encounter with the Cubans'
self-prescribing enthusiasm. 'Two capsules to start with and
then one every four hours,' she said. 'Also, an aspirin each time
you take a pill. With this One Hundred Eleven you have got to
meet force with force.' I thought of how aghast our family doctor in New York would be at the use of such strong antibiotics
for anything but serious infections, and set off for the big pharmacy on Leyte Vidal.

It was a busy, well-stocked pharmacy. Cuba, of course, has
no basic chemical industry, and the subsidiaries of foreign

pharmaceutical companies before the Revolution confined their operations to simple subdividing, tableting and packaging; now the National Laboratories have taken over such operations, buying the raw material from Europe and the socialist countries. The government also maintains a joint venture with the Italian firm Carlo Erba for products not obtainable from socialist countries; Italy has no patent laws and its firms are free to produce, without royalty payments, medicines first developed by firms in other countries. Thus, Cubans have no trouble obtaining medicines whose original patents are held by American firms that are not allowed to trade with Cuba.

Next to me at the counter was a Negro campesino woman who protested when she was given injectable procaine penicillin. 'But that is what your doctor prescribed,' said the pharmacist. She shook her head. 'Listen, my son is only eighteen months and I will not give him any but the potassium. This other is an oil suspension and it raises a bump on his tender little buttock – no, give me the potassium, it dissolves faster.' The pharmacist agreed, took away the procaine vial and brought her what she wanted. When my turn came, I found out that the revolutionary government requires pharmacies not to dispense drugs without prescription, but he gave me the tetracycline when I said that it was a doctor who had recommended it.

At six I was lying in bed in my room number 1 at the Bitirí, when Dr Padrón knocked on the wooden jalousie window and asked me how I felt. I opened the door for him and told him I was now on tetracycline. He nodded. I asked him if he didn't object, and he shook his head and said the tetracycline would clear up my trouble quicker, especially since I probably did not have a simple congestion. 'Do you know Victoria, the waitress?' I asked. 'She prescribed the tetracycline.' He said that he did not know which of the waitresses was Victoria, since he always ate at the hospital, but that any Cuban would have done as much. 'Every Cuban is a doctor and every Cuban home a pharmacy,' he said, and smiled to show me he knew what was on my mind. We were friends from then on.

Padrón lived in room number 3 at the Bitirí, since he had decided to let the other bachelors on the staff have the only available house for hospital personnel in Mayarí; the motel room was adequate for sleeping, and he did all his research and reading at his office at the hospital. I had not noticed him until that day because he walked to the hospital at seven, returned at six in the afternoon to shower, and then went again to the hospital for dinner and another look at his patients and a last conference with the administrator before getting into bed about ten to read. On Sunday mornings he woke up at five, got into fatigues, denim shirt, boots and an old hat, and joined the volunteer group from the hospital to cut cane until noon; Sunday afternoons he made another visit to the hospital but did not do the rounds, except to look in on a serious case.

That night he got to talking about the self-prescribing habits of Cubans and did not go to the hospital for dinner, but stayed with me at the Bitirí. 'I have had a woman – not an unusual case either – come to me with her child and say that she has noticed little white worms in his faeces which she felt certain were parasites. So I would start to tell her that as soon as I got a faecal analysis done, I would prescribe, but she did not let me go on. No, no, doctor, she said, I have already given him such and such for twelve days – twelve days is the full course of treatment, right, doctor? I have brought him to you, doctor, to see if he is anaemic as a result and if you would like to prescribe vitamins or some other course of rehabilitation.'

Padrón brought his hands together and laughed. 'And of course, they are usually right. They have recognized the symptoms and discussed them with a neighbour who has already had some experience with a particular medicine.' At Cayo Mambí, where he had spent the previous year, his consultation room had two doors; one of them, which was kept permanently closed, was at the end of his desk and he could thus hear the people on the other side of it who were waiting their turn. 'I could hear them there consulting with each other and recommending to each other what medicine they should ask me for. It was hard to keep a straight face with the patient who was in the room, and should I by chance, in reply to someone who already knew me and asked how I felt, say I had a cold or a stuffed nose, they immediately recommended all sorts of remedies without the slightest self-consciousness.'

I said the revolutionary government's decision to put medicines on prescription must not have been popular. 'Oh, you should have heard the grumbling! What is this nonsense, doctor, about getting a piece of paper from you to buy medicines? In our house we have always been used to having tetracycline, penicillin, cortisone – oh how marvellous it is for bone-aches! – and intravenous dextrose, wonderful after a purgative or a bad digestion or vomiting – it revives you so!' Padrón laughed – loudly for him – at this. The pharmacies were full of dextrose bottles and there was much indignation when they began to be taken off the shelves. 'It was the custom for people to come home feeling worn or dispirited and suspend the bottle after inserting the hypodermic. Twenty-one drops a minute, and soon they were feeling fine and that was that, ready for a good time!'

Padrón found all the idiosyncracies of Cubans delightful, but he could also be caustic and critical. 'Of course, with all this expertise about medicines, some of those people still think an X-ray is some sort of cure.'

Although he stayed with me for dinner, Padrón returned to the hospital as soon as it was over, and I told him I hoped he would have time for a little chat when he returned. He did. We sat outside my room in the high-backed chairs of the motel and talked; it was to become a habit with him to do so, except when he saw I had another visitor: he understood that I was working. Later he made a little joke about the number of people that would sometimes be out there with me; he said he was going to arrange for a little plaque, such as one house on each street has, saying, *Here Meets the Committee for the Defence of the Revolution of the Bitiri.*

I remembered that at dinner he had said that all his education, prior to the Revolution, had been Catholic, and I asked him if he still believed in God.

'Yes,' he said without a pause, 'I still believe.'

'Then you are not a Marxist.'

'Oh yes, I am a Marxist-Leninist – I am a revolutionary.'

I looked at him questioningly, and he smiled and nodded firmly.

'Do you go to church?'

'There is no time,' he said.

'If there were time . . .'

'I would have to see . . . if I had the time and there were a church, I would have to see if I would go.'

In December, when he had a whole month of vacation, he was godfather at the baptism of a classmate's son in Havana. He sometimes still saw the old padre, a Marian, who had been his adviser. He was an Argentinian, but he had not left Cuba.

I asked, 'Did he approve of . . . ?'

'Yes, he approved. And although he is old and could retire and go back to Argentina, he will not.' Padrón paused and looked at me, as I was to observe him doing with patients, to see if I understood. 'All these things are the process of the Revolution. It changes you. I sustained some great shocks – the invasion of Playa Girón, the October crisis. I lost a dear friend, a compañero I loved, at Playa Girón, and that made me think very deeply about the Revolution and what it is worth. And why we are hated so much by the United States. It changes you.'

I pointed out to him that there was a Catholic church on Leyte Vidal, and he said he had seen it. 'I also saw – from the outside – that it is full of those old maids who you can be sure are reactionaries, all making believe there is still a middle class.'

He regretted his waspish response and added, 'When you

work in a hospital, when you are so close to life, you see what it is, you see what reality in truth is. And so you cannot be as religious. Not when you see how you can help, how you can save life – you cannot be so religious.'

His father had owned a little land in Pinar del Rio where he planted tobacco. He kept his family in Havana, but he worked on it himself and hired others; some years the crop was ruined, others he could not sell his produce, and Padrón believed that 'it was because of this suffocating life that he died of a heart attack'. And although there was no money in the family – there were three boys – Padrón went to the best Catholic schools on scholarship; a black boy among the sons of the wealthy, but he made many close friends until the Revolution began to break up those relationships. To some he said good-bye with equanimity; with others he stood at the airport with arms crossed watching them go with an implacable look. Unlike Morales, he did not argue with them – 'If Fidel did not convince them, how could I hope to?'

His room-mate and closest friend at boarding-school did not leave, nor his friend's family, and the friend, unlike Padrón, is a member of the Party now. This relationship with the good families of Havana and Pinar del Rio still shows in a certain snobbery that only talk of the exiles can unleash. He then half closes his eyes and says, 'When I see some of these nothings leave for your overdeveloped country, I say, What can they be thinking of? They are unequipped – why, they will be unable even to walk down your streets, they will slip and fall!'

Padrón didn't begin his medical studies until after the Revolution; he was quite proud of being a member of the first class to begin its studies at the reorganized Havana University and, on graduation, to have climbed El Pico Turquino (the highest mountain in Cuba; climbing it has become a revolutionary ritual) with Castro and other important members of the government. They were a symbol of the new type of doctor the Revolution would develop: they had abjured going into private practice and had voted as a group to spend two years in the countryside, wherever the Ministry of Health sent them, before returning to Havana to specialize. The first decision has become official and the second a prerogative of each class binding on all; last year's class voted to spend three years, for the expansion of medical services throughout the country has created an enormous demand.

Padrón's class began with six hundred, but by graduation there were only four hundred. Some had been unable to keep up with the studies – 'Others saw which way the wind was blowing and were leaving with their families. But we did not fool ourselves, even about the four hundred who graduated. It was a long, hard climb up to Pico Turquino, it took a full week to do it, and when we got there, Fidel told us that he knew that we were not all revolutionaries, that there were those amongst us who would desert the Revolution. There were. They were just waiting to get that medical degree.'

Of the four hundred some forty have left or put in to leave. Unlike other Cubans who apply to leave, doctors cannot go until the Minister of Health himself releases each, and they are expected to remain at their posts. Young men up to the age of twenty-seven who have not done their three-year military training cannot apply either. Padrón commented that it was a pity that during the class purge, before they received their degree, the forty who eventually were to leave had not been found out.

'Purge?' I said, my voice betraying my alarm. 'You had a purge?'

Padrón described a closed meeting attended only by members of the class and chaired by its leaders, in the main members of the Young Communists. The leaders gave a report on those who throughout the years at the university had not shown themselves to be revolutionaries or sympathetic to the Revolution; some fourteen were named and discussed. They could speak and defend themselves, and others also could speak in their defence or add their comments. It was a tense meeting, and some of the accused did not bother to speak – evidence,

Padrón thought, of the rightness of the accusations. He insisted that only students who were actively anti-revolutionary were purged – some were accused of counter-revolutionary activity, such as placing petards in the lavatories, as had occurred a couple of times – and Padrón felt that because students neutral to the Revolution or apathetic about politics were not questioned, those other forty got by.

I said that I thought the only gauge the medical school should have for dispensing medical degrees was how well the student had mastered the courses. Padrón was genuinely astonished. 'Do you think the Revolution should waste its resources – the people's resources – on training young gentlemen and young ladies too fine to serve the people, who are going to take that diploma as entrance into your imperialist society? No, you cannot think that! Medicine is a vocation, and the Revolution has made it impossible for any to be happy in it who do not come to it as a vocation – to serve the sick.'

When he got to know me better, he would say I was thinking like a capitalist, however minor the argument. He was scoring rhetorical points, or simply having fun: in a group he would suddenly turn to me and say, *'Los malos como ustedes'* – bad guys like you people – and end the sentence surprisingly, 'make the best stethoscopes'. He had lost his Tycos and longed to get another. It is a tradition in Cuban hospitals that any doctor may pick up any stethoscope left carelessly around, and no questions asked. If I started to protest, he would cut me off with an encomium to American medicine. Once he came in jubilant with an enormous tome on haematology, a translation of an American book he had ordered, *'Lo hemos fusilado!'* he announced. 'We have executed it and we are going to keep executing any we need. I am only quoting Fidel!' Some 'executed' books are published in English, photo-offset editions of the American ones with the simple tag line on the title page: *Ediciones Revolucionarias.*

But he reserved his most withering criticism not for the imperialists – his only word for Americans – but for Cubans who were lazy, incompetent, apathetic, a manner of Padrón's that may have been strengthened by his working with Che Guevara, known not to have suffered fools gladly. Before the Revolution Padrón had attended the Instituto of the Marian fathers – it was there that his room-mate and he stored explosives in their room for the Movement – from which one came out with a teaching degree. He was, therefore, prepared to direct an evening workers' school after the Revolution while studying medicine during the day, and the 'godfather' of the school – all schools in Cuba now have a godfather from the Army – was Che Guevara. It is mainly an honorary position, but Guevara took no job lightly, and he came to the school frequently and discussed its problems carefully with Padrón. 'I do not mind telling you,' Padrón said to me, recalling Castro's speech announcing Che's departure from Cuba, 'that when Fidel read the letter from Che and the television camera showed his wife dressed in black, I do not mind telling you that right then and there I burst into tears. I am not ashamed to tell you that.'

When I returned from my Sunday with Soní and El Moro and reported El Moro's news about the emergency aqueduct that in seven days would get us water, Padrón said, 'Do not count the days. I do not disbelieve that they are building such a connexion to the Guayabo – I have been told that too – but every morning I call up the Municipal and ask where the water is. That is my routine and I do not intend to stop until I see the cistern at the hospital filled.'

His routine! One Monday morning, I got up at seven and set off to the hospital with him; on foot, for he had no car at his disposal. The administrator, Joaquín Oquendo, an indefatigable man, was already there, and around the entrance were weary-looking campesinos. They had spent the night crouched on the sidewalk, or across the road, sleeping where they could, and although each one would have liked to question Padrón, only one did. He wanted to know how his father was. Padrón asked him if he had got the previous evening's report at the window next to the entrance and the campesino said yes. 'Then you know as much as I do. I shall be seeing him soon and you will have the report at eleven o'clock. But there is no need to worry, he should be better today.'

Inside, Padrón explained that when a campesino entered the hospital as a patient his closest relatives camped outside until he was released, and evenings his friends would come, though it might not be one of the visiting days, and stay outside with the relatives. They tried to discourage this but had not had much success; they were forced to have reports down at the entrance twice a day to satisfy the relatives. 'Rather detailed ones, too,' said Padrón. 'They will not be satisfied with less.'

To Oquendo, Padrón directed his first question: How was the water situation? Oquendo, a man in his late thirties, small, slight like a campesino from Oriente, his voice high and worried, told him that the Municipal had promised trucks by eleven. That meant that the morning clean-up had to be done by the women carrying the pails from the cistern in the yard as far as the third floor. Hygienic conditions, Padrón said, were kept up, but the thorough kind of cleaning that can only be done with plentiful water, also hot running water, had not been done since he had been at the hospital. It was a preoccupation that never left him.

Like the laundry. Mayarí had no mechanized laundry to do the linens of the 140-bed hospital, but nearby Central Guatemala, once the sugar-mill town of United Fruit's largest mill, did (an inheritance of capitalism, I used to say to kid Padrón), and they had taken on the responsibility of doing Mayarí's laundry. It was an extra load and sometimes they were late with their deliveries. 'They also chew up the linens,' Padrón would say, and he carried on a constant battle with the director of the Guatemala hospital about the situation; he also kept up a constant demand for one to be built in Mayarí, and at the moment had thought up a manoeuvre for joining forces with the horticultural school being started up at Los Pinares to get a new laundry which would supply both.

Padrón told me this while we were at breakfast (one egg,

bread and café au lait) in the tiny dining-room of the hospital, and when he got back to his office he called up the Guatemala hospital and talked to the director there, a young man of twenty-four whom I was to meet later. The linens, he insisted, had to be delivered that day because they would run out by the next; Guatemala was four days late and the previous day Padrón had, in desperation, commandeered a truck and sent one of his men to pick up the laundry when the Guatemala truck had not shown up. He now wanted to know why the truck had to return empty, and the Guatemala director told him the linens had been ready but that the truck had not shown up there. 'Do you know that the man I sent with the truck is a member of the Party?' Padrón said. 'Are you telling me that a Party member lied?'

When he got off the phone, I asked what the Guatemala director had said. 'He said that he must have been given wrong information,' Padrón said.

'A Party member never lies?' I said.

Padrón shook his head and Oquendo did too. 'He would lose his militancy,' Padrón said, by which he meant that at the yearly review of his Party work he might have his Party card withdrawn and some control task given him before he would be accepted back in. I looked sceptical, and Padrón got his haughty look with the half-closed eyes and repeated, 'A Party member never lies.'

The man Padrón had sent with the truck was not in fact a member of the Party, he was a candidate for it. A party nucleus had not yet been formed at the hospital, but almost four months earlier local Party leaders had called an asamblea of the 139 employees (which included the medical staff) of the hospital to propose that a Party cell be started. The assembly was composed of absolutely everyone at the hospital, from the director to the cleaning-women, and they agreed to the Party proposal and, after much discussion, nominated twelve people to the Party. (One cannot apply for Party membership; one must be nominated by one's fellow workers at one's place of work.) The Party then proceeded to interview each of them and to investigate them thoroughly. It was expected that any day the Party would call another assembly and report back to all 139 workers and ask for their support of the Party's decisions.

The only doctor nominated had been the former director. Oquendo too. The others were nurses, laboratory technicians and maintenance workers. Some did not get the nomination not only because of objections raised by their fellow workers but because they disqualified themselves on the basis of certain requirements they knew the Party would be checking in their investigations. To become a member of the Party one has to be a member of the militia, to have gone through the sixth grade, to have had no connexion with the Batista régime nor voted in its fraudulent 1958 elections; it is expected also that one engages in voluntary work, has a good fraternal attitude toward neighbours and fellow workers, is a member of a mass organization, such as the Committees for the Defence of the Revolution or the Federation of Cuban Women.

At the hospital assembly, religious beliefs were not mentioned, but Padrón feels certain that the reason he was not accepted into the Young Communists on the two occasions when he was nominated was this: 'I do not lie to the Party,' he said, 'I did not conceal my religious beliefs and they were too fine to tell me so directly in the final interview, when those who were not being accepted were being told. In the list of things which are considered weaknesses the compañero said that one must be a materialist. For believe me, until they come to their conclusions they investigate even the colour you defecate!'

After Padrón finished talking to the director at Guatemala and was assured that the laundry was on its way, he went over with Oquendo some of the work that had to be done that day. Oquendo was not certain when the Army planned to bring its draftees for their medical examinations nor how many there would be, but he promised to have someone contacted by the time Padrón finished his *paso de salón*. Then they went to the pantry of the hospital kitchen to look at the supplies that Oquendo had purchased. There was one item Oquendo wanted his approval for: six long strings of garlic that he had been able to obtain on the free market; they were very fine but they would cost forty-five dollars. Padrón said no, and Oquendo said he would return them that day.

The kitchen, the pantry, the dining-room, the emergency entrance and treatment room, like the outpatient clinic and the offices, were all on the ground floor; and since he had a few minutes before he was due at the third-floor wards, Padrón showed me the autopsy room at the back near the ambulance entrance. He said post-mortems were done on all cases, even when they were rather certain of the cause of death. I thought it unusual that the families, particularly of campesinos, would agree to autopsies, and Padrón informed me that they didn't consult the families. He did not see my point about their right to decide: autopsies were invaluable for acquiring medical knowledge, a benefit that would accrue to all the people.

At the Guatemala hospital, however, I was to find out that they obtained permission from the families first. The autopsy room there was a wooden shed separated from the hospital, and this made it impossible for them to conceal post-mortems from the families. In no case, however, had they been unable to get permission. 'In some cases,' said the director, 'I put it to them very simply. Do you want us to be better doctors? Do you want us to learn more so that we can work better and save more people? They always give in.'

As soon as we walked into the first male ward, I learned that Padrón only liked to appear highhanded, for at the slightest appeal from a worried patient, he was compassionate, friendly and full of little jokes that made them feel better. Before we walked into the ward, he was met by the floor nurse. 'Is everything ready?' he asked. She said yes, meaning that the floor had been scrubbed, the beds made, breakfast served and cleared, and that on the chair by each bed was a clipboard with the patient's clinical history. Because two nurse's aides were down with One Hundred Eleven, Padrón excused the floor nurse from accompanying him on his rounds. He pointed this out to me. 'I do not want you to think that I just go by, talk to the patients and write their progress on their record. I always have a thousand questions to ask of the nurse and a thousand orders as well. Today she shall have to read each progress report I write with extra care to make sure she has it all.'

The men's wards were large rooms that accommodated six. The beds were skimpy, the solitary chair by each somehow making the room look barer, for there was no such thing as a night table or a vase with flowers or a stand for books. And it wasn't until we got to the women's ward that I saw a hospital bed, one that could be cranked up or that looked more substantial than a fold-away extra bed one keeps in a closet. It bothered me that the clinical record was left on the chair next to each patient and that the patient could, if he wanted, read it. But Padrón said they knew they were not to read it and they did not; he did not say that probably most were not that literate.

As we walked into the women's wing on the same floor, a frail old woman was being guided by the nurse to one of the rooms. 'Oh doctor,' doctor,' she said, frightened and happy, 'I did not think I would last until I got here!'

'But you see, you have,' said Padrón, following her into the room. 'Now give me your little hand, just put it here. There is no need to be nervous any more.'

She looked up at him while he took her pulse – an old white woman at this young black boy – with complete faith that he was already making her better.

The woman in the same room with her was an asthma patient and she had doubled her pillow to hold her head higher and breathe better. She also had an upraised arm under the pillow, and she looked uncomfortable. 'I am going to show you something,' Padrón said to her, and cranked up the bed. 'Now you can smooth out your pillow and be comfortable.'

Particularly on the patients' floors, the hospital needed painting. There was never, it seemed, a single empty bed, and the hospital, though built after the Revolution, had been in use several years. The plaster must have been very cheap, too, for the edges of doors and entrances were dented and crumbling, so that wherever your eye roamed there was some deficiency. The women's wing was made up of tiny, two-patient rooms, and they all led into a very large room which one first entered from the corridor, totally bare except for two or three straight-backed chairs against the walls. It made no sense and I told Padrón.

'The hospital was designed by some Mexican architect who I hope is back in Mexico,' he said. 'Imagine building a socialist hospital with private rooms! That is what these rooms were. When I came last month I had them tear out the doors of each one, so we could put one more bed in each room. Now there is this big room ... if only we had some furniture, it could be used for ambulatory patients. But you know what it was supposed to be for? – the visitors' room for the patients in private rooms!'

We were on the third floor almost three hours, and during that time Padrón saw some twenty-five patients. They were not all his patients, of course, but every day he reviewed their cases, as he had just done, and other doctors on the staff who had admitted them and first prescribed the course of treatment also came up to see them during the day. There were sixteen doctors on the staff, of whom only four were doctors who had already been practising before the Revolution; the rest were all in their first or second year of rural medicine. Attached to the outpatient clinic were also two dentists – an innovation in the countryside, for before the Revolution only people in the big cities went to dentists.

All treatment at the hospital was free, as was all the medicine that was given there. But outpatients were supposed to pay for the medicines prescribed for them; the exceptions – pregnant women, accident cases, children with infectious diseases, hardship cases – were so many that it was easy to get medicine free. 'As a matter of fact, our rule is to give a prescription to be filled free if we suspect that they are not going to buy it for financial reasons,' said Padrón, and the tetracycline I bought was one fourth the price in the United States, even at the unrealistic rate of exchange of one peso to the dollar. Once when I was sitting in the mayor's office, kidding him about the emergency aqueduct, which had just suffered another breakdown, an old lady came in and handed him a piece of paper which he signed while exchanging greetings. If I had not asked him after she left, I wouldn't have found out that he was approving her prescription for non-payment at the pharmacy: she was retired on a little pension and paying for the medicine would have been a real hardship.

From eleven fifteen to twelve o'clock Padrón handled a stream of callers in his office. One of them was the young Army man whose responsibility it was to see that new draftees were examined; as director of the leading hospital of the region, Padrón was a member of the military council of the region and had to arrange for such examinations, using his hospital staff or drawing upon that of three other hospitals of the region. The young man turned to me and said, 'You are the American? My aunt told me you asked about me.' He was the young man in the famous photograph of the nationalization of the United Fruit Company in 1960 whom I wanted to interview; and for a moment Padrón's office became a place for shoulder-slapping and purposeless talk. Roberto Silvera promised he would come to the Bitirí and have a real talk with me, and although I got to know him well enough to call him Robertico, he never stayed still long enough to give me a formal interview; just as Robertico was not to get the photo from Padrón that he needed to make up Padrón's military identification card. But they did settle the question of the recruits.

There was one moment, as Padrón was setting aside some medical magazines that he wanted to read later in the day, when I found time to ask him if he did not mind, as director, the existence of a Party nucleus in his hospital who in a sense were above him and might even dictate to him. 'There is nothing I would like more,' he said, with the patient manner that I called his *docencias* – his professorial lectures. 'Do you know what it means to me to have someone in the laboratory who has been made a member of the Party? It means that I have to worry much less about the work of that laboratory – that there is someone there who is totally devoted to the work plan.'

'Yes, but will they not be dictating to you what the work plan should be?'

Padrón had enormous eyes and he could open them very wide when he wanted to show you had said something outlandish. 'Do you think that any suggestion for the hospital would be made without prior discussion with me or with Oquendo? What do you think being a member of the Party means if not to achieve and surpass the work plan of your work centre?'

At noon we had lunch: nondescript, but it included meat, rice, vegetables, a sweet and a demitasse of coffee. Padrón was the only Cuban I met who did not drink coffee. At twenty after twelve we were back on the third floor, on a little balcony off the main corridor. He dragged a chair there and three other doctors did the same; none of them had outpatient clinic duty that afternoon, so they were gathering, as they did several times during the week, to discuss in detail some case in the ward complicated enough to have medical interest. That day Padrón had the assignment of doing the summing-up. He asked each doctor what diagnosis they would have made of the case and what treatment prescribed, and then began so detailed an analysis that he spoke for three quarters of an hour. One of the complications of the patient was that he had hypertension, and so, for my benefit, Padrón threw in: 'Reserpine sells by the ton in the Unites States where life is so suffocating that hypertension is common.'

Between two thirty and three thirty, Padrón took Oquendo

around the grounds discussing the kind of clearing and planting that had to be done. He once came back from an inspection of a small clinic in the region very depressed because there were chickens running around in the yard and no grass or shrubbery, no trees planted. 'There is more to a hospital than dispensing penicillin.' And he had plans of all sorts for the Martyrs of Mayarí Hospital. A week later I found him conferring with the gardener of the Bitirí about where one could obtain a certain kind of grass that he admired at the Bitirí because it had remained green throughout a winter month of no rain.

At three thirty he was back in the office where the paycheques were being distributed by Oquendo's office. Padrón earns $305 a month and pays $2 dues to the union. His base salary is $225, but he is given another stipend for being in his second year of rural medicine and another for being director of the hospital, so that his $305 is more than most doctors his age earn. He sends some money each month to his mother, whom he supports with the help of another brother. He saves some money just in case it should become possible some day to buy a car, for that is all he really misses. 'It would be a diversion some evenings or Sunday afternoons to take a drive around the region.'

That afternoon, besides going over the medical magazines, he worked on the preparation of final examinations for the nurse's aides who were finishing their first year's training at the hospital. He was not pleased with the course of training that they had had, nor with the method of selection, for quite a few had dropped out, and he had plans for the new class which would be selected in a few weeks from candidates to be proposed by the Committees for the Defence of the Revolution. Everything was to be more rigorous, now that he was in charge.

'I know I am considered a terror here because I am so demanding. I know I am an obsessive-compulsive, but I do not care, nor whether they like me or not. I do not get angry or raise my voice for I am incapable of that, but I simply keep instructing, Miss, this has to be done this way and that another. I keep repeating and repeating, as many times as necessary. I have had nurses who started their turn with me by saying, Doctor, I understand I am going to need skates; and I say, Not skates, wings. I got a new cleaning-woman for the third floor, a good one I noticed in the kitchen, and I have begun teaching her. Fidel says we need administrators, and to get them from the new generation is a slow process – yet of course, there is no one like a Cuban in an emergency.'

I followed him out of the office and stood talking to Dr Jimenez, a young doctor who was attached to the regional staff of Public Health, while Padrón asked the girl at the reception desk for some papers. When he returned to us, Jimenez said he thought that Padrón, as a new director, ought to be able to get permission to hire another office girl to be at the emergency entrance to keep statistics on everyone who came, so that not only the cases that were admitted would be recorded.

Padrón was very cool with him. 'There is no room down there for it,' he said.

'Oh, a little table would do,' said Jimenez.

'This is no time to hire extra people, when we need so many things for the hospital.'

Jimenez suggested that he transfer the girl from the reception desk in the lobby down there so she could do both jobs. 'You treat all those people who come, but if you keep no statistics, no work has in fact been done.'

'You show me how she could do both jobs down there,' said Padrón, unable to entirely control his annoyance.

Jimenez shrugged his shoulders.

'Statistics is not the job of a hospital,' said Padrón, half closing his eyes, 'If they had been treated, I am satisfied that the work has been done.'

To get away from Jimenez, and because he had no consultation duty, he decided to take off early and go back with me to the Bitirí. We went out through the corridor of the outpatient clinic, and it was as full as the morning Morales had taken me there. Five days a week, there are five doctors on duty mornings and afternoons, and the reception clerk is allowed to give as many as thirty appointments for each doctor in the morning and thirty in the afternoon. 'You get so many people all the time?' I said.

Padrón nodded, still aloof as the after-effects of his argument with Jimenez. 'And they said the campesinos would not come for medical treatment!'

Walking back, he suddenly relaxed and said, 'You see that Dr Jimenez – a doctor of hygiene! – well, that shows you that not all the young doctors are revolutionaries. Take old Dr Panades, he has practically given up his private practice. He only sees people at his private office who beg to see him, for there are still fools who think that if you pay a doctor you are going to get better attention. Dr Panades gets up every morning at five and cuts cane for two to three hours before he comes to the hospital.'

He said no more about Jimenez. I knew that Jimenez spent most of his time at the Bitirí reception desk talking to the girls there. He did not cut cane, he did no volunteer work.

Having changed his routine, Padrón asked me to go to the movies with him, an English film whose Spanish title he said was *The Crying of the Idol*. He came back from the hospital before eight, and the film turned out to be *This Sporting Life*, one which I'd missed in New York and was happy to see because I was told it was a powerful story about English working-class life. We came in towards the end of the first showing, and immediately Padrón was called out. When he didn't return in five minutes, I went out and found him in the lobby talking animatedly with a tall girl with light chestnut hair.

'This is Xiomara!' he said excitedly; I knew it was the medical student who had spent last year's month of volunteer work at the hospital at Cayo Mambí. She had just arrived and was being taken to her assignment at Marcané in a Public

Health jeep; but she had called him out to greet him during the few minutes she had in town. She was handsome and charming, a city sophisticate, and they didn't stop talking until the jeep came.

I was left with Padrón and another fellow from Public Health on the sidewalk after she drove off, and I said, 'It seems to me that Xiomara holds more than ordinary interest for you.'

'She is married,' Padrón said.

The Public Health fellow said, 'You do not know? They are separated, I think they may even be divorced.'

Padrón did not say anything for a moment, and then when we went back into the theatre, he said, 'I think Xiomara was ashamed to tell me.'

The audience did not understand the violence and tragedy of the English worker's life, didn't see that the ethics of professional Rugby brutalized him, and that his love relationship with the young working-class widow was killed by this and the mean inheritance of a life without love. They laughed at it; there was no tension in the theatre, none of that concentration there would have been in a New York art house. Their presence made me see that for all its artistry (the editing was particularly fine) it was a false picture of life: those country people knew that the easy-going goodness of people was missing from it, that it allowed no avenue for joy, such as they know exists as soon as any bar to its enjoyment is let down. Nor does it take a revolution to know this, just a bit of living.

Walking back with Padrón and the anaesthetist and his wife, they agreed that the hero and heroine were two psychopaths. Padrón said, 'It was a very well-made film. The actor was fine, really fine: you saw him change before your eyes, saw him really lose his teeth, get ugly, all that. But the fact is that it was not real, that is the problem. After all, when a widow has a man come live with her she has a husband again, and they lived as such, did they not? Why all those quarrels and pulling apart? They were each psychopaths in their own way, so that the film had no theme, you could say it had no social reality.'

He sat with me in front of my room while I had my last cigarette, and talked about how he planned to ask Public Health to get a group together to go up to Marcané on a Sunday. 'It is a politeness we here owe young students like Xiomara when they come to the countryside.'

'Ah ha,' I said.

After a while, he said sadly, 'I am a prisoner of my religious education. I do not drink, I do not smoke, I do not go in for the pleasures other men have, which are commonly called vices. The younger generation does not have these inhibitions or habits of mine – they are open to more of life. I wish I were not like that, but that is the way I am.'

4. Some Complaints

The wire hangers the manager of the Bitirí promised me the first morning never, of course, showed up. They were not mentioned again and I never asked: a good look at the shops in town made me feel I had been indiscreet. Amelia, the chambermaid on duty from two in the afternoon until ten at night, told me she would find me some, and after two days of searching at the Bitirí, she returned with two rachitic ones. I took them and went searching for more on Leyte Vidal, finally finding four at a *quincalla*, a kind of notions store, so tiny it was literally a hole in the wall on the side of Leyte Vidal that would some day be torn down. They were home-made hangers, put together with a wire that was not entirely straightened out and a little slat of raw wood on which my shirts and pants frequently caught: a little irritant that was a symbol for the much graver ones that people in Mayarí lived with.

With the hangers I was now able to empty some of my suitcase – I learned to fold two pants on each hanger and three shirts over them – and place the suitcase on a stand inside the clothes wardrobe to act the role of the nonexistent dresser. The writing surface screwed into the wall next to the door was no doubt meant to be a vanity, for there was a mirror above it that could not have been set there to help writers ruminate. I placed my typewriter, notebooks, books, magazines, pencils on this small surface, and in the early afternoon, when the room had finally been tidied by Angela or Margarita, I sat on a backless, slatted bench to work. In the doorway, one of the girls or the dentist's boys usually leaned, watching me. If I picked up a book to read, the girls would say, 'Oh Jose, you are studying!'

When Amelia filled the carafe each night with cooled water,

I tried not to drink any, for I needed the whole amount to brush my teeth and shave each morning. A full carafe, as my expertise increased, became a luxury. I learned not to flush the toilet until morning, for the water was turned on only in the late afternoon or early evening. And if I didn't get to the Bitirí during the one- or two-hour period when the water was on, I stood outside my room and called, as loudly as anyone else, 'Amelia, my love, a bucket of water for my bath!' She would lower a bucket on a rope into the cistern behind the kitchen and bring it to me with many sighs about the number of buckets she had carried that day.

You didn't sympathize with Amelia; she was a notorious whiner. When she arrived at two, she was already tired, and spent her first hour sitting in the office on one side of the reception desk listening to the radio. She too was separated or divorced; one didn't look into that too closely because often there had been no marriage – they had been *arrimados*, had 'come close', and now were no longer. She could well have been tired, for she had a four-year-old and a seven-year-old at home (another was in the country with her mother and the oldest, who was fourteen, in Havana on scholarship), and she had already done a good deal of housekeeping before she arrived at the Bitirí. But aside from filling the carafes and carrying buckets of water for late-comers, there was not much else she did but gossip and complain. If one of the early-shift chambermaids was out and there were two or three rooms still to be tidied, she was expected to do them. Then she grumbled all afternoon, her face folded up with self-pity, and it was touch and go whether the carafes got filled.

The early-shift chambermaids did work harder than Amelia, but they were not any speedier. They began fixing the twenty-one rooms before eight in the morning, starting at the apex of the triangle and working down, so that Angela, who worked my side, didn't get to my room until after lunch. Until they did, the used linens sat on the high-backed chairs outside each room, and I couldn't, as I wanted, go into my room and work uninterruptedly or lie down and take a nap. So I sat outside with a clipboard and took notes and listened to Angela and Margarita call out to each other while they slowly worked. Margarita was bolder than Angela; she joked with the clients, and whenever she saw two people or more standing together, she would run over and get into the conversation.

'We have so much fun with the guests,' Margarita once said. 'When they stay here more than one day, they become like family.'

Essentially that was the problem with the service at the Bitirí: most – not all – of the girls felt they were at home serving some member of the family. Consequently, a bedroom didn't need to be ready for use until it was time for bed, and food made its appearance at the table when the cook got to it. They had all gone to a training school in Holguín before the Bitirí opened, some five months before I got there, and they were very proud of their training; but it sometimes seemed that they had simply picked up some frills there that they added to their natural friendly manner. They walked very erect, and whatever they carried from the kitchen to the dining-room, whether a small dish with plantains or a tray with three meals, they held at shoulder height on one hand, and walked swiftly, their heads up, a slight smile on their lips, delighted with themselves.

The Bitirí was the newest, most modern motel and restaurant in that whole region of northern Oriente, and as with any small-town girls it pleased them to be where the action was. Victoria, one of the girls who took your order, would often be there on her off hours in her best clothes. 'There is no other place to go, so I come here to be with my friends,' she would say. Victoria was the most correct and efficient in her manner, and so the girls once elected to send her to Santiago to a meeting of the *gastronómicos* – the restaurant workers – to discuss service and other problems. At the meeting she got up and said that at the Bitirí they were unable to give the good service they would like to because of the lack of water and the inadequate kitchen. 'We have only one cook and an assistant,' she said.

Sometimes, after half an hour had passed and no food had come, one of the girls would come over and commiserate, but only if you complained. Otherwise they hoped you would not notice. If you did, they would say, It is terrible, *mi hijito* – my little son – but the cook has not got your order yet. If you persisted, as did many who came through the Bitirí on official work, the girls would have a frank, open argument, but a family argument. It was only with the two Russian farm technicians living at the Bitirí, who when impatient got an arrogant tone, that the girls would become coldly angry. They could understand someone getting up and leaving without warning after they had waited a long time, but arrogance – anything other than equal treatment – would infuriate them. Whether the customer was right was a matter for discussion.

Soon after I arrived, the Bitirí got a new manager and one of his innovations was to have breakfast served daily – until then it was unpredictable – at the four tables at the bar. Benilda, who had only worked in the dining-room serving bottled drinks, got the assignment. (She used to ask with great aplomb, 'Will you have bottled water or from the faucet?') It was too much for her. She was a thin, nervous girl with a shrill voice and the assurance that she could do no wrong. A cup of coffee and bread and butter took a half hour, and she did not find the time to wipe the table of the debris left by previous customers. She copied out the order in front of you with great difficulty; she wrote it in duplicate and spelled out the name of the Bitirí at the top laboriously and her own full name with a great flourish at the bottom. She made so many useless trips to the bar and kitchen and back that she was ragged at the end of her two-hour duty.

One morning three young men from the National Film Institute, in a hurry to get up to Los Pinares where they were making a newsreel short, tried to find someone other than her to complain to, and they had a strong exchange. When they left – without breakfast after three quarters of an hour – Benilda explained the whole thing to the customers in her shrill voice. 'And the little one was the worst of all,' she said. 'He had the nerve to bring up the Revolution. What does he know about the Revolution! You can be sure he expects us to smile at every customer as waitresses used to have to do in the old days!'

Being served breakfast by Benilda was no way to start the day. But she was aware of her deficiencies and when there was enough of a pause, she would apologize. Once I saw that the carbon she used to make duplicates of orders was completely worn and I brought her some from my room. There had been no coffee that morning – half the week there was none – but she served me some that one of the girls had brought from home. And I noticed in the dining-room at lunch that she had shared her new supply of carbons with the two girls who took orders.

'Sometimes I think that the real test of the Revolution has been the shortage of coffee,' said a revolutionary to me in Havana. 'When you think how used we Cubans were to stopping a thousand times during the day for our sip of coffee – it is marvellous how we have put up with so little coffee.'

This was not the case in Mayarí; in the mountains near by coffee was grown, and many had relatives who sent them fresh coffee-beans. In fact, some did not bother to use the ration book for coffee, since most liked to make it according to their own recipes. Amelia used to bring me coffee from home, and she explained that it was dark the way I liked it because she always toasted the beans with brown sugar, then ground them fresh each day. (That method, I was to learn, was typical of northern Oriente.) Coffee was the only thing Amelia did not complain about. She was not typical, but it was through her that I became immediately aware of the hunger for consumer goods that for so long had not been available.

Amelia arranged to take my laundry to a neighbour's, and the first time she returned a bundle and laid it out on my bed, she let her hand run over each shirt and murmured her appreciation. 'Now that is my favourite colour,' she said about a blue one. 'And that one, oh that one is the finest, most delicate of all!' It was a wash-and-wear shirt; it had a hole made by a hot ash from one of the many cigarettes I smoked, and I told her she could have it. 'Oh, it is too fine!' she demurred, but kept her hands on it. I told her I meant to throw it out. 'It will make a divine blouse!' and she folded it over one arm and ran out of my room.

'Jose, Jose, you have turned her head completely with that shirt,' said the girl at the reception desk when I went out later.

'You will need a factory to supply us all!' another called.

'Jose, Jose, never throw out a shirt, never!'

It was not just curiosity, then, that had made Angela call Margarita over to my room. 'Oh, look how curious that is! How charming!' I heard them exclaim in the room at one possession and another while I waited outside impatiently for the room to be tidied, my eyes half closed with the desire to lie down for my siesta. They never, of course, took anything, but once when I sat at my improvised desk, I noticed that Angela had tested one of my ballpoint pens by drawing a couple of lines on the margin of a newspaper. Those two lines wriggled with life: what a release of wonder they contained!

One day as I walked by the reception desk on my way out the back exit, little Miriam who took care of accounts asked me if I would allow her to use my nail clip. I told her that she would find it on my desk and warned her that it was a man's clipper, perhaps rough, and the file too strong for a girl's nails. 'Oh no, it will be fine,' she said. It was not until I was on Leyte Vidal that it occurred to me that Miriam had never been in my room and that she could only know about the clip because my possessions must be a subject of discussion.

Walking on Leyte Vidal, I sometimes thought that the only way people could tell I was not Cuban was by my shoes, for my pants were not tight and I let my shirt hang out as Cubans do. The men sitting on the sidewalk at the bank, waiting for their bus to arrive across the street, often did not look up further than my ankles. The ration book allowed for one pair of dress shoes and one pair of work shoes each year, but not enough showed up at the shoe-stores and many had been unable to buy a pair of shoes for two or three years. 'We Cubans have a certain national character, I must admit,' said a Mayarí revolutionary to me; he said it as if confessing to something bad, for in Cuba the phrase 'a national character' carries the sense that it is a weakness. 'We like shoes and we like to dress well.'

'Everyone does,' I said.

'No, we put a special emphasis on it,' he said. 'We think about it too much.'

Since Christmas no clothes or shoes had arrived at any of the stores on Leyte Vidal, and one of the young men who had not bought any since rationing began – 'I would not stand in line for anything!' – said that there wasn't a pair of men's pants to be found in all of Oriente, except olive-green or khaki ones. He was a *disgustado* – one of the unhappy – but no one contradicted the statement when I repeated it.

Jorge, one of the town boys, a plumber's assistant, was very concerned about this, for he wanted to marry a girl in Victoria de las Tunas, and to ask for her hand he had to appear presentable. 'So here I am in Mayarí this weekend when she expected me to talk to her father tonight,' he said. 'I sent her a telegram telling her I would come next weekend.'

'Because you do not have a good pair of pants?' I said.

'Look at this one, look,' he said, and showed me the frayed pockets and the worn crotch.

'Well, if you would keep your hands off your cock!' said one of his friends, and we all laughed. Cubans quite unselfconsciously make adjustments in public, or pat it affectionately or simply check that it is still there.

'I do, I do!' Jorge said, 'for pants are not the only thing there is a shortage of!'

We had been standing in front of INDER, the sports organization headquarters in Mayarí, and when Jorge walked on, Eider Cesar, a sports teacher, said, 'Jorge is a good boy but *muy enamorado* – too apt to fall in love.' Jorge had taken up baseball a year ago and had done so well as a pitcher that he went as far in the eliminations as the provincial team. He was nineteen and everyone expected him to make the national team the following year. 'If he sticks to it,' someone added, 'for he is very flighty.'

'Well, I can understand him,' said a sober young man of twenty-six. 'I remember when I was his age I was terrible.'

Two nights later, Jorge – his friends called him *Manguera*, garden hose, and when I asked why, they burst into laughter and pointed at Jorge's crotch – picked up the theme again. He and a friend walked by the Bitirí and joined me and some others outside my room. Jorge would not sit down; he was too restless. He stood on the lawn and, as he talked, went through the motions of pitching.

'Oh Jose, it is *de alma* in Mayarí for young people!' he began; *de alma* – from the soul – means rock-bottom bad, for the birds. There is nothing to do, no girls and no clothes, ah man! *Jebas, jebas* – chicks, chicks – that is what I need. My insect is rotting away. Forty minutes ago I gave myself a hand job. No, do not believe that. But it *is* rotting away. When I take a bath, I do not touch it or it stands up like a rod!

'I have to get married quick, I cannot wait. Sometimes I am busy kissing my girl, my arm around her like this, and a jeba goes by and I turn my head and look and my girl says, Jorge! I have got to get married even if I do not have any clothes.'

He came out of the wind-up and watched the imaginary ball he had pitched streak home. '*Etrai* – strike!' he called, and got ready for another pitch. 'Next year I make the national team. Imagine, Jose, my father had twenty-nine children with several women. He was strong, he was tall, and he killed himself, because he had sugar in his blood or something like that, I am not sure. So you see how I am this way – I must get a jeba.

This year I am going to make the national team and I am going to get to Havana and then it will be like in the Army – jebas, jebas, jebas! That is all I want – jebas and money for rum!'

Dr Morales had already worried about Jorge's problem during that first week when we were together so much. 'Listen,' he had said in a very serious tone, 'they have a problem about sex and it is going to get worse – just think about the coming agglomeration of twelve thousand women at Los Pinares! And here in Mayarí there are no *posadas*, inns where men can rent rooms by the hour or day; the nearest is in Holguín. So they do it in cars or out-of-the-way places they go to on foot.' He smiled at me – the smile of the Havana sophisticate – as he said 'on foot' and then admonished me, 'Do not laugh, you old man. It is a serious problem.'

Even the head of the Ministry of the Interior for the region had talked about it, though he did not view it as a problem. He came to the Bitirí looking for me my first Sunday in Mayarí, and I was called out of the dining-room. He was in uniform, and again I thought this was Roberto Silvera, the young man in the photograph of the nationalization of the United Fruit Company. He was twenty-four, handsome and amiable, and I laughed out loud when he told me that he was the head of the Ministry of the Interior.

'Of the dread secret police?' I said.

He nodded and laughed too.

He came to tell that he had heard of the work I was going to do in Mayarí and to assure me that I had complete liberty to go and inquire wherever I pleased. I smiled. He smiled. I said, 'How about the library? Can I read old magazines there?' And he laughed out loud. He said it should not happen again, at least not with the police.

'We are not a repressive organization,' he said. 'For example, there are no posadas in Mayarí, so any couple can park anywhere they want and make love with the knowledge that they will not be bothered. Our men know better than to go look at a car parked in some out-of-the-way place at night. We know couples have registered at the Bitirí as husband and wife who in fact are not. But we do not consider that to be any of our business.'

What if there is a scandal?

'Well, yes, scandalous behaviour,' he said. 'But even then, not in an official way. Someone at their work centre – it does not even have to be a member of the Party – would worry about it and draw the person aside and advise him. That is what would happen, most likely.'

There was to be something of a scandal at the Bitirí – it involved Angela and is a story that comes later – and although it went to court, the police never got involved except to make the initial arrest.

Meanwhile Jorge did not have a pair of pants to ask for his girl's hand. 'And socks, socks too, you cannot get enough of them,' he said. 'And listen, Jose, when you go back Up North, can you send me a pitcher's glove, a left-handed one?'

Everyone had something they wanted from Up North; it came out sooner or later. How soon depended on the strength of their revolutionary convictions, and many were only able to ask because they felt certain I would not judge the Revolution on this basis. Dr Padrón would become stiff and icy when he heard Amelia come out of my room saying, 'Oh Jose, is that atomizer you have in the bathroom a deodorant? Oh how fine it is, how delicate! If only I could buy one here! I need one.'

When she left, I said, 'Do not worry, Padrón, I know Amelia is no revolutionary and that is why she acts the way she does.'

He gave me a grateful smile. 'I am very pleased you have observed that.'

Amelia was saved the care and education of her oldest son by his scholarship to a Havana school, she was given a new stucco house in the 26 of July project when the hurricane swept her old house away, and the job at the Bitirí made it unnecessary for her to wash clothes for a living. But she never volunteered a good word for the Revolution. When I asked her if she thought, as the government promised, that rationing would some day be ended owing to the agricultural projects already begun, the best she would say was, 'We shall see, we shall see.' One of the revolutionaries thought hers was a good attitude. 'She is right in a way – let the Revolution prove itself, let it solve problems, not just explain them.'

Angela with her sliding gaze, her suggestive ways, had good things to say about the Revolution; all in her own good time, however. If she lived with her aunt and uncle, I asked, why did she send her sixteen-month-old baby to the Círculo Infantil? 'Because there they get all the food you sometimes cannot get for them because of the rationing.' She stopped to watch Margarita across the way speaking to a guest. Dreamily she returned to her train of thought: 'The reason we need the rationing – besides the fact that we sell food to other nations for the things we need – yes, the reason is now everyone has money to buy the things that used to be so plentiful. You open a store like that now – ha! – and there will not be one person on the sidewalk studying the goods in the window. They will be inside buying them.'

One of the boys treating me to coffee at El Parque Cafeteria said something similar. 'If everyone in Mexico could afford to buy a pair of shoes, how many do you think would be left in the stores?'

He was wearing an old-fashioned pair of pants of white wool with a thin black stripe; at the ankles they belled out a little; they were obviously an inheritance. I told him that pants like that were very much in fashion Up North, and he looked at me sceptically, somewhat hurt that I might be making fun of him. 'I mean it,' I said. 'That is the latest fashion.' He smiled and said, 'You do not say!' and walked off home for lunch, more jauntily, I thought, for the knowledge.

At one time, he would have taken me home to lunch too. But rationing makes such hospitality impossible: you see the thought occur to every Cuban you talk to, the invitation is on the tip of their tongues, and then you see them reject it. Consequently, you cannot pass a coffee stand when coffee is being strained without being offered a sip, or stand at a bar without being bought drinks, and often strangers sharing the table with me at the Bitirí insisted on paying for my lunch or dinner. The knowledge of what the rationing costs them as sociable beings inhibits you at first in asking specific questions.

After I had been in Mayarí two weeks, I finally walked into Oficoda, the rationing office, and went over a food-ration book with them and noted down exactly what each person is allowed: rice, 4 lb. a month; lard or oil, 1 lb. every 21 days; beans, ¾ lb. per month; butter, 2 oz. a month; *malanga*, a potatoelike vegetable, 2 lb. a month (although the availability of vegetables is unpredictable, there are often enough, so that the ration book is seldom used); coffee, 1½ oz. weekly; soap, 1 bar a week each for bathing and washing; milk, 1 bottle fresh a month, a varying number of cans for children up to the age of thirteen, and 4 cans for adults over sixty-five; tomato puree, ½ can a month; salt, ½ lb. a month; onions, 1 lb. a month; 1 chicken per month per family; and ¼ lb. meat per week. Anything not on this list, they told me, such as bread and fish, is not rationed.

In Havana I knew the ration of meat was ¾ lb. a week, and they explained in Mayarí that this higher ration was due to its being difficult for Havanans to get to the countryside and buy from campesinos on the free market. Neither can city people raise their own vegetables or chickens or pigs. The prices of rationed goods have remained more or less the same since the Revolution, but most campesinos charge up to three times the official price; a practice that the government does not like, but it only tries to persuade them to sell at official prices. You can buy a pig or a chicken from a campesino, but not portions of either; this and the resale of such purchases are economic crimes.

A group of us left early one Saturday morning for a day at the beach, and as soon as we reached the official outskirts of Mayarí, we were stopped and the trunk of the car searched by soldiers. If we had been transporting more than twenty-five pounds per person of such purchased goods in total, we could have been arrested for black-market activities. With the exception of me, most in the car were doctors from the hospital; one of the soldiers knew this – he had been treated by one of them – but it did not make the checking less thorough. No one in the car minded, either.

I was studying the list of rationed goods from Oficoda at lunch, trying to imagine what a housewife could make of it, and I finally asked two of the waitresses standing near me, 'Is it very hard to make do with the rationing?'

Both got a look that said they were sorry I had brought it up. Then with a self-pitying grimace one said, 'Oh yes, Jose, it is very hard.'

The other nodded. 'What is the use of pretending?'

'But Fidel never lied to us about that. He said there would be times when there would not be enough and times when we would have all we want. Fidel never lied.'

After lunch, when I stopped at the juice stand for my usual drink, Jaime Hernandez, who was always extremely courteous, broke off a conversation with me for the first and only time during the many we had. 'Will you please forgive me,' he said, and pointed across the street, 'but our butcher shop has opened and I must get there quick to see we get a good cut.'

If you were so disposed, any day in Mayarí would do for noting scarcities, inconveniences, irritants of all sorts. Just by looking you knew there was a shortage of paint. After I left Mr Hernandez, I had an hour before they would be straining coffee at El Parque – I was already inured both to such a wait and to the lack of coffee at the Bitirí – and I used it to look along Leyte Vidal for three things I needed: ink, envelopes, notebooks. The book-store was open – that was a surprise, for it was seldom open during my stay, a casualty of the harvest – but though their stock of books was good, they had none of these things.

'You know, children get their supplies at school,' the clerk said, and I took it as a warning.

I found a tall bottle of ink at the quincalla, an import from China, looking as if it had survived the hurricane. I took it to Despaigne, the gardener at the Bitirí, to help me open it; he had considerably stronger hands than I, but he had to find a pair of pliers to loosen it.

No envelopes. The post office sold stamped ones, though there were days when they too ran out. Dr Padrón found an old college notebook, cut out the first ten pages of notes – 'I never throw out anything' – and made me a present of the rest. A week later at Central Guatemala, where I spent a few days, they sold me a school notebook at the general store; I thanked them elaborately because I knew they were making an exception with me: notebooks were for students.

I got to El Parque with my bottle of ink just before the coffee was ready, and joined the taxi drivers who always hung around the counter while waiting for customers. One, with a double-breasted blazer thrown over his shoulders, was very angry. 'It is not just the fucking bother about the tyres – why do they force you to have that painter they selected to paint your car? Just let them give us the paint. We can do it better ourselves or get someone we want!'

'Do not act innocent,' said an older one. 'It is the same thing as with the tyres. They give you tyres so you can give service – not to make a business of reselling them.'

'But they do not let you rent them even!' said the indignant one.

The older one looked at me and winked. 'But you can lend them,' he said. 'I have one on my car that a friend lent me.' He chuckled and shook his head to show that he had, of course, bought it.

The serving of the coffee interrupted that argument, and the older driver and I found ourselves together at the inside counter. First, we had to shoo two little boys wrestling on the sawdust-strewn floor; the black one got up and said to the other, 'That will teach you not to mess with a Negro!' although he had not been doing as well as the white boy; and they went off together happily. I said to the taxi driver, 'You have to be a North American to appreciate that.'

'Yes, I realize that you have no problems about tyres,' he said, missing my point and thereby proving it, 'but the fact is they are pretty fair about the few tyres we get. After all, the man in charge of distribution is just down the street. He can see with his own eyes the new tyre on my car – you think he believes I have it on loan?'

You have to apply for new tyres and wait your turn. When they come, they can be either Cuban, Czech or English, and the price can be as little as four for $74. But they bring up the value of your car by $1,000, for a new tyre is worth $250 on the black market. That is why the taxi drivers, who get preference on distributions, are not allowed to sell their cars when they get new tyres, or at least not with the new tyres as part of the sale.

'Private individuals are the ones who have it good,' said the driver. 'One doctor here recently made a big profit – he sold his car as soon as he got new tyres!'

He said it tolerantly, and thought about it a moment. 'A friend of mine recently paid seven hundred dollars for three new tyres for his taxi,' he added. 'You have to work very hard to pay that price, when you consider that all you get for a ride to Nicaro is five dimes.'

I was to find out that was the normal cost when six or seven people got together at the taxi stand. When, as happened with me, you wanted to take one alone and in a rush – I had to catch a plane at Nicaro airport – it could cost ten dollars for a fifteen-minute ride.

At the Bitirí I sat outside waiting for Angela to finish; Margarita leaned against a pole near the door and gossiped with her. Suddenly, at the reception desk across the lawn, the shrill voice of the dentist's wife began. Angela came to the door to see what had happened. 'She still is going on about the rat,' said Margarita. 'What a beaky woman she is.'

'Of course she got a rat, it was bound to be,' said Angela.

The dentist and his wife and two little boys lived in a double room, and she had brought in two burners to make coffee, since they could get all their meals from the hospital for five per cent of his salary. But she had taken to cooking meals on the burners. 'One whole wall is greasy from her cooking,' Margarita said. 'I could stop that, I am in charge of the cleaning and it is against the rules.'

It was the dentist's wife's belief that there was a nest of rats in the flower bed outside her room, and her complaints would worry Despaigne, the gardener, because he suspected she wanted the flower bed levelled. Already, in order not to walk the half block to the entrance, she left the Bitirí through a hedge near her room, and had knocked down a tall cactus to make a path.

'Oh no,' said Margarita, 'listen, she has lost something again!'

The chambermaids were not allowed in her room to clean because when she first moved to the Bitirí she had lost something and had decided it was best if she took care of the room herself. This time she had lost a box with a notebook and two pencils. El Gallego, the new manager, kept turning away her anger by joking; he was young and handsome and good-humoured. In a moment, her voice softened and she kept assuring him, 'I am confiding, I am. Do not say I am suspicious.'

At one time or another, all the girls at the Bitirí discussed the dentist's wife with me that day. Most of them had decided that the woman should go back to Havana and 'stay in that fine house she talks about so much' and let her husband finish his rural duty in peace.

'Has she told you about her fine house in Havana, Jose?' Margarita asked, and sniffed.

Angela half closed her eyes, a gesture which gave whatever she said a suggestive ring. 'It is her fine husband she worries about. . . .'

Mercedes, an older woman who worked the other side of the triangle during the day, came over to escape the argument with the dentist's wife. She raised her eyes and commented, 'It is not right for a woman to follow her husband around. She has her children. My husband lives up at Los Pinares all week. The devil take him – who cares what he does!'

But Mercedes did take the rats seriously; she had recently had a terrible experience with 1080, the name for a poison that was now illegal to use but which killed them instantly. She had noticed a hole under the fifty-gallon drum in the yard where they kept their water, and had spread a little 1080 on a piece of bread and pushed it into the hole. The next morning there were ten rats – 'stiff as wood' – lying around, not more than two or three feet away. 'That is how fast that poison works,' she said, and looked around and lowered her voice.

But that same day her granddaughter's puppy began to act strange. They laughed at it, they thought it was having bad dreams. At night it began to foam at the mouth, and Mercedes gave it milk with oil, warmed up. 'But it did not help him and by morning he was dead. And then I went crazy, for my granddaughter had been playing with the puppy and what if she had touched the dog's saliva? I washed her hand over and over again. I even used alcohol!'

A neighbour's chicken died and they came to ask her if she knew whether someone was using 1080, but Mercedes believed that the chicken and the puppy must have picked up the poison elsewhere, for she had buried the bread deep in the hole. 'I am not using 1080 ever again, as God is my witness.' Then she laughed.

I asked, 'Why did you laugh?'

'I said God, it is a habit. They do not believe in God any more.' And she giggled.

At night, sitting outside my room, I could see the rats run from one flower bed to the other. If I stayed quiet enough, they carefully came over to within a few feet, then scurried. Sitting in the dining-room, waiting for dinner, I had to stamp my foot to discourage one from entering. There were flower beds around the dining-room and also inside, and the rats waited there to get at the crumbs that fell on the floor, for the dining-room was not swept until morning. The waitresses laughed at my manoeuvre; no one was really afraid of rats.

'It is just that they will eat up any food they can get to, and God forbid that you have left a piece of clothing lying around with a grease spot on it!' said an old man with whom I occasionally had a drink at a little bar on Maceo. He was a night-watchman, and every day before he went to work, he set up a wire trap in his home.

'It is a little enclosure, my trap, like a bird cage,' he said. 'At the closed end I put a piece of cracker and as soon as they nibble on it, the door behind them closes. Every day I catch one, sometimes two. It never fails to catch one. I come home in the morning, empty the trap into a bag and give it a couple of blows. Some people burn them; I do not like to do that. I have not kept count but I have caught hundreds now. There is no shortage of rats.'

'You would think Hurricane Flora would have drowned them all,' I said, for our conversation was caused by my having seen two dead on Maceo that morning, the result of torrential rain during the night.

'Oh no,' the old man said. 'They float, they hang on to bits of wood. You could see them doing that during the hurricane. All those animals came down from the mountains along with the top layer – well, not of soil but all those things on top that make good food for them. As a matter of fact, it is since the hurricane that we have so many rats.'

El Gallego, the new manager, didn't know what he could do about the rats at the Bitirí. 'I do not dare use 1080, though I can assure you it would wipe them out,' he said. He grew up in Nicaro and had been a Rebel in the monte, so the idea of such direct action appealed to him, but he was a Party man and he wasn't going to break the law. 'What if one lives long enough to run to the cistern and drop in!'

'I do not know if it is the law,' he said. 'I do not care so much about that, it is contaminating the water that frightens me.'

I believed El Gallego, for he had once gone against the Party's instructions when he believed it was in the wrong. That was about four years ago when the Party was first being formed and was called the Integrated Revolutionary Organizations (O R I) and Anibal Escalante, a leader of the pre-revolutionary Popular Socialist Party (Communist), was trying to set up a sectarian, authoritarian party. 'You remember that Fidel finally broke that up and Anibal left the country,' El Gallego said. 'There were a lot of extremists in those days, and at Nicaro they sent me to talk to a woman who had moved into one of the good houses that had become empty, with all her children.' He was to persuade her to move out, and although he told the Party he didn't agree, they insisted he go talk to her. When he went to see her, the neighbours gathered round, and instead of urging her to move, he got up and made a speech that this kind of action was not what he had been taught in his classes on revolutionary orientation.

The woman was allowed to keep the house, but El Gallego was asked to leave the Party. 'It was only a week or so later that Fidel made his famous speech,' said El Gallego, 'so you see I was right. And the Party invited me back!'

What El Gallego really wanted to do about the rats was shoot them. He had stayed overnight at the Bitirí and had seen them in the darkened dining-room in the middle of the night. 'If I could bring my rifle and sit there quietly and knock them off one by one – ah, that would be something!' El Gallego liked to talk, but he had to go home to shave. I offered him a blade – 'if you do not mind accepting it,' I said.

'If I do not mind!' he said. 'If you knew how I have plotted to ask you for one!'

When I saw him later clean-shaven, he said, 'What a difference to the Soviet Tatras. I can use it many more times.'

From then on, I would give a blade to men I met and the response was always the same. I gave a package of five to Dr Padrón and he was quietly thrilled. 'I think I can make them last until Christmas if I use them right. Look at the shave I got – I do not think I have to shave for the rest of the week. I even cut myself because my beard was so thrilled that it got goose pimples!'

What girls most wanted was hose – 'fine hose', as they called them – although in a tropical country the lack was not a real hardship. At a mid-semester show at the Frank Pais Elementary School, one of the teachers, a Hungarian girl who had married a Mayarí boy when he was in Hungary studying, showed up in a pair of white string mesh stockings, not as outré as windowpane stockings, but certainly very stylish. 'Oooh, ooh,' said the other teachers, 'how beautiful! You got them from Europe!' She shook her head and said she had got them in Havana when she was there for the gymnastics course. 'I must go to Havana and get me a pair!' one teacher exclaimed.

She may not have meant to go to Havana just for a pair of 'mayas', as these stockings are called, but some people do make the trip just to shop. Havana has more entrepreneurs making scarce goods and more black-market activity. One young man in Mayarí wore very nice loafers with a deep-blue canvas top whose soles were of wood: when flat on the ground the soles looked like a solid piece of leather, but when he brought his foot up and bent it, you saw that the sole was made of quarter-inch strips of wood cleverly fitted together to give the shoe play. He had bought them in Havana from a shoemaker whose speciality this was.

The owner of the shoes was a defender of the Revolution;

the admirers of the shoes were young men very conscious of the lacks the Revolution, they felt, made them suffer. 'It only takes a little imagination,' said the owner of the shoes. 'You can get what you want if you are sufficiently interested.'

Jorge got his pants. The Saturday night after I had last talked to him, I ran into him on Leyte Vidal at the ice-cream parlour. He was with friends who, like him, were wearing starched bright sports shirts hanging out over their pants, shined shoes, and their hair slicked. There was not too much light on that corner, but his pants looked presentable.

'I am going to Tunas next Saturday, Jose,' he said. 'I sent her a telegram. I bought a pair from a friend who had no use for the ones that were distributed at Christmas.'

'And what are you doing tonight all dressed up?' I asked.

Jorge's friends laughed. 'I am doing a *cochinada*,' he replied.

'A *cochinada*?' It means, literally, a piggish thing.

Jorge began to get restless; he swung his shoulders and his hands reached for his crotch. 'Watch out,' said one of the boys, 'you will wear them out.' Finally he confessed: 'Sweet talk with a girl at the other end of Leyte Vidal. She is a decent girl and it was only talk, that is all I went for. It makes her feel good and it keeps me in practice!'

No more rats got into the dentist's room and he never complained – at the cane cutting on Sundays he was one of the most cheerful – but his wife's voice, as she called after the boys during the day, got shriller as time passed. July and the end of her husband's rural duty must have seemed very far away. Except for Margarita, who for a bit of talk was willing to forgive and forget (old Mercedes said about her, 'You cannot keep that girl out of anything but work'), the dentist's wife and the girls at the Bitirí seldom talked.

By that time Angela was no longer at the Bitirí, and old Mercedes now cleaned the rooms on my side. She was faster and more efficient, and took to telling me things. She was telling me about Holy Week – it was Good Friday – when the dentist's wife threw a fit at one of the girls. 'On Holy Friday people did not sweep out their houses or bathe, because you would break out in scabs. You ate *caballero* beans and yams with sugar and you prayed all day,' she was saying. 'And there was Sunday of the Palm Leaves, you put them behind the door at home for when it thundered –'

At that point the dentist's wife began screaming. 'Oh, oh,' said Mercedes, 'Nereida must have gone over to tell her not to walk out through the shrubbery!'

The dentist's wife's face was scarlet. 'Who are you with your fresh face to tell me what to do!' she screamed.

Nereida, a quiet, somewhat supercilious girl who worked in the office, backed away and then simply listened.

'I am going to walk wherever I please!'

We did not hear what Nereida said to that. 'What a beaky woman,' said Mercedes.

The dentist's wife leaned forward, almost as if she were going to – incongruously enough – 'touch toes', and from this position she was able to fill her lungs and scream louder. 'If you are such a revolutionary, why do you not concern yourself with the way I am forced to live here! I have suffered a lot for the Revolution, I have to put up with a lot – I make a thousand trips a day because there is no water. And I am going to walk out wherever I please – right now, watch me!' And she took one of her children and headed for the short cut, but she changed her mind and came back. 'You ought to occupy yourself with making this place livable for me!' she yelled again, and this time Nereida left.

A moment later, Margarita went by dragging two huge cacti for Despaigne, due later in the afternoon, to plant in the path the dentist's wife had made. 'Why did she say that about the Revolution?' Mercedes asked.

'That is what Nereida wants to know,' Margarita said. 'She never gave her a chance to say anything more than that she should not destroy the shrubbery.' Margarita shrugged her plump shoulders. 'What does the revolution have to do with it?'

I went for my third haircut in Mayarí that afternoon; ordinarily I would wait longer, but you are self-conscious in Cuba with shaggy hair, and in any case, Columbie was a pleasure to listen to. 'How are things at the Bitirí?' he asked, for a start.

We were now friends, so I said, 'There is a lot of coming and going of all sorts of officials. I like the campaign against bureaucracy, Columbie, but' – I tried out the phrase for the first time – 'it seems to me that you are in danger of getting an ambulant bureaucracy.'

Columbie took a step back so I could see him well, and clicked his scissors, a signal that I should listen to him.

'All these people running around doing and producing nothing cannot continue. This matter of the per diem has to go. Why, there are people who earn six and seven dollars a day who have a per diem of twelve! The hotels and motels and INIT resorts which were built for tourists are not being used by tourists but by all sorts of delegates and functionaries on per diem. These are resorts to which I cannot go, or at least only for a day, and whenever you go to one you find them full of such people who pay for it with the resources of the state – we do not even call it that, we call it the resources of the *people*. You see all those soldiers and Army officers driving around in cars doing nothing and eating at the Bitirí where the food is good but is also costly – it has got to stop, for it makes a mockery of the Revolution!

'It is true that you do not find Party leaders living that way, but that is no more than as it should be. The one hope I see is in the fact that the Party and more and more leaders are being selected by the people, that what defines a Communist is not based on an education that for the moment could only have been acquired through a certain privilege – no, it is based on what you do and what you are. It is also a good thing that these ambulant bureaucrats, as you call them, are forced at certain times to go cut cane. Cutting cane is a brute's job. I am a barber, I cannot cut cane, but I cut and will cut cane because it is right that we all do it. And if we all do it, then we all produce for our country and that production must not be wasted by people running around with little brief-cases and eating at the Bitirí and staying at the hotels on per diem!'

He went back to cutting my hair, and I could hear him breathe hard from his monologue. Then he clicked his scissors again.

'There is one thing the Revolution lacks and that is a con-stitution, such as the Soviet Union and other countries who have made the social revolution have. A constitution that writes it out clearly for everyone what one can do and what one cannot do, what rights one has and what one does not. Even for Fidel himself, so that he too knows what he can do and what he cannot. Fidel made this Revolution and he leads us, as is right, but he too needs to know what his limitations are. So that he cannot take millions of dollars and invest them here or there and then have the whole thing fail and the effort lost.

'I shall tell you why we need such a constitution. It is true the government leans on the 1940 constitution, but it does so when it wants to, which means that it uses it only when it pleases. Well, Batista did that too. We need such a constitution so that these boys in Orden Pública cannot act just as it pleases them. Do not think I say this to you alone. I say it to the delegate of the Ministry of the Interior too. As it is, Orden Pública picks up a man and throws him in jail and one week later says to him, Well, *chico*, there is no evidence, so you can go. So you can go! But they need to be held responsible for depriving that man of his liberty for one week. That man has the right to take *them* to the courts and say, You have held me illegally and you should suffer for your error. For we have a lot of impassioned men who need a constitution to calm them down. I do not mean by this that they are not good men – oh yes, they are, and they have fought for the Revolution, but they need to be held to the letter of the law. That kind of thing cannot happen in the Soviet Union because they have a constitution and respect it.'

When I got back to the Bitirí, I found Dr Padrón waiting outside, not betraying his impatience but put out that the Army doctor from Santiago who had made a date with him and the head of Public Health had checked in at the Bitirí and then disappeared. Since it had worked so well with Columbie, I told Padrón that the army doctor was just another member of that new phenomenon, the ambulant bureaucracy. Padrón's eyes opened with delight. 'That is good, that is very good,' he said. 'Why, you are getting as smart as we Cubans!'

I did not have to wait for Soní and El Moro, with whom I was hitching a ride to Central Guatemala. I did not try out my new phrase on them, but I told them I had heard from two or three people that many of the thousands who were waiting to leave or had left did not do it simply for political reasons or even primarily for anti-communist reasons: they were tired of the rationing, the scarcities, the terrible difficulties of living from day to day.

'Soní, do you remember the patched pants?' El Moro said, as if he had not heard me. 'Remember all those men in town with pants so worn and mended that you did not know what the original had been like?'

Soní nodded; he knew what El Moro was going to say.

'And when they walked away from you, you did not even have to turn around,' said El Moro, 'because you could bet that the seat of their pants was one big patch.' El Moro turned to me. 'Have you seen one man like that in Mayarí? Have you seen one of the patched?'

I shook my head.

'And about the rationing,' El Moro said, 'Soní and I are not good persons to ask whether it bothers us personally. Soní and I would be with this Revolution if the only thing to eat was yams. But the people who tell you different – the people who leave – you know what bothers them? What bothers them is social equality. They do not like to see Soní and me working together. That is what really bothers them.'

5. In the Fist of the Revolution

The American executives of Central Guatemala – in the days when it was called Central Preston – lived on La Avenida, a street lined with regal coconut palms along the blue-green Bay of Nipe. Their Southern homes with long, wide, curving screened porches were cared for in each case by a cook, a cleaning man and a gardener, from a monthly allotment the company paid its executives. At the railroad crossing behind La Avenida and at the avenue's start near the sugar mill, there were always guards to keep out Cubans who were not on specific errands. Now the pavement is cracked, the gardens unkempt, the white paint on the houses peeling off, and three of them have burned down. Luis Chao, the Chinese who had worked for the United's administrator when the vice-president was not there to claim him for his kitchen, stood at the Visitors' House, formerly the administrator's, and exclaimed, 'Bad, bad, bad, they do not know how to live here!' For in 1960, when the sugar mill was nationalized, the poorest of the poor, those with the largest families from the neighbourhood called Brooklyn, were moved to La Avenida: two families to each house, where seldom more than two or three persons had lived. They have made it their own: the children of *los tiznados* – the sooty, the old epithet for the poorest workers, who were also apt to be Negroes – play ball on the street; and there is now elbow room to raise chickens, goats, cows and pigs. The calm of that street is gone for ever.

La Avenida is now called Katanga, but the other neighbourhoods of the *batey* – the name for towns around a sugar mill – are still called Brooklyn and New York, and this is where most of the six thousand residents of Guatemala live. New York lies on the other side of the railroad from Katanga, and here in the best houses near the Administration Building formerly lived the Cuban office workers; in lesser houses away from the offices, the skilled workers at the mill. Brooklyn also has two sections: on one side of the railroad, two-family houses of three rooms each; on the other, barracks-like buildings called *barracones* – a name descended from the days of the slave quarters, which were built on very much the same principle – composed of some twenty rooms measuring ten feet by ten feet, one family to a room.

I had caught a glimpse of all this on the fifteen-minute ride from Mayarí to the town square of Guatemala. We left Mayarí on the bumpy gravel road of the neighbourhood called El Naranjal, going north until we reached the new smooth highway leading to Nicaro; we crossed it and continued north-west on another good road leading directly to the little peninsula in the Bay of Nipe on which Guatemala lies. Just before the land flattened out at the isthmus and the road turned to gravel for a stretch ('The harvest stopped the work on the road,' said El Moro) we passed a lovely, round, unmenacing hill. 'Guanina?' I asked. El Moro nodded.

It was here on 30 December 1958, two days before Batista fled Cuba, that the four hundred men of the Mayarí Army command, frightened that the Rebels ruled the surrounding country, themselves tried to flee. They marched down the road, feeling protected by the daylight and the knowledge that they were heading for a town which could hardly be said to be Cuban. The United Fruit Company owned everything in it, every piece of land, every house; even its police – the *guardias jurados* – were company guards. Not only did the private railroads, spread out over the 330,000 acres of cane-fields which made the Bay of Nipe (twelve miles long and eight miles wide) a private lake, come together at the isthmus of the little peninsula, but beyond the sugar mill there were the private piers where the freighters came for sugar. The soldiers expected no trouble in getting a ship from there to take them where things were safer: probably Havana. And they would have had no trouble if a group of young Rebels had not descended the lovely hill at Guanina and routed them all.

There was a little home-made arch into Guatemala, perhaps more unprepossessing for being so far away yet from the centre of town and from the towering sugar-mill itself. But the arch set the tone for the days I was to spend there; it said: *We are going to convert all the cane into sugar this Harvest VII*. It was a small arch and did not have enough space to refer to the harvest as the Harvest of the People, as was usually done, for in fact this year's was the ninth since the Revolution but the seventh since the sugar mills were nationalized.

Just beyond the arch, in swampy land, was Brooklyn, so dismal in appearance even from the street that ran along the railroad that one look down a side street from the car was enough to embarrass me in the presence of my Mayarí friends. Like Loma Rebelde, I knew it must hurt them. In a minute, however, we were in New York, and although the houses here were all painted the same mustard-yellow colour that La United painted everything – except the homes of its American executives – the difference was startling. These were wooden frame homes, each with its front porch and fair-sized plot of ground; and although the scarcity of paint had made it impossible to paint them for many years, the lush shrubbery, the flowering trees gave them some colour and individuality.

Two months later, when I came again to say good-bye to the friends I had made in Guatemala, I hitched a ride with Dr Padrón and others of the Mayarí hospital staff who were seeing Guatemala for the first time. They had known other bateyes and so they did not flinch when we went past the arch and could see the barracones down the side streets. But when we got to New York and took the long way round to get to the Guatemala hospital, skirting at one point a little inlet where the houses faced the water, they turned to one another. 'Charming, charming!' they said, and were so pleased with it that when I pointed out that it was like a Southern town in the United States, they said yes, it reminded them of ones they had seen in the movies, and forgot to answer me with mock disdain.

Off the charming town park which had been completely redone after the Revolution, in an old wooden building, was the office of the Administración Regional, and here I was left in the hands of Juan Paredes, the equivalent of mayor in Guatemala. He was a little wiry man with darting black eyes, full of delight about untoward events, such as getting an American in Guatemala, and he was, in any case, very happy that day because the work plan for the town had been met a full three days before the end of the month. He wore dungarees and a denim work shirt, and I got behind him on a motor bike, the only vehicle at his disposal but which delighted him as much as if it were a Cadillac, to go to the Hotel where they hoped there would be a vacant room for me.

The Hotel was at the furthest point of the peninsula which is Guatemala, but a block before we got to it, we passed the mill's Administration Building and as soon as I asked about it, Paredes stopped. 'Let us go in and meet the people there,' he said. 'You will want to know them, and there is plenty of time.' Paredes was not one to pass up anyone, so he stopped at the office on the ground floor of the two-storey building and introduced me to Cutier, a light-skinned Negro who had worked for La United all his life. This was the personnel and engineering office, and next to Cutier's desk was a blueprint map drawn years ago by La United's engineers showing the holdings of the company, the cane-fields and sugar mills surrounding the Bay of Nipe. Here and there was the laconic statement: *Owned by Others.*

'The policy of La United was to divide the workers into classes and races,' said Cutier, and it was he who first gave me a run down of the old neighbourhoods. He raised his eyebrows each time he made a point, and paused to let it sink in. He stood at his desk and accompanied his florid talk with gestures. 'If someone got together enough money – which did not happen often, I can assure you, for everyone was always in debt – to buy his own home, there was none he could buy here. He would have to go to Mayarí or Guaro – here at the Central everything was theirs and they were not selling. They had their own little empire and they were creating it in the image – you will pardon me and I count on your understanding that you are welcome in socialist Cuba – in the image of the society from which you come.'

Paredes, for whom speech did not come with such ease, looked at him with admiration, as if he might applaud if Cutier continued. It embarrassed him, however, when Cutier ended with so pejorative a statement about the United States; he looked down, then looked up with a serious look, having thought it over and decided it was not an unjust statement. He was relieved and overjoyed that I understood. It made him laugh.

Upstairs, the secretary to the administrator, an elderly man named Paco Ortega, took us right into the administrator's office. A Party official, the chief of engineers, and other men from the mill were having a meeting with the administrator, but they were willing to chat. Behind the administrator's desk was a large photograph of Camilo Cienfuegos, one of the original twelve who began the insurrection in the Sierra Maestra, who died when his small plane was swept to sea in the first year of the Revolution. He was a tall, handsome young man with a face which can only be described as beautiful, and its smiling gaiety greets you all over Cuba. Above it and to the sides, in smaller prints, were Martí and Maceo. I asked them if these last two had been there when La United's administrator occupied the office. They all laughed.

La United had left little behind. They knew what was coming when the Revolution triumphed. In 1959, with the Agrarian Reform, they lost their cane-fields; in 1960, they continued milling, but by the time the mill was nationalized in the late summer not a single American executive was left; the houses on La Avenida were empty. At the time of the nationalization, La United's administrator was a former assistant in the accounting department who is now in Miami. 'One Suarez by name,' said the administrator.

'My brother-in-law,' said Paco Ortega, as if he did not want them to spare his feelings.

'He is still one Suarez,' said the administrator. 'It has nothing to do with you.'

Ortega recounted how La United at its sugar mill at Banes had left an engineer in charge, a young Cuban who had studied in the States. He stayed on as administrator after the nationalization, and they discovered one day that he was calling headquarters in the United States every afternoon to tell them how production was going.

'Imagine!' said the administrator.

Ortega, a stickler for details, said, 'But he turned out all right. He works in Havana now for the Revolution.'

'Yes, he did not mean badly,' the administrator confessed. 'He simply could not imagine that the Central really no longer belonged to La United.'

'The mentality of the past,' someone said.

Little Paredes nodded and repeated, 'The mentality of the past.' Then his lively dark eyes looked around. 'But who would have thought it, eh!'

Someone there told me the story about Roberto Henderson, one I was to hear often in Guatemala. Henderson was the chief engineer at the mill, a very fine man; he was the only one to answer the angry statement of the American administrator that the Cubans would be unable to make sugar without them. He told them the Americans had never made sugar; that had been the work of the Cubans. 'He told that last administrator to his face and that man was bad amongst the bad!' Henderson was now in Havana; he had been important in the organization of Acopio, the distribution organization for food.

Someone smiled: Henderson first went to the United States with the other executives and then returned.

'It was his Cuban wife,' Paco Ortega said. 'She was the one who wanted to go Up North. He divorced her. He said, Well, we have been here three months, I am going back. But she finally rejoined him and they are now remarried and living in Havana.'

This story about Roberto Henderson was told me so often, with embellishments to broaden it and speculation to give it depth, that Henderson became a myth to me. Until one day, looking through a weekly, I came across a story on Acopio and in a photograph of some of its officials saw a fair, thin, middle-aged man identified as he. But as soon as Henderson was mentioned again the story filled out Henderson, who had diminished on being a man in a picture, to his proper dimensions. That double view is the vision of all Cubans: their heroes walk about them as human beings and legends; and the street one lives on and the place where one works are the settings of lived history.

The administrator told Paredes the Hotel was no place for a writer – it was full of young men, skilled workers, who had come to the Central to work in the mill during the harvest – and advised him to take me to the Visitors' House, which is at the disposal of the mill and the Party to house men coming through for a day or two on business. 'A writer needs peace and quiet,' he said to me. 'Luis Chao is in charge there. He is a superb cook and worked for the Americans. I dare say his political opinions are not of the best, but he is a good cook. It is a pity you will not have an opportunity to find out.'

Guests at the Visitors' House now had to go to the Hotel or to the new counter cafeteria on the town plaza to eat, but Luis Chao always had coffee warm on the stove, though he wasn't drinking it these days because he had been suffering from a pain in his stomach and was watching what he ate. I never went in or out that he didn't offer me some or that I didn't accept, as both Paredes and I did immediately the first day. Paredes worried about Luis's health, and asked him how old he was. He was seventy-three, was born in Canton, and had been living in Cuba for forty-six years; he was all alone, all his relatives had died, and he only had a couple of contemporaries left in Havana.

Unlike other Chinese I met in Cuba, Luis spoke a pidgin Spanish, short declarative statements, always in the present tense. It must have struck Paredes for the first time, for he asked Luis if in Asia only one language was spoken. 'No, no,' Luis said. 'In China many languages. China only one country in Asia. So they speak many languages.'

It delighted Paredes to learn this. 'Of course, of course,' he said, 'I should have known. Even in Cuba they have different words for things in Oriente than they have in Havana. *Es de carajo* – it is a hell of a thing, eh!'

I pointed out that in Cuba and other Latin American countries the second-person plural of the familiar form – *vosotros* – is never used.

'Oh yes, that is for courtesy,' said Paredes illogically but nevertheless correctly, for *vosotros* does have for Latin Americans a more pompous ring than the more grammatically formal *ustedes*. 'President Dorticós uses it a lot. He is – well, a lawyer of profundity. Not like Fidel, who tells you clear this is this and that is that. It is very interesting. I hear some speakers say "idiosyncrasies" and I run to the dictionary and find out what it means. Deformed habits – that is what it means. Such as if I die and leave my little son and he forms idiosyncrasies. That is something, that word, eh?' He laughed at having talked so much. '*Es de carajo!*'

The Visitors' House, formerly the home of La United's administrator, stood at the head of La Avenida. There was one more building beyond it – the school for the children of the Americans – but it was reached by the road behind the houses on La Avenida. Across from the Visitors' House, there was no home, and it consequently had an unobstructed view of the bay, green and endless in the distance, with bending, picture-postcard palms in the foreground. The house was, strictly speaking, a two-bedroom home, but so large that the dining-room now had eight beds, the second bedroom six, although the double bed in the master bedroom sat in lonely splendour. Six rattan easy-chairs and three small tables remained in the porch from former days, but they took up only one corner. Luis lived in a small servant's room behind the kitchen.

When he saw me looking at the view from the porch, I said, 'The water looks wonderful.'

He raised a warning finger. 'You be very careful. You put foot in water. Shark bite it off. You do not put foot in water. Too many sharks!'

I said I noticed his neighbours all raised pigs. He shook his head. 'Bad, bad, they do not take care of the garden.' I said the pigs helped supplement what they got at the store. He raised a warning finger again. 'You be very careful. You not kill pig to sell. You kill pig to eat yourself – all right. But not to sell, you be very careful!'

I asked him what the Americans were like, and he spread out his forearms from his waist, a happy gesture for remembering the good old days. 'All good people. You sure of their word. They say, Okay Luis – it is done. Not now.' He pointed to a group of men extending the street beyond the bend toward where, two or three blocks away, were the piers for freighters. 'See those fellows. They working. They say they finish tomorrow. They never finish. You not sure. Americans say we do this, you be sure they do it.'

But when you took Luis out of his own situation – that is, of what it had been like for him personally – then he had good things to say for the Revolution: that everyone worked now, everyone made money, all the children went to school. And concerning a project like Los Pinares, he spoke lovingly of the tomatoes they grew there. 'Each one wrapped in a piece of fine paper. Packed fine. To sell to other country. Very good.'

We had many talks in the big kitchen of the house while I drank Luis's excellent coffee, sometimes when his assistant, a thin, deferential Cuban who admired Luis enormously, was there, and Luis never censored his criticism or tempered his recollections. Luis would tell me how much meat you could buy for fifty cents in the old days, and his assistant would look down and say yes, yes, there was a lot of food in the stores then. 'But of course, no one had money to buy it,' he would add, and Luis, a fair man, would nod and say yes, that is true.

Sometimes Antonio El Japonés would join us for coffee. He was the Japanese gardener responsible for the neat, manicured town park with its many varieties of shrubs and trees. You admired the park and whoever you were with said, 'That is Antonio El Japonés for you, a tremendous gardener.' Antonio always asked Luis first how he felt, then told him how his own aches and pains were doing. Anything we said he nodded at; everything had equal interest for him. Luis's assistant always asked Antonio about the movie he had seen the night before, and the critique of it consisted in pinning down for certain whether it had been Hungarian or Bulgarian or Czech or Italian. Antonio went to the movies every night, even when the programme had not changed.

It took me a couple of days to find the pattern to Luis's responses: whatever the Revolution had done that was new, he admired; whatever the Revolution took over, whether distributing shoes or making sugar, he found deficient. A generational difference. But when the subject was, for example, the production of sugar at the Central – the major subject of conversation at Guatemala – that involved not only a comparison with the old days but between Cubans and Americans, his response was practically automatic: the Americans did better.

La United's administrator must have known better; there never could have been any doubt that Central Guatemala would continue to produce sugar. From any spot in the batey – even across the bay – you could see its two belching chimneys. It is one of the giant mills of Cuba, with a capacity for grinding 15,400,000 pounds of cane a day, 450 loads from the huge iron cages of railroad cars that go miles beyond the isthmus of the peninsula to bring in the cane from the fields. But whether the mill operates efficiently – or rather, as efficiently as before – was the subject of debate; it was usually – though not always – an index to the politics of the speaker. It took, consequently, many conversations to get to the niceties of all the arguments.

Luis Chao put it starkly: La United with its short, ninety-day harvests produced almost as much as the mill does now with seven months of milling. The mill had often produced 13,000 bags of 250 pounds of sugar a day; now it was averaging between 8,000 and 9,000.

Luis's assistant nodded. 'Yes, but –'

Luis interrupted. 'The Americans make everybody work very hard, very hard. But they make more.'

So began the distinctions that I gathered for five days from everyone I spoke to in Guatemala. The equipment at the mill is old and does not work at maximum efficiency; when a breakdown occurs it must usually be remedied with repaired parts, not new ones as under La United. La United had 850 railroad cars at its disposal; Minaz (the Ministry of Sugar) has lent 200 of these to other centrals. The grade of sugar produced now is one step away from refined, white sugar; La United produced only crude brown sugar.

Everyone agreed, however, that most of the problems derive from the cane-fields, not the mill. La United could easily find, in a countryside where only a minority had steady jobs, 14,000 full-time cane cutters; many were heads of families and their wives and children helped them clean, gather and pack the cane at no pay. Until the forties, boat-loads of hungry Haitians were brought in at harvest time to cut cane. Everyone admired their endurance, and from their performance comes the saying: To cut cane you need only a *mocha*, a yam and a Haitian. (A *mocha* is the Cuban version of a machete.) The life in the cane-fields was supervised by the *mayorales* and the *guardias jurados* (the overseers and the company guards), and their performance has given a sinister resonance to these words.

The mayorales of La United would stop and start the cane cutting so that it was always freshly cut when it

went to the mill, a practice they could afford because cane cutting was piecework. And since sugar quotas set the limits of
each harvest, not all the cane was cut, so that they could pick
and choose which fields to harvest that would give the best
yield. The Sugar-cane Workers Union was able to win gains
for the workers in the mill, where the workers' skills and
ability to close down a mill in a strike gave them a certain
power, but the campesinos in the fields were totally unprotected. As Columbie, the barber in Mayarí, said, the Rural
Guards did not have to force anyone to break a strike in the
cane-fields – there were always enough hungry campesinos
eager for the work.

Neither the cane-fields nor the cane cutters have disappeared. As all over Cuba, there has been new planting to en-
large the supply, for by 1970 the government wants to reach
a harvest of ten million tons of sugar. There is even fertilizing
of the cane and weeding of the fields; the new planting is more
scientifically planned, for they have found that rows of cane
in a particular relation to the sun result in better cane. But, in
a sense, the cane cutters have disappeared. There is now full
employment and this brute's work, as Columbie called it,
has become the responsibility of the entire population.

After a morning of stripping the cane of its leaves and
stacking the stalks, later to be packed in trucks or railroad
cars, I was dead of exhaustion and my charley horses were not
to leave me for several days. Trujillo, a maintenance man at
the hospital by whose side I had worked, laughed at the sight
of me climbing into the truck taking us back to Mayarí at
midday. 'Now you have learned the lesson of all the city volunteers,' he said. 'You have some idea of what it is to be a campesino.'

As with so many other experiences of the Revolution, they
have put this problem to ideological use, giving force to the
egalitarian push among the masses of people. But the problem
in the cane-fields remains, for the Soviet-designed machines
for cutting the cane, after five years of use and experiment, do

only a tiny proportion of the work; and there will have to be considerably more redesigning before anything more can be expected of them. The cane must be cut close; no more than an inch of stalk must remain above ground or the new shoots will be thinner and shorter; and at the same time the machine must also lop off the tops of the stalks. This means the machine works only on level ground and with even-growing cane, whereas many of the cane-fields are hilly, and the cane, one planting of which will last ten years, often grows at an angle and keeps resprouting that way.

The cane-cutting machines and the cranes used for gathering and packing the cut cane in the cars bog down in the fields after heavy rains. 'Wait until the days of rain come in May,' volunteers said to me. 'You will see us slogging around in the fields fighting the mud.'

Although half the Army now cuts cane during the harvest, there is no choosing your labour pool for the most propitious time: the cutting by full-time cutters and volunteers who go mornings and weekends or for two weeks or a month at a time has to be continuous. So the cane often lies in the fields a couple of weeks after cutting and stacking, its juice drying and its acid content rising, and when it arrives at the mill its yield is lower.

Late in the afternoon, on my first day at Guatemala, I left the Visitors' House by the back street which led directly to the railroad crossing on the way to the Hotel, where I planned to have dinner. There were three long lines of railroad cars filled with cane waiting to be shunted into the mill. They perfumed the air with the sweetish smell of cane, and I stopped to have my first look close up. The cane was packed helter-skelter, as the machine dropped the stalks into the car, and this made it impossible to pack as much into one car as when it was done by hand; it also sometimes created a bottleneck inside the mill when the cars were tilted to empty the cane on to the belt lines that carried it to the choppers and grinders.

The flagman at the crossing was a young campesino, and he

called out to me, 'Not so good, eh?' I asked why and he got up and limped towards me, the limp explaining why he held a job that was so undemanding. 'It is dry,' he answered, and reached for a stalk in the nearest car. 'See the ends ... they are dry. It means they have lost a lot of juice.' He threw the stalk back into the car; if it had been fresher, he might have peeled it and chewed the white pulp for its sweet, cool juice.

I got to the Hotel before the dining-room opened, and stood at the cigarette-and-coffee counter with others who were waiting like me. Most were young men but one of them was older, and when he mentioned that the water pressure had again been low that day, I asked why and he began an explanation of some of the problems at the mill. 'This water pressure I am talking about is the salt water used at one point in the process,' he said, 'and you have to dredge in the area to keep it up.' I told him I expected to see the mill that night and that it would be the first for me, and he began to explain something of the eighteen-hour process that it takes to make sugar from the cane dumped on the belt lines. At Guatemala no one tired of hearing about it, and the group at the cigarette counter got larger.

He had got on to some of the matters that affect yield when the Party man I had met in the administrator's office that afternoon came to buy cigarettes. 'It is shortsighted not to clean the way the Americans did,' the man was saying when the Party man stopped to listen with me. 'Every week they stopped everything and all the machinery and vats – everything – got a thorough cleaning.'

The Party man got a serious look. 'Listen, compañero,' he said, and I could see he did not know the man who had been talking. 'I must remind you that in Cuba we cannot afford the luxury of such interruptions in production because it means the life of the Revolution itself. Sugar is our economy, our life, and its production cannot be stopped.' He had coloured by the time he finished.

The other looked around with an embarrassed air. 'I think

there is some confusion,' he said. 'I have worked many years in the mill and I still do and I am a revolutionary.' He looked around to see if he were going to be challenged, and the Party man nodded, as if apologizing for the tone he had taken. 'I am aware,' the man continued, enjoying the complete attention of our group 'that the Americans did not care about cost the way we do, that they did not repair parts but simply replaced them, that they did not care how much oil they used to run the furnaces whereas we run them with *bagazo* alone – I know all these things. I am saying that clean-up is very important in order to keep the yield up, though I repeat I am aware of all the reasons why we do not do it.'

One of the young men spoke directly to the Party man: 'You see what he means? We clean every ten days or less often – it is not frequent enough.'

'I am glad to hear this,' the Party man said. 'I am interested in these problems.'

I spoke up for the Party man. 'He did not want me to get the wrong impression,' I said. 'I am a North American.'

It made them all laugh, but the millworker saw his duty: he listed all the accomplishments at the mill. The finest grade of sugar was now made; the furnaces to supply steam were run only with *bagazo*, the dried cane fibre; the *cachaza*, a black, spongy substance which is the last impurity extracted by the clarifiers before the crystallization process is begun, was once simply carried away and dumped, and now it was used as a fertilizer; the tasteless syrup removed from the crystallized sugar by the centrifuges in the last stage of the process was now packed in drums and exported for use in feeds and for the manufacture of alcohol and purgatives, a syrup with a marvellous name: *la miel final*, the final honey. 'These were all things that did not interest La United,' the man said. 'But the most important thing of all is that we now work for ourselves.'

He forgot one innovation that I saw that evening when Paredes took me to the mill: air blowers that untangled the cane in the tilted railroad cars on the occasions when tilting alone did not persuade the cane to drop into the runnels leading to the choppers. The three or four men showing me the mill – Paredes, the administrator's assistant, the head of the trade union – looked at it with pride: something La United's executives would not recognize if they were to walk into the mill today. Two hours later, after walking throughout the mill talking to the operators and workers – following the fascinating process until the sugar tumbles out of the centrifuges and slides into the funnel which automatically fills each bag with 250 pounds – after all this, we were at the entrance to the mill with a group that had formed around me, and almost every man that joined us asked, 'Did you show him how the cane is unloaded now?'

The group around me grew; it included the Party man, Paredes, the assistant administrator, the chief of Orden Pública (a young man of twenty-three named Jose Fuentes), workers in the mill, militia, all of them friendly, curious, calling out questions. It was my first such experience in Cuba, and it was puzzling that it should happen at Guatemala where they had known many Americans; perhaps they were testing how it was to talk to an American as equals. Some who had come out of the building to buy coffee at the stand within the gate paused a moment, got a question in, then tore themselves away to take coffee to others who could not leave their operation. Certainly, out in the balmy night air, with the extraordinary activity of the mill behind our shoulders, it was exciting to stand there and engage in a group interview. For one moment I thought I understood what feeds the public personality whom one sees in photographs and newsreels walking amongst the curious, bantering, being created by the shouted greetings, the outstretched hands.

They wanted to know my impressions of Cuba, my opinion of the Revolution – not of the Revolution in the abstract but of the public projects, the education programmes, of Fidel; they wanted to explain all of them to me, too. I had heard much of what they said, was familiar with the questions they posed. I objected that they were not supposed to interview me and they laughed at that. But the questions continued; they wanted to know:

1. What did Americans think about the war in Vietnam?
2. Will the truth be told about Kennedy's assassination?
3. Will the American Negroes rise and make a revolution?
4. What do Americans think about Cuba? What do they say when they hear Fidel's speeches?
5. What will the United States government do to me when I return? Will they let me write the truth about Cuba?

The chief of police, young Jose Fuentes, watched me with dark, intense eyes. Finally, he could contain himself no longer and explained that he knew the American people were not responsible for the actions of the government; they had not wanted the war in Vietnam. 'You have been here in Cuba for some time and you know we do not hate Americans, but' – he paused to put his question reasonably – 'but why do young workers – why do Negroes go to fight in Vietnam? Why do they not refuse to commit such crimes?'

The group of thirty or so became quiet for my answer. I told them that the soldiers sent to Vietnam were not told that they were going to fight for imperialism. 'They are told that they are going to help a small nation that is threatened by Communist imperialism,' I said. 'They are told that this people struggling to maintain a democratic society have asked our help against the attacks of outsiders. It is in the name of democratic ideals that American young men are sent to Vietnam. And if anyone says that it is economic imperialism, the State Department can laugh at you. They will say, What profit can we hope to make out of a poor country like that? How can we hope even to make back all the money that helping the Vietnamese has cost us?'

When I finished, everyone was still quiet, and Jose Fuentes looked at me with a bitter half-smile. 'Do you see?' I asked him. He would not say yes or no.

Then little Paredes broke the strained silence. 'Those imperialists are a clever bunch!' he said.

'But it is a crime,' Jose Fuentes said.

'Yes,' I said, and everyone relaxed, reminded that I was not a State Department spokesman.

Then someone began to speculate about the American people as being afraid of communism as they (the Cubans) had been. 'You remember all the propaganda?' he said. 'We feared communism.' I had heard this from others as explanation for why they had been anti-communist before the Revolution, and this time I asked why their fear of communism had not kept them from supporting the Revolution as it became more and more socialist. I kept going from one to the other and asking each individually why.

One old man volunteered: 'I had another fear – the fear that my son would be assaulted and killed by those Rural Guards of Batista's, that my daughter would be found attractive by one of them. That was one fear. That my son would grow up without an education or a job and turn into a marijuana smoker and my daughter end up in a brothel. That was my important fear.'

'What happened to them?' I asked.

'Both are now in a university,' he said. 'Only a rich man could have given them the careers they will now have.'

'Come,' someone said, 'they are straining coffee at the stand.' The proper way to end a good talk.

The next morning, after Luis Chao's coffee, I set off to look at Brooklyn close up. At the railroad crossing, the flagman on duty was a darkly handsome middle-aged man who had never done any more than nod at me before; today he squatted at his post with an old man who was keeping him company. I looked down the three lines of railroad tracks, and except for a few cars which had made the turn into the mill, they were clear all the way past Brooklyn.

'Where are they?' I asked.

There was something about the way the flagman looked at me as he got up to talk that revealed he now knew who I was. He shrugged to show disgust, and told me one of the belt lines had had to shut down for lack of cane.

The old man also advanced on me. 'It is the usual inefficiency,' he said. 'They cannot do anything right!'

All the belt lines were being fed a couple of hours later and there were filled cars waiting their turn, but the flagman and his crony, eager to talk to someone new, went into a thorough denunciation of every aspect of Cuban life. 'I tell you,' said the flagman, 'if fifty ships appeared in the bay right now, they would sink from the number of people who would try to leave on them!'

'Why fifty?' said the old man. 'Even if the entire bay was full of ships it would not be enough!'

It was difficult to ask them questions once they saw that I wanted to listen. They spelled each other like a vaudeville team, so happy to be complaining that they could not stand still but moved about and waved their arms. Everyone is starving, they said. 'Coffee and bread is what you eat for lunch and dinner,' the old man said.

'If they run out of wheat, people will faint in the streets!'

'There was always corn, you could always get corn,' said the old man. 'There is nothing special about growing corn. So where is the corn?'

'There is nothing special about cutting cane,' the flagman said. 'You can see for yourself they cannot get it done.'

I finally got a word in. 'But they say there used to be more experienced macheteros cutting cane in the old days.'

'They say, they say!' the flagman answered. 'They say they are planting more of everything all over Cuba – so where is the food?'

The old man waved a hand irritably. 'There are more cane cutters now. The whole country is cutting cane, the shops are closed all the time so they can cut cane, but they cannot do anything right.'

The flagman explained. '*They* do not know how to cut cane. The macheteros are all in the Army.'

'But the Army is cutting cane,' I answered.

'Why should they cut cane,' said the flagman, 'when they do not get enough to eat?'

'But the campesinos are still here and they know how to cut cane,' I said.

The flagman got red with anger. 'The campesinos are sons of whores!'

This was real blasphemy: in a sense, the Revolution had been made for the campesinos. It made all three of us quiet. The old man looked at me to see if the flagman had gone too far. The flagman looked away. To break the tension, I asked them how much money they made. The flagman earned $4 a day; the old man, a retired machinist, came over and wrote on the palm of his hand, so that only I could read it, $2.80.

The old man's pension was more than twice what he would have received before the Revolution, but there was no rationing then and the stores at the Central were full of goods; also, the campesinos and the fishermen sold their products even cheaper than the stores. Now the rationing was honest and the prices at the government stores were more or less what they were before the Revolution, but the campesinos usually sold their chickens and vegetables at three times that. If you had a regular job at the mill in the old days, as the flagman and the old man did, you might be deep in debt when the short harvest rolled around but you could get your staples in greater quantities and with much more ease than you could now. They must also, I imagine, have had the sense, since so many were so much worse off than they, that they were doing quite well.

During the harvest the sugar-mill workers worked seven days a week and could get, at a cost of $5.71, the following extra ration per month: 5 lb. rice, $\frac{1}{2}$ lb. beans, 1 lb. lard, 1 can of Russian spam, 1 can of Russian pork, $\frac{1}{2}$ lb. sausage, 1 lb. cornmeal, 1 can of frankfurters, $\frac{1}{2}$ lb. codfish, 1 lb. coffee, 2 cans of milk and 2 cans of squid. Nevertheless, a housewife spends a great deal of time on the look-out for the vegetable truck supplying her store, and the best thing even a revolutionary will say for the rationing is, 'We get along, we have to sell what we produce to pay for all the building and development the Revolution is doing.'

Past the Administration Building, walking through New York, a lady called me from her porch. I did not recognize her until she told me she was Juana Poyato. I had seen her at the mill the night before, and had stopped to talk to her because it had been a surprise to find a woman – especially a grey-haired one – working on the 7 p.m. to 3 a.m. shift. She was fifty-six, the mother of eleven children, and her job was to wield a long heavy broom to keep the *guarapo*, the cane juice, with much of the fibre still in it, flowing. When I asked her if it wasn't a hard job for her, she exclaimed, 'Oh, I wish I were younger, that I had another twenty years to work for the Revolution!'

Her husband was with her on the porch, and two of her daughters, one with a child in her arms, came out; also a son who now lived in Havana with his young family but was released from his job there during the harvest to come work in the mill. Until four years ago they had lived in the three-room places in Brooklyn. 'Now look at my palace!' she said. They had planted vegetables in the back yard and shrubberies all around, and every day they scrubbed down the whole house, as one daughter had just finished doing, to keep it shining.

'There were times,' Mrs Poyato said, 'in those three rooms in Brooklyn when we were eighteen persons in all, because of relatives or because the older children married and had babies. I do not know why I call them three rooms. They were three divisions really, three tiny divisions. One of the rooms was supposed to be a kitchen, but as the children came I used it for them and we took out the stove and put it in the little yard. We built a little two-by-four for it – you know, just to keep the rain out – and the company guard came around, sir, and said he did not want to see it the next time he passed. I myself had to tear it down. Oh how that hurt me – to tear down something we had built.

'I left the stove out there and cooked out in the yard, in the rain and all, for I could not take the space away from the children. After some time passed I said I do not care, I am going to build it again, and so I did. Another guard came around and I myself, sir, asked him to get out, so I could show him our three rooms. "Now sir," I said, "do you think I should cook where my children are?" Do you know what happened? He told the company and they sent for me to go to the big offices and there they talked to me about what rights I did not have!

'You see my husband, he used to work at the mill ten days a month during the harvest as a clean-up man. At other times he made charcoal and he sold candy from a cart and he also shined shoes. Once he had just got home and he was sitting out on the porch with his shoes off to rest when a sergeant of the guards came by and called him from his jeep. He got up to serve him, sir, for one had to, and the man slapped him hard on each cheek. I was watching from inside and I ran out and said, "What are you doing? Do you want to kill him?" And the sergeant said, "That is not a bad idea."

'I threw out my arms, sir, and I yelled, "Well, kill me and then you can say you have killed a woman!" There was a neighbour of ours who saw me and he grabbed my wrist and said, "Come with me." He pulled me to his house, for he feared that I might keep on talking and they really would kill me. That night we took our clothes and went to stay with an aunt who lived in the hills, but we had to come back, for the company sent a note saying my husband could not leave his job or would lose the house.

'My husband used to have trouble with his candy cart because the guards decided he was carrying messages to the Rebels. He had to avoid passing their headquarters, though it was here in the centre of the batey by the park and that was where there would be likely to be more people to buy candy. A couple of times the sergeant called him inside, sir, and made him empty the candy on a table. They would eat some and look for messages and then the sergeant would tell the others to dump the candy on the floor and my husband would have to pay for the broken candy. Those were the company guards.

'And then, sir, there were the Rural Guards who belonged to Batista. One day my nephew, a darling boy, was coming along the road with nine others to the batey after cutting cane. A jeep with Rural Guards came up and ordered them to remove a trunk of a tree that had fallen on the road and when they had done so, the soldiers herded them into a field and told them they were going to shoot them. Drink some water if you want, they said, for you are going to die. Some of the boys said they were not thirsty – they thought the whole thing was a joke. But the soldiers shot them, sir, and two had their heads blown off entirely. Three of my nephews still have pieces of iron in their bodies from those days. My own children I never let out of my sight after six in the afternoon.

'See my little old man there, he has had such trouble raising this big family I gave him. He was twenty and I was sixteen when he married me and I always said I would not marry a man who was a drunk or lazy or no good. But he has always been good. Look at him, he was beautiful, just like his son here – a pretty man he was! And if, as they say, I extracted the meat from him in all these years, then I have to make do with the bone now!'

'Ha!' said Mr Poyato. 'She held me with flattery!'

Mrs Poyato drew up her legs and hugged them like a young girl.

I asked her about the rationing. 'I do not know if it is bad – I tell you frankly – because I always had it bad,' she said. 'How can I tell you I do not have ham when I never had ham? You know, sir, when I had ham? One of my sons used to work for the Americans in their garden and when they had ham and had sliced all the meat from the bone, they would wrap up the bone and give it to him and say, Here, give it to your mother. I would throw it in a pot with water and vegetables – and beans if there were any – and hope it would fill my children's stomachs.'

When I left the Poyatos, it was already time for lunch, and I put off Brooklyn and decided to have lunch at the counter cafeteria facing the town park. I bought the 'special' which, like the one at the Hotel, cost $3.80, more than the old man's daily pension. It included soup, bread, salad, rice, steak or lobster or pork chops, a bottle of beer and cake. At the Bitirí it would have been better prepared but it would have been much more expensive, for there a steak, à la carte, cost $5.50.

The manager of the cafeteria came over and introduced himself; his wife was one of the librarians in Mayarí and she had told him about me. They lived in a house off the town plaza and everyone called him Chanda; everything he said made people smile, and men immediately came over because they knew he'd soon be telling a joke. He had managed the Cuban office workers' club in the days of La United, and belonged to the middle class of the batey – he had even, I heard, been a *garrotero*, a money lender – but he was happy about the Revolution without talking much about it. It gave him a kind of nobility that he enjoyed: there was hardly an eating-place in the region that he hadn't managed since the Revolution, and he was to become the manager of the new pizzeria in Mayarí after it opened.

Someone made him try out his English on me, and that reminded him of his first job with Americans. He was a young man then and knew no English, but a friend gave up a job as a waiter for an American bachelors' quarters at Guantánamo. It all happened very suddenly; he had about an hour's warning before he had to serve breakfast and no one had tested his English. Two Americans came down to breakfast just after he had consulted a dictionary, and he said to them. 'Juice yes? Coffee yes?' And the American answered in perfect Cuban,

'Coffee with milk and bread and butter – and for God's sake do not try to speak English!' Chanda slapped himself with delight and everyone laughed.

After lunch I walked to the other end of the park, admiring Antonio El Japonés's gardening, and climbed up to the high porch of the pharmacy to take a photograph of the park. In a moment I was talking to the pharmacist and the four women who waited on customers. Having just come from Chanda, it was the pharmacist who interested me, for he too should have been a candidate for the trek to Miami; he had been the pharmacist at Guatemala for thirty years, had lived in one of the houses in the preferred section of New York, and had even once been the president of the executive committee that ran the Cubans' private social club. He and Chanda were friends; also Paco Ortega and his wife, whom I had met in the accounting department at the Administration Building the first day: a diminished group at Guatemala, for so many of their old friends had left, they were a mystery to me.

The first time I asked the pharmacist why he hadn't left, he thought I was joking. 'But you cannot be living as well now as then,' I said.

'We live much better,' he said.

'I mean you,' I said. '*You* cannot be living better.'

'You see that beautiful park out there?' he said. 'It was a scraggly place. There used to be two enormous eucalyptus trees and the men used to sit under them for shade. Well, La United had them cut down because you know what unemployed men talk about when they get together.'

'At least you do not eat better now,' I said.

'You mean that you cannot get steak,' he said. 'Yes, at ten in the morning in the old days you could still find steak at the butcher's. Why do I say ten? – any hour of the day! They used to rot there.'

I did not want to say that he and Chanda and the Ortegas were a mystery to me. Instead I said, 'Well?'

'Listen, in this life you have to be human,' he said. 'What

was the use of eating well when around you hundreds were starving?'

I asked him what there was about the Revolution that was good for him personally. 'Everything,' he insisted. I threw up my arms. 'All right, I shall tell you what I like,' he said. 'I love construction and when I see the construction of houses and schools – oh, wait until you get to Levisa near Nicaro and see them building a whole new city! – when I see our great projects I am thrilled.'

He took a deep breath and smiled. 'Now you have me started, let me tell you what we spent our time doing in the old days. What did we spend our time doing? – and remember I do not blame La United for anything, I blame the government – why, we spent our time juggling for position. To get out from under the barracones – yes, people lived *under* the barracones in Brooklyn and put up cardboard and sacks to make walls! To get out from under the barracones and into the ten-by-ten rooms. To move from Brooklyn into New York and then to get a house in the better section or to get a house on a street that was lighted, for there was always some little thing that made someone superior or inferior to you.'

By this time we were in the stock-room of the pharmacy and there were several people with us, for the pharmacist believed in live examples and kept calling in customers to tell me about their case. 'The ones who leave – those old friends of mine – do not know why. Yes, I speak to them. You are not being thrown out of your job, I say. No, they say. I ask them, Do you dislike the system of education? No, they say. Do you think the new houses for the poor are a bad thing? No, they say. Do you think year-round employment bad? No, they say. Then what do you object to? I do not like it, that is all. So they really do not know. It is like the gold fever you used to hear about in the last century. There was a gold strike and everyone took off and almost no one found gold. They do not know why, for there is nothing concrete that they do not like.'

A light-skinned Negro woman said, 'What they really do not like is social equality.'

'And then they get there to your country and they find their tongues. They say people are starving and that there are so many dead that we do not bury them but throw them in the Bay of Nipe.'

A man laughed. 'That was Eliseo Reyes. We heard him on the radio!'

The pharmacist had one hand on a muscular young man whose happy pectorals threatened to tear through his shirt. 'This is Alcides Salazar – last year he got to be national wrestling champion in the third category and second in the second category. Alcides lived in Brooklyn with fourteen others in three rooms, and during the day he was one of the grass pickers in the park. We called them grass pickers because they chewed on a blade of grass once in a while and waited for the caller from the office to pass through, hoping he would say he had work next week for them. That is what Alcides did in the old days and now he lives in a big house in New York and works all year round as a solderer and is big in sports.'

The pharmacist was so inspired that day that I did not get to Brooklyn, but I did sit with Alcides Salazar in the house his parents had moved to in New York. It faced, across the railroad tracks, the entrance to the mill, and the porch was a bower of vines and shrubbery. We had mutual friends in Mayarí; for one, Eider Cesar, the light-skinned Negro at INDER, who had taught Alcides wrestling. 'But I taught Eider weight-lifting,' said Alcides proudly. 'We are brothers.' I did not want to point out that Eider was a Negro, so I said they did not have the same last name. Alcides explained: 'We are *hermanos de crianza* – we were brought up together.'

I said I had heard that Eider believed in witchcraft, and for a while I thought I had made a mistake, for Alcides did not answer me. I talked about my visit to the mill. Then Alcides said, 'There are people who believe that harm can be done to people by spells and witchcraft and all that.' I nodded and said I had heard that in Oriente there was much of that. He explained that spiritualists were people who believed in spirits, witchcraft meant putting the spirits to work, and *santería* was a way of curing people by witchcraft. 'Here in Guatemala?' I asked.

Alcides looked behind to see if there was anyone in the living-room and then spoke in a subdued voice that was not usual with him. Occasionally he became embarrassed and paused for a moment.

'When I was a boy,' Alcides said, 'there lived a fellow with us, a good fellow. My parents, seeing that he was a good fellow and had no place to stay, had asked him to live with us. That was in Brooklyn. He was a campesino from Los Pinares and he was completing a fifteen-year sentence by the spirits to do works of charity. Such a sentence meant that he was not to work but only to go about doing good to people without charging money, and he was to live by whatever people gave him. It was not only from him that I was to overhear this but also from his parents and they were good people, people who do not lie.

'When he was young he had believed in nothing, and worse, he had made fun of such things. Then one day he suddenly began to spring about in the house, and they said he jumped from floor to ceiling and out the window to the yard and there from the ground to the branches of trees. They were enormous leaps that no ordinary man could do, as if he were a bird. It was then that he believed and got the sentence and began to go from place to place helping people and taking no money. He became what is called a *santero*. At our house in Brooklyn they brought people to him and he cured them.

'One of the people he cured was my uncle. They brought my uncle from Nicaro where he worked and he was completely mad. The woman he lived with had given him a *bretage* – a potion made from herbs – because she thought he was going to leave her for another woman, and he sat in a corner and seemed to notice nothing. He did not seem to hear anything either and sometimes he just babbled and it did not make any sense. In three sessions the santero cured him.

'They began to do things to my uncle in the house and I would go away, so that I cannot say what the santero really did. I did not like those things and I did not like such people, though this man was a good man – yes, he was – and he did cure and do things you cannot explain in other ways. I think I did not like the whole thing and went away from the house because such people were always lowly and depressed. They did nothing to better themselves, they were poor and limited and had no horizons. Do you know what I mean? Yet the santero was real – sometimes he went into a trance and spoke foreign languages that people who knew them could understand.

'Once I myself had an experience of a person who had such supernatural understanding. It was the first time I went to Havana to look for a job. I was seventeen and all by myself. There was a big fat woman sitting on the other side of the bus one row ahead, so that she could not see me without turning her head. I was sitting there quietly, talking to no one, for I was preoccupied, and then the woman said, "Young man, do not worry about your mother any more, she is all right and nothing is going to happen to her." And she told me about other things that were on my mind and tried to reassure me. I had an opportunity to go to your country then and I had started to get my passport and such things, and that Negro woman told me about that – "But whether you are going to go or not I do not know," she said. And it was true – I was undecided and never did go.

'There are people in Guatemala who still believe in spirits and talk about it, but there is little santería now. All that is dying out. Maybe because there are few such people left and young people do not care for it. Myself, I do not know, though I cannot deny the things I have seen. I think I believe in the good, in doing good. All that about bretages and putting curses and doing evil, I do not believe in. I believe in *lo bueno* – the good.'

'I notice that you bought some medicine at the pharmacy,' I said. 'So the santero did not have much effect on you.'

Alcides laughed at that. 'The Revolution has given people other things to think about,' he said.

'What happened to the santero?'

'Oh, he got married and he lives at a collective farm,' said Alcides. 'My family still sees him but he gave up all that. I guess he served his sentence.'

The Hotel at Guatemala was a wooden, three-storey structure at the tip of the peninsula. There were grounds going down to the water, and it bordered on the extensive landscaped grounds – once better kept than now – of the home reserved for the vice-president of La United. The vice-president's home was used for a Party school, and everyone pointed out to you that now it could put up almost one hundred students whereas in the old days it was only used two or three months out of the year and then only by the vice-president and his niece. But the Hotel was modest, the kind that still survives in some small American towns: a small porch out front with rockers, a small lobby inside, the reception desk a small cubicle facing the door. One wing of the ground floor contained the dining-room, and in the passage before you got to it was the coffee and cigarette stand where the guests and diners gathered before and after dinner.

They were in the main young men and at first I thought they were the drugstore-corner cowboys of the town. The first conversation I overheard was about the price of American cigarettes paid to the English, Greek, Spanish and Bulgarian sailors whose ships come to the ports in the Bay of Nipe and Nicaro; they engaged in a semantic discussion on 'can', 'should' and 'would' and the law. But I soon learned that they were all married men, each a technician of a sort boarding at the Hotel for the harvest; on Saturday afternoon they all headed for home and were back on Sunday night.

And their conversation about black-market cigarettes ended on a note peculiar to Cuba. 'It is not just because the government loses revenue that it is illegal,' said one. 'But because it also adds up to exploitation and that is one thing you cannot find in our country any more – exploitation!'

'Listen, there is still exploitation,' said the young man who worked in the pastry shop across from the Hotel. 'So long as there is rationing there is exploitation, so long as there is shortage of any kind there is exploitation –'

'No, how can you say that!'

'I say so long as there is a single campesino working the land, breaking his back while others work in offices – there is exploitation!'

A fellow who worked on the pay-roll at the Administration Building embarked on an explanation for the shortages and inequalities. 'I know, I know,' said the other. 'Some day they will all end. But then we will be at full communism and *then* there will be no exploitation!'

The group at the cigarette stand before dinner was not always the same, but there was a core of us who came early because there were seldom more than a dozen 'specials' in the dining-room. The special was the most expensive dinner, and you had to buy a chit for it, as well as for the one or two others listed at the last moment on a blackboard inside; the special cost $3.80 and the others $1.60 and $1.80, the difference being in the bottle of beer that came with the special and in the main course, which, with the special, consisted of lobster, pork chops or steak and with the others, of spaghetti, eggs, liver or tripe. If you did not get in line at the cashier's as soon as the doors opened, the dozen chits for the special would likely be sold to those ahead of you.

My third night there was steak, and the young man from the pastry shop cursed that he could not afford it on his per diem of six dollars. One of the men who worked at the mill was a little impatient with him. 'For steak I do not mind spending some of my own money,' he said. 'I too get only six dollars.'

We sat at a round table, and the conversation seemed naturally to be directed to a young man about thirty; he was mild-mannered and unassuming, but he was also a master machinist at the enlarged repair shop of the mill and the others worked with him. A man in his thirties who joined us halfway through the meal explained, 'Juan here has been teaching us all at the shop. We gave him a fiesta a week ago in his honour.'

Juan said, 'It was just an excuse to kill a couple of pigs and eat a lot.'

The older one, Ventura, laughed, 'Everyone knows I like to eat a lot, but we really meant to honour him.'

But throughout dinner, and later when we walked to the park and talked there, Ventura kept returning to the subject of his appetite. He was eating at the Hotel because his wife had taken their two boys to visit her mother in the country, where she meant to buy food from the campesinos. 'The boys are like me too,' he said. 'I have a sow and three pigs and one of the boys was feeling one the other day. "I think he is fat enough," he said, "we will have the boiling water ready tomorrow when you come home from work!"' He laughed. 'I love pig. I wish the hair were edible, I would eat that too.'

'Do you get enough to eat with the rationing?' I asked.

'I do, but do not ask me – I am one of the privileged,' he replied, and when I raised my eyebrows explained, 'I work in the repair shop and make ten dollars a day. So I run around to all the grocery stores and buy the extra rations from people who do not want them. I can eat five pounds of shrimp at a time.'

One of the others pointed out to me, since they knew I was interested, that Ventura had been the union delegate from the mill for a long time. 'Is that so?' I asked. He nodded but kept his eyes veiled. 'In the days of La United?' He nodded again. 'Why not now?' I asked. He shrugged and seemed uneasy, but then got a bold, smiling look in his eyes and said, 'There are some qualifications I do not have. I do not belong to the militia.'

Then he told me what a fine man the master machinist was, and the others joined in. Ventura said, 'He is teaching me all I know.' Then he laughed. 'In the old days no one would do that for you.' The master machinist looked down modestly and while the others said complimentary things, Ventura looked at me and smiled with his eyes long enough to make me suspect for a moment that he felt the master machinist was foolish.

When it came out that I was a writer and that I was interested in life in the batey in the days of La United, Ventura began to tell me about the credit system. During the dead time, workers with regular jobs would be given credit at the stores, later to be deducted from their pay by the company, and the union endorsed the credit. Without the union's endorsement, you could not obtain credit. Then there were the individual garroteros, the money lenders, who as their name suggested squeezed enormous interest from the workers. 'Some of them are still around,' Ventura said. 'There is one who at pay-day – they used to hang around the pay window on pay-day – once held a gun to one of his debtors and threatened to shoot him if he did not pay. He is still around and has a good job too. We all know who he is.' He laughed and the others looked a little embarrassed.

I knew he meant Chanda but did not ask. Instead, I said, 'Do you think it was a good idea for the union to be part of the system that got the workers into debt?' To get money, workers would buy a household appliance they didn't need and go to Mayarí and sell it for half what it cost in the stores. They got into debt, but the interest – the forty to fifty per cent difference in the price they would pay out of future salary – was less than they would have had to pay a garrotero.

Ventura overreacted. 'Of course it was right. Who would

have spoken up for the workers if not the union?' Then he smiled and confided, 'When the Revolution triumphed, I was $1,800 in debt of that kind to the stores!'

One of the boys told me that during the short harvest, some often drew blank cheques at pay-day. 'There would be little stars on the cheque where the figures ordinarily appear. Someone like that we called a *comandante* – as if he had a military rank!'

After dinner, the group of us walked slowly to the town park. On the way, I told them a story Paco Oretega's wife had told me. Mrs Ortega, a cultured middle-class lady who supplied me with books on the Revolution that she thought would help me, worked in the accounting department, a job she had held many years. I had hoped she would find a copy of the booklet on how to treat Cubans that La United had distributed to the American employees recently arrived from the States. That such a booklet, unavailable to any Cuban, should have been printed by La United seemed outrageous to those who had told me, and Mrs Ortega said, 'It is extraordinary, you agree, that they should have special instructions about us Cubans? Extraordinary. I knew it existed but they never let it out of their hands. Actually, friendly relations with Cubans were looked on with great disapproval.'

I did not tell her that the booklet was probably an attempt to guide Americans in ways to avoid hurting the feelings of Cubans, something usual, in the post-war period, with American corporations that had subsidiaries abroad.

'There was a young engineer, a most delightful person, who came here to become the replacement for the head of a department who was due to retire. He was very friendly with us. Every night after dinner he came to have coffee with us. Also with the pharmacist whom you met. "Bill," I used to tease him, "please remember that we will not mind when you cannot come see us any more. We will understand." Bill would laugh and say that would never happen. But of course it was not long before he stopped coming to our house. Or to the pharmacist's. In the office he continued to act as if nothing had happened. And we of course acted as if nothing had.'

When I finished, Ventura said, 'I do not know about that, but I can tell you that American played baseball with us – he was always friendly. As for Paco Ortega, he was always at the Americans' dances dancing away all night. Of course, Mrs Ortega was always more revolutionary than he. They lived in the A section of New York – they still do.'

We had reached the town park, and we stood in the corner by the movie house where the buses from Mayarí end and start, and watched the townspeople walking in the park. The chief machinist took a deep breath and said, 'I love this sky, I love this weather, I love being in shirt sleeves at this time of year. I could never leave Cuba. Sometimes one has to get away from talk of politics and just live peacefully. I am like that.'

'I do not know how my wife can talk of leaving with the boys,' said Ventura.

One of the fellows, a Negro, recalled how the sky had been different up in the mountains when he lived with some campesinos during the alphabetization campaign.

'Now there is where I think Fidel has made a mistake,' said Ventura. 'I think he has given the campesinos too much wings, too much their own way.'

'They have learned a thing or two with this Revolution,' said the Negro. 'I do not blame them. For one thing they can now read and write. I can too. You know what it is to walk around and be able to read the signs! Remember how there was always a bunch of people at the bus stations asking each other where the bus was going to – because they could not read what it said in big letters at the front?'

The master machinist reluctantly came back to politics, though only to talk about the literacy drive: 'I must admit I enjoyed the alphabetization campaign. It is true that sometimes I had to remind the campesinos that I had come to teach them to read and write, not to work on the farm. But you know what a feeling it was when I would sit down to eat and find that there were three or four extra meals there for me that the different families had sent!'

'Yes, it was a wonderful thing,' Ventura admitted. Then laughed. 'Some of the girls came back pregnant. Those campesinos would sit next to them while they taught and say, Look, my chick, look how my cock is acting – how can I learn while it is this way?'

All of us burst into laughter at once, and became conscious that people turned to look at us. I saw then a fat woman, who had been pointed out to me as someone who had applied to leave, take the arm of a man who came out of the Mayarí bus; both of them were looking at me, probably because I had been pointed out to them as being an American, a future compatriot. I asked my companions if it were true she was waiting to leave. The master machinist didn't know, but Ventura and the Negro said yes. 'She makes a living selling candies – behind the Administration Building.'

I asked them if they thought she would speak to me if I went to their home. The master machinist said, 'I do not know,' but his face showed he would be loath to do it himself, not because he was intolerant of people who went into exile but out of delicacy of feeling. The Negro said, 'She has a good job in the office here and he a good one at Nicaro. They always had it good, so you can imagine what they will say to you.' Ventura was excited by my question, but he only said, 'You might try it.'

Before they all went in to the movie, I asked them a final question: Had they been surprised when the Revolution became socialist? I did not make a note of their replies, so I only remember Ventura's. No doubt because of what happened the following day. He said that he remembered that soon after the Revolution triumphed the administrator of La United took him aside – they were friendly because they had been involved in a lot of union negotiations – and showed him a copy of the *Reader's Digest* with an article that said Raul

Castro and Vilma Espín, his wife, were both Communists and had both been to Moscow before the Revolution. The administrator warned him that the Revolution was Communist. 'I have to admit,' said Ventura to us, 'that the Americans were smarter about that than we.'

The next time I saw Ventura I was on the road behind the Visitors' House heading towards the railroad crossing, and he could not see me. The flagman on duty was the one who hated campesinos, and the old man was keeping him company again. They got up from their haunches to greet him and they had a friendly exchange that I could not hear. Before I got to the crossing, Ventura had ridden off on his bicycle; across from the Administration Building, he turned and saw me and waited.

'Have you talked to her?' he asked immediately, and nodded down the side street where the woman who was waiting to leave the country lived. I told him I was on my way there, and asked him what he was doing here in the middle of the day. The repair-shop workers get an hour and a half lunch break and he was going to the big store around the corner to see if canned milk had come. 'Good luck,' he said to me.

At the house, young people on the porch told me that the family of the name I mentioned lived on the next block. It puzzled me, and I decided to go to the Administration Building and ask Mrs Ortega, whose house was on that block. Mrs Ortega told me that I had been to the right block but the wrong house. 'I am glad you are going to see her,' she said. 'She is not one of those foolish extremists who will tell you lies or who will exaggerate. We are good friends and I shall miss her. I maintain such friendships; we simply do not talk about politics. Why cannot our countries be like that – have normal relations and not interfere with each other's politics? Then I could see my daughter and two grandchildren in Florida . . .'

I was in a hurry and did not stay to talk; I planned to leave on the bus next morning, and so wanted to see Brooklyn during the day. I also wanted to get to Party headquarters near the arch and obtain from the First Secretary, Alfonso Ricardo, a copy of a food-consumption study which, he said, showed that people ate more now than they did in Batista's time. Thinking about this, I went back to the original block and knocked on a different house this time; it was large and well-kept, and it occurred to me that there were probably residents in Brooklyn as eager for them to leave for Miami as they were. A group of men repairing the street watched me. There seemed to be no one home, and as I came out the gate I recognized one of the workmen as someone I had met at the pharmacy.

'They are not at home,' he told me. 'They went out an hour ago. Maybe they got their notice!'

Across from the Administration Building, Ventura leaned on his bicycle and watched me come towards him. He moved around the corner and waited for me there. 'There is no one home,' I said.

He looked at me closely. 'I guess it must be difficult for you,' he said. 'People are probably afraid to talk to you.'

I said I had not noticed that; it seemed to me that Cubans never hesitated to say what was on their minds.

He smiled and veiled his eyes. 'Are you sure?'

I said that the one thing writers must trust is their ability to tell when people are being frank.

'Well, you have made a good impression here,' he said, still holding fire. 'You do not go around with a little notebook writing down names ...'

I waited.

'Last night ...' he said, and narrowed his eyes, 'would you say I was being frank with you?'

'About sixty per cent,' I said, and suddenly we both laughed at the tension my reply released.

'You are right,' he admitted. 'I am one of the disgustados – one of the unhappy. There are many things I do not like.'

I asked him what.

'Did you hear me last night when I said my wife and children were going to leave?' he said. 'I let it drop but you did not ask anything. Did you already know?'

I said I thought he had been joking.

'I tell you one of the things I do not like. They are trying to force my children to join the Pioneers and I do not want them to. I went to the school and spoke to the director and reminded him it was supposed to be voluntary. He admitted they were doing everything to persuade them to join. I do not want the boys to be ruled by anyone but me. I do not want anyone to say they should be at a certain place when I want them to be at another.'

Was he really going to let his wife and children go?

'My wife has family in Puerto Rico and they have put in for her and I finally said to her, You can go. It is hard, I know, but I think I shall let them go.' He stopped and peered at me. 'Maybe later I shall become enthusiastic and follow them. What do you think of that?'

I said nothing. I was thinking that he of course had already decided to leave and that they were doing it in this order because of the Cuban government's regulations. Once an applicant has completed the forms requesting permission to leave and has met their qualifications (doctors and men of military age excepted), a copy is sent to his place of work. He immediately loses his job. The only job he is allowed to hold is in agricultural production, a fate that the great majority of would-be exiles are desperate to avoid, and during the long wait that follows – due, say the Cubans, to the clearance procedures of the United States – the applicants go through a difficult time. They cannot sell any of their household goods to maintain themselves, for at the time their applications are accepted an inventory is made of the home by Orden Pública with the help of a neighbour who belongs to the Committee for the Defence of the Revolution; the latter's job is to check whether any major household items have been sold in the previous year. And when the telegram arrives with instructions on the flight the applicant is to take, a new inventory is held, to see that nothing is missing from the house.

There are some exceptions. I knew of a man in the New York section, widowed a year earlier, who decided to leave because his only son was in the States. He had been waiting several months for the final telegram, and he was allowed to keep his job at the mill. Everyone felt sorry for him. 'You cannot really say he is a *gusano*,' Paredes explained to me; *gusano* – worm – is the epithet for exiles. Cubans approve of any action if it results in keeping a family together, whether in Cuba or the States. Yet the administrator of the Nicaro plant, telling me of his belief in letting all go who want to, said with ironic disdain of his mother: 'The author of my days left a month ago to join a brother who lives alone in New York City – I shall learn to live without her.'

Since Ventura had made no application to leave, none of these regulations applied to him, and therefore his wife and children would not suffer during the long wait. Since he had earned a high salary, he would not find it hard when it came time for him to wait alone. I asked, 'Has there been any trouble since they applied?'

He shook his head. 'No, if someone asks if it is true, I say yes, they want to go and I am letting them go.'

It was out and he had to justify himself. 'Listen, I agree that I should not be a union leader, though I was elected each time by a majority of the workers. A leader should be a member of the militia. Anyway, I am not good at being a leader of this kind of union. I am used to arguing and negotiating with the company for benefits for the workers. Now the union and the company are the same thing, they pursue the same objectives. And in 1960 I did not like what they did to remove the union leadership. They came to the top man and said he had to leave, that there would be new elections. They did not arrest him but there were militia standing by. What do you think of that?'

He had been in the 26 of July Movement, so I asked him when he began to be disappointed with the Revolution. 'At

Playa Girón,' he said. 'I dropped out of everything after that. I did not like the exchange of prisoners. If they deserved jail or execution, then they should have got that. They should not make deals with human lives.'

I asked him about other things that the disgustados complain about, but he did not always go along with them. 'When it comes to the barracones, the bad housing, you cannot blame the Revolution for that – they are the fault of La United.' Or: 'They do not bother me at work. I have one of the best jobs and there are even Batista followers working at the mill. So long as you do your job they do not care what your opinions are.' Or: 'I do not know if I would like the United States, for I hate capitalism.' When he said that last, I laughed aloud and he smiled slyly, as if admitting that he was disingenuously presenting a complex picture of himself by exonerating or praising the Revolution.

It was this lying, this cat-and-mouse game he played with me, that made me dislike him, and it must have showed, because he tried another tack. 'I like Soviet Russia,' he said, nodding. 'I do. You know, they do not trust the old Communists here.' I nodded. It seemed to me Ventura was a man who, after those years as a union leader, was unhappy about not being 'in'; yet he had no heart for the dreadfully hard work and devotedness of the Cuban Party member: there was simply no juice in it for him.

He put a leg up on his bicycle; he had to go. But he was unhappy, and also worried, about the impression of himself that he was leaving me with. 'Listen, what do you think of their throwing people who want to leave out of their jobs?' he said. 'It is inhuman.'

I said nothing. 'I am sure you think it is unjust,' he said. 'Is that your opinion?'

I told him I was a foreigner and my opinion was not important.

'No, I would like to know. I have been frank with you –' He laughed. 'Really, what do you think?'

I said, 'I may change my mind but right now I think that if a man abandons his country, his country has the right to abandon him.'

The shock made him look away. 'You would not leave your country . . . even if its politics went against you?' he said.

He grabbed the handlebars of the bicycle and held them tight. He did not look up to see me answer. When he finally turned to me, his eyes were lit up with deception; he was his old negotiating self again. 'You are right,' he said. 'I will not leave my country. This Revolution goes forward – nothing can stop it!'

Ventura went off to the mill and I headed for Brooklyn the long way round, along the sea wall on the eastern end of the lip of land. There were stucco houses here built since the Revolution and the old Cuban office workers' club which was now a nightclub. Across from the houses facing the water little sail-boats were tied up, and in the inlet the land turned marshy before it rose to the smooth level of the old golf club. In the marshy area some of the people living nearby kept pigs; they had been taught to do this by the Administración.

On the old golf-club turf, there was now a baseball field, and I watched Jose Fuentes, the police chief, warming up to pitch a game. Beyond the field were the emergency houses, neat and painted, built for those who lost their homes in the hurricane. There were also the more substantial stucco houses built in the first years of the Revolution, and across from the hospital a small project of seventy-five apartments was going up. I walked past all this across an open field that dipped where it had once been all marshland and was now half filled with rubble and cachaza, the fertilizer from the mill, and entered Brooklyn from the back. I stood in the first shade I came to, a kiosk in the centre and dead end of a Brooklyn street.

The man who ran the kiosk had a wooden leg and he made room for me on the stoop, and soon we were joined by a black Negro and a young mulatto. There were whites in Brooklyn but the view was of varying shades of coloureds, all lively and talkative and convivial. From my position on the stoop I could see that the barracones were built on four- or five-foot stilts and that it was possible to have set up a kind of home under them. Most of them were sixty years old and consisted of the original ten-by-ten rooms for each family, ten rooms back to back with ten others to each barracón. There were public latrines nearby and also sinks to wash clothes in and separate showers for men and women. Around the buildings were cement drains for the rain water; everything else, including the streets, was dirt.

Besides the houses in New York and Katanga that became vacant after the Revolution, only 175 new units (plus the 75 apartments to be completed) had been built, and the authorities had only been able to tear down three barracones. Two more could have been demolished, but at first the authorities did not know that if this was not done the moment the families moved out, others, eager for more living-space, would move in. 'And the Revolution does not evict anybody, you know,' said the kiosk man.

'Remember Sanchez?' said the Negro. 'He was one of the company guards who used to police the area and run out people living under the building. Well, he retired and they threw him out of his house like they did everyone who retired or the families of those who died. Yes sir, he ended up living under a barracón!'

Everyone had added a ramshackle porch to their quarters, but that was all the expansion possible. There was a strike in the forties to get electricity in the barracones, but it was not until the Revolution that running water became available inside the rooms. The young mulatto had moved to one near the kiosk when the family there was given one of the emergency houses; he was married and had a little daughter, but until then they had lived with his family in another barracón. 'Oh, how I wish there would be an end to these barracones!' he sighed.

The kiosk man said, 'There is so much to do they cannot get to everything. They will not paint the barracones not only because of the shortage of paint but because what they mean to do is tear them down.'

I asked if there was a rat problem in the barracones, and the young mulatto leaned away from me to get a better look at the man who was naïve enough to ask such a question. Then he laughed.

The kiosk man said, 'I got bit on my one ankle last night.'

The mulatto had found two in his traps that morning, and a neighbour's chicken had had her crop chewed out while she slept in her nest.

'We keep all our food in bottles,' said the Negro. 'Peña was saying the other day that his damn goose was no good at hatching and then he took a closer look at the eggs and found they were all perfect empty shells. It is a marvel how they can suck out an egg through a little pinhole!'

It made them all laugh.

'There are two men walking around here who had the heads of their cocks chewed off in their sleep,' the kiosk man said. 'El Chino had to be rushed off to hospital when he finally woke up!'

The Negro laughed. 'I tell you, those rats anaesthetize as they chew. Of course, those two were old men!'

The young mulatto looked at me. 'You know, there are still many filthy people around,' he said. 'Sometimes you go into the showers and you find shit there.' He sighed. 'How I wish we could see the last of the barracones!'

I asked about the food. 'We manage,' said one, and the others nodded: the sign of good revolutionaries.

When I got up to leave, I stood next to the Negro and noticed a necklace of small black beads under his shirt. We were standing apart and I asked him what it was. He turned his face away from the others and said, '*Eso es de Regla.*' It belongs to Regla, he literally said: the Virgin of Regla around whom rituals of African origin are practised; she is, in fact, the African goddess Yemayá. We nodded and smiled and shook hands, and I did not ask against what particular ill black beads afford protection, for his friends were not of the faith.

Alfonso Ricardo, the Party Secretary, was not at head-quarters and it was closed. I waited because I wanted to see, if the study had been found, how they had determined that people ate more now. I was joined by a fifty-two-year-old woman, with her young grandchild, who had come looking for the girl in the Party office; she hoped there would be a reply to her youngest daughter's application for a scholarship on the 'rescue' programme, one designed for teenagers who had dropped out after the sixth grade. Neither of us got what we wanted; the Party Secretary told me he had been unable to find the carbon last night and informed Luisa Duran, when she introduced herself and asked about the office secretary, that the office would not open again until the next day.

'I fear my daughter is not going to get the scholarship,' she sighed, 'for she is not one of the lucky ones.'

'I am surprised she did not get one last fall,' he answered. 'There were seven hundred from here who did.'

Luisa shrugged, and the Party Secretary turned to me: 'I saw you in Brooklyn but I could not stop. You know we are going to eradicate all those barracones. All but one – it is going to be a museum because it was there the old revolutionaries used to meet and plan strikes.'

Luisa gave an unbelieving smile. 'When it comes to housing, it is still the same here as before the Revolution.'

I asked her why.

'Let me not talk,' she said. 'What is the use?'

The Party Secretary urged her.

'Listen, I have been here before,' she said, 'and I have been to the Administración innumerable times. I wish Fidel would come here, I would tell him. I am not afraid, for I do not lie.

I am a revolutionary, an *old* revolutionary, a communist of the old Socialist Party, and I tell you it is a shame what they have done to my old man that he is still living in Brooklyn.' She had told me she had four children, her husband was retired, and they lived in one of the three-room houses.

'But that is our problem,' the Party Secretary explained, 'that we need houses for everyone and that it takes time. Now at least we can say everyone has hygienic conditions.'

'Hygienic?' she said, and gave him a disgusted look. 'You want to see the house I have lived in for twenty-six years? And do not talk to me about gastro-enteritis! A new word they have given us with the Revolution! It is vomiting and diarrhoea and all it amounts to is bad digestion. I know, I know, you are going to tell me that having a pig causes gastro-enteritis. Let one of those new little doctors come and tell me that and I shall tell him he lies!'

'Let us not argue about that. It is something the scientists tell us, and you and I have to accept it,' the Party man said, not too enthusiastically, for he had been a campesino until a few years ago and it must have cost him a great effort not to raise a couple of pigs around the house.

'All I can tell you is the Revolution does not care for us old folks,' Luisa said. 'My old man is retired three years with a miserable thirty-eight dollars a month, when he worked all his life and earned two retirements.'

The Party man said he could not be getting that small a pension if he had been a stevedore.

'I know, I know,' Luisa said. 'He retired before they passed the law increasing them. I tell you, if you are an old man, they do not care about you. I was a socialist before you were, and you have to have been a socialist in those days to know how hard they were.'

The Party man smiled and paused as if he held another opinion of old socialists. 'So it comes down to the fact that you want to move to a better house,' he said. 'But people who are in worse conditions get precedence, you know that.'

'You know who gets the houses,' she said disdainfully.

I said there were large families on Katanga.

'That was at first,' she said in a kind tone because I was a newcomer. Then she gave the Party Secretary an accusing look.

'It is true that we have to give the technicians some of the new houses,' he said.

'Aha!' exclaimed Luisa.

'They are people who live in their own homes in Havana and we want them to come here with their special knowledge. We cannot offer them the worst we have!'

'Where do you live?' Luisa asked, with narrowed eyes.

It turned out the Party Secretary lived in the emergency prefabs beyond the ball field. His place consisted of two bedrooms, a tiny living-room and a kitchenette. It gave Luisa pause; then she said, 'How many are you?'

'Eight,' he replied.

'Then you must know those houses are no good,' she said. 'I would not live there.'

'You would not live there!' he exclaimed. 'You must have had privileges in the old days. You say that you had no trouble getting treated at the hospital – what about the people from the country who did not have the kind of relationship you had with Dr Ruiz that got you that privilege?'

'Listen, I do not lie,' Luisa said. 'I was a socialist long before you, and I do not lie. The only time I lie is when I see a Negro and I call him a mulatto and when I see a mulatto and I act as if I see nothing. Dr Ruiz never failed to treat me or to give me medicine when a ship had not come in.'

'And how long were the periods when ships did not come for sugar?'

'There was one time when a ship did not come in for three months and twenty days,' Luisa said. 'But Dr Ruiz and Raspail at the grocery treated me well. Raspail gave us credit, and now if you do not have twenty cents you get nothing.'

'And in the old days could you have stood here on this street and criticized and complained?' the Party man asked. 'I do not mean to an official, just to your neighbours.'

'Listen, there must be something to luck,' Luisa answered, 'for I have never kept quiet. And I do not lie.'

'All right, I do not ask you to lie,' he said. 'I ask you to say that the campesinos could not get the credit you did or treatment at the hospital.'

'What if I told you that the campesinos always got treated free at the hospital?' Luisa said.

The Party Secretary coloured and got angry for the first time. 'I will tell you about my sister. We brought her on our backs in a hammock because she was so sick we thought she was dying and because there was no ambulance, nothing at all with which to bring her across country. And when we got to the hospital your Dr Ruiz – who is so kind and is now Up North – said, "Lay her down there, we cannot admit her unless you pay $175 now!" And we ran around like madmen borrowing the money.'

'But she got treated?'

'Yes, and we sold every animal we had to pay for it.'

A stocky, bald man carrying a lantern had been listening to their exchange, and he told Luisa and me he had begun working on La United's railroad at forty-five cents a day and after years of work got to $1.10; now he earns $6.50 and works all year. The house he lived in burned down and he got into the prefabs.

'That is because you are working,' Luisa said. 'If you were retired like my old man you would never get a house.'

'Now tell me,' said the Party Secretary, trying to be calm. 'You have four children, one girl married in Havana and working in the hospital, one son working at the mill, one daughter a teacher and one applying for a scholarship?' He turned to me. 'You are going to see how much money is coming into that house.'

Luisa protested that the daughter and son who were married could not help support them, and the teacher only cleared $86 a month.

'Isn't your son in the militia?' said the Party man. 'I think I know him.'

He was, so were her daughters.

'And you, you would carry a gun, right?'

'If they came, if they invaded? I would cook for the soldiers, I am too old to fight.'

It made them happy with each other. I asked Luisa just what her house was like, for I hadn't yet been in that part of Brooklyn. She took her grandchild's hand and started to walk off. 'Come with me and I will show you,' she said, aggrieved again.

It was a miserable place. A narrow porch which four people could crowd, separated by a low wooden railing from the one for the other half of the house. Each room was tiny; a bed took up most of the living-room. But it turned out her married son lived in the other half of the house and the daughter who taught was moving soon to be near where she studied nights. They would then be only three: a glorious situation compared to the barracones.

The grandson jumped over the wooden railing and pushed open the door of his side of the house. His mother came out: tall, slim, light-skinned but undeniably Negro. She said hello to me and to Mirda, the daughter who taught. Luisa did not respond to her daughter-in-law: she was one of those mulattos that Luisa flattered by not seeing.

'I told the Party official right to his face,' Luisa said to Mirda. 'We have been treated very bad.'

I asked Mirda if she felt like her mother. She was wary and said no. I asked if she liked the Revolution. She said yes. 'I have not had the experiences my mother has and I like this. It is what I know.'

The daughter-in-law nodded and smiled and went inside with the baby.

Luisa looked away and said to me, 'Old socialists to them are people to hold tight in their fists.'

'Well, Mother, it is your present stance that counts,' Mirda said. 'Not what you were.'

'You are very fresh, Mirda,' her mother said. 'Some day you will grow old and not count in production.'

'And when I do they should throw me aside.'

When I left, Luisa said, 'If you are a writer, you must live in Havana?'

I said I lived in New York and that I was a North American, and I could see that though this interested her enormously – I had to answer the usual questions about what they would do to me when I got back – Luisa was disappointed that she had been talking to someone who could not help her get out of Brooklyn.

At the railroad end of the dirt street where Luisa lived stood a tall Negro in dungarees. As I walked toward him, he kept waving to me and calling, 'Well sir, well sir, do you remember me?' in a sweet Jamaican English. I said I did but he could see that I wasn't sure. 'I met you at the mill the other night and my name is Roland H. Miller.'

He had come to cut cane forty-six years before and stayed. 'But first I saw almost all the world working on a ship and I fought for the British Empire in the Arab lands. That was at the beginning of the First World War. And for the last thirty years I have been driving the railroad cars.'

I asked him how old he was.

'I am seventy-three today,' he said, and burst into laughter. 'I am already retired and I am still drawing my salary until the pension comes. Isn't it fine of the revolutionary government to do that?'

I said I was leaving on the next bus and asked if I could take his photograph. He threw his shoulders back and posed, then peered when I wrote down his name. 'The name is Roland H. Miller,' he repeated. 'It is a name Fidel knows.'

I looked surprised, and he explained. 'I knew Fidel and Raul and their old man too. I worked for him in Birán when they were boys, and look what a wonderful man Fidel has become. I am retired at higher pay and I can keep my house. I can keep my house! They will not throw me out, think of that! Isn't that a fine thing? Say it is a fine thing, man.'

6. The Girls of the Bitirí

'Oooh Jose! We thought you had forgotten us in Guatemala!' squealed Miriam at the reception desk of the Bitirí. 'You did, you did, you forgot us!'

Minín, the waitress, joined in. 'We asked, "Where is Jose? Where did he go? He does not love us any more!"'

There was no question that I was a member of the family now. I had lived there, I had gone away, I had come back: it made all the difference. Despaigne, the gardener, straightened up from his task of cutting the lawn with a simple pair of clippers, and waved at me. Angela came out of one of the rooms on the other side of the triangle and nodded and smiled slyly. Plump Margarita (Dr Padrón called her The Bulk) skipped down the walk to the reception desk, her breasts and thighs bouncing. 'There he is!' she called. 'There he is!'

'Never mind,' I said, 'I only went away while the emergency aqueduct was being finished. Now that I can take a shower any time I want I shall never leave again.'

'Oooh Jose,' said Miriam in mock-abashed tones. 'There is no water ...'

Minín laughed.

I pretended to be shocked. 'There is no water!'

'They got all the pipes connected,' Miriam said, 'and the water was running fine for one day –'

'The cistern was getting filled up,' Margarita interjected. 'Then they covered up the ditch and smoothed down the ground with a tractor – and it broke all the pipes!'

'I want you to know,' I said, 'that at Guatemala there was not only water all the time, there was also hot running water!'

'Oh, that Guatemala is full of gusanos,' Minín said. 'That is why Jose likes it.'

'You have nothing to worry about,' said Margarita. 'You want to take a shower right now? You go right in and get ready in your bathroom and I shall bring you a pail of water!'

Minín covered her face with her hands and shrieked, 'Margarita!'

When I got to my room, Angela was leaning against the pole on the walk. 'Now that you are back, I shall put linens on your bed and mop the floor,' she said.

'You have had almost a week and it is not done!' I exclaimed, and, using a phrase I picked up in Guatemala, added, 'There is no affection here – *no hay cariño*.'

'Oh, oh, things must have gone very well for him in Guatemala,' Angela said, half closing her eyes, and went to work on my room.

I sat outside and listened to Despaigne improvising a song. Or rather, composing one. Despaigne was a black man in his forties and for many years had been the florist of Mayarí. He still kept his shop in his home, but he now spent most of his time at the Bitirí, whose grounds were large and whose lack of a lawn-mower made it necessary for him to spend hours bent straight down from the waist cutting the grass, as he was doing now, with a large pair of clippers. I first got to talk to him the day I told him that his name was the French for 'From Spain'.

He had not known and it didn't interest him too much. What interested him was flowers and shrubs. And popular music. I did not learn about his composing from him, but heard about it in Guatemala from someone who, like many others, worked there and lived in Mayarí. But the garden of the Bitirí was always on the tip of his tongue, and my having approached him gave him the opportunity to tell me about the pests which were attacking the shrubs. He took me around the grounds, pointing out the blackening ones suffering from fungus. 'They will rot,' he said, pulling out a few. 'And these – see those white little spots?' – have *huahua-chincha* and they too are dying.' Pesticides were not available; he had even gone to Holguín but had found none. 'I could cure them if I had a little copper sulphate, not a lot, just a little. I know how to make the mixture.' Then he said, as if it had just occurred to him, though I suspected it had not, 'Do you think the hospital might have some in their laboratory?' Despaigne was not the first to try to approach Dr Padrón through me.

That day I returned from Guatemala, Despaigne was composing a *guaracha*, a traditional form suitable for satirical comment, and he already had the line on which each stanza was to turn: *Se acabaron los colchones* – There are no more mattresses. A subject that should have been popular in Mayarí, for Hurricane Flora had destroyed every mattress and although the government had distributed many, there was probably no home that could not have used one or two more. A week earlier the furniture store on Leyte Vidal had received some, and they were being rationed very strictly. As I walked by, a frustrated-looking man came out of the store and addressed me as if he knew me: 'I shall never get one!' I asked why. 'They refuse to sell me one because I live in Nicaro and Nicaro never gets a damned shipment!'

Without stopping his cutting of the grass, Despaigne sang his key line over and over, trying to find rhymes that made sense. *The Manager says/Don't make a queue/You'll break the show window/And there are no more mattresses!* But he had stretched the melodic line and so he would try variations, shooting them out like machine-gun firing. In a while he gave up the guaracha and worked on a bolero with the key line, *I am the king of the bongo drummers!*

'There is no affection here,' I called impatiently to Angela.

She strolled out. 'It is done,' she said, and held out a hand for me to see. 'My rheumatism is holding me up,' she explained.

'What rheumatism?' I said. 'You are only nineteen.'

Tomorrow, she said, was her twentieth birthday, and she showed me that she could not straighten the pinky on her right hand and insisted all her knuckles ached. 'At night I sometimes cannot sleep because of bone-aches,' she said. 'Maybe you could ask Dr Padrón about it?'

Before she finished describing her symptoms, Padrón unexpectedly came by to pick up something from his room. I told him about Angela while she stood listening as if she were not the subject of the conversation. 'Do you get short of breath?' he asked her, and she nodded vaguely. He told her to come to his next consultation, two days away, and he would make sure to see her that day. 'That is a very real illness,' he said.

When Padrón left, Angela said she didn't know how she could get off from work to go see him. I encouraged her, and reminded her of her appointment when I saw her again the next day before she finished her shift early in the afternoon. I also gave her a birthday gift. I mention this because the gift emboldened her – later that day – to ask me to a party in the evening that Basilio, the friendlier of the two Soviet technicians staying at the Bitirí, was giving in their room: it was Basilio's birthday too. I had already heard about the party at dinner from a young man who was invited and who was to get into all the trouble with Angela that, I liked to think, would have been my lot if I had accepted her invitation. I was to find out, however, that there were several other men who felt they too had just escaped.

The young man was named Granda, and he was temporarily working at the Bitirí to help improve the service in the dining-room. El Gallego, the new manager, had begun to make changes, and he had got Granda to spend some time at the Bitirí advising them before Granda took on the job of preparing the new pizzeria and its raw, new staff for the grand opening. Granda had been trained at the best restaurateur's school in Cuba and had worked at the top restaurants in Havana and learned from the old-timers there. He liked nothing so much as to talk about the different types of glasses for wines and liqueurs or to tell about organizing, on two days' notice, a banquet for three hundred at an inadequate location in Holguín.

What was really remarkable about himself seemed to have

escaped Granda's notice, and it was only because I recognized
his accent that it came out that he was an Asturian from Spain.
He came from Arriondas, a little town near Oviedo which I
had once visited, and we exchanged notes about people there.
Granda had left Arriondas in 1960 to go to Guatemala where
an uncle who had several small businesses had offered him a
job; on the way he stopped in Cuba to visit a cousin he had
not seen since he was a boy, and he never got to Guatemala.
He loved the Cuban Revolution, though all he really liked to
talk about was restaurant service.

He told me all this because I happened to mention, when
he took my order, that I was happy the dim coloured bulbs in
the dining-room had been changed; I could now read the menu
at dinner. That had been one of his innovations, and he
pointed to the bottom of the menu where it now said that the
Bitirí offered its guests a free liqueur after dinner. 'Nothing
like a little friendly gesture like that just before you get the
bill,' Granda said.

When El Gallego passed by, he interrupted himself just a
moment to say that he had accepted an invitation from Basilio
to have a drink in his room to celebrate his birthday. 'I did
not feel I could refuse,' he said, obviously not intending to go
if El Gallego disapproved. El Gallego told him he had done
right. The next time I saw Granda he wore a bandage that
covered almost the entire left side of his face, and he was looking for Margarita to give him an injection of penicillin.

After dinner, I sat in front of my room waiting for the
schoolteacher whom I had met the first night in Mayarí, and I
saw Basilio in a clean shirt, though it was only the middle of
the week, running back and forth from the bar to his room at
the end of the triangle, carrying bottles of beer. He looked
happy, and not morose as he and his room-mate invariably
did mornings, when they also drank at least two bottles with
breakfast to carry them until lunch. Angela showed up dressed
in a short sheath, and she told me that she had had to return
to get permission from El Gallego to be off the next day for

her appointment with Dr Padrón. It was then she invited me to Basilio's party. 'He says I have to come because today is my birthday too,' she said.

The schoolteacher of course did not show up. I was used to Cubans not keeping casual appointments and did not fret, for I knew the young man would not either if he showed up later and did not find me there. There had been no after-dinner coffee at the Bitirí, so I went on my usual walk to El Parque for my demitasse. On Maceo, Jaime Hernandez, the man who kept the juice stand, called to me and crossed the street excitedly. 'She made it, she made it!' he said, and it took me a moment to remember that his daughter had taken the examination for the nurse's aide course at the hospital. 'My wife is happy too, but she says now both our children will be gone, and I remind her she will be living here in Mayarí and can drop by in the evenings.'

I said that Dr Padrón probably had a very full and strict schedule planned for the new group, and he nodded and nodded. 'Yes, yes, that is very good,' he said. 'My daughter is very serious about this – it is a vocation with her and I am happy to have a daughter who is like that. She has every intention of continuing and becoming a full nurse.'

At El Parque one of the men from Public Health treated me to coffee, and I walked back to the office with him a block away. They were possibly going to leave soon on an inspection tour to Cueto. Beto Maseto, a truck driver about whom I'd heard, was at Public Health, standing in front of his nineteen-year-old truck; he hired himself out with the truck but had been working mostly for Public Health this year. He looked the way his name sounded – a massive man with a round happy face – and when we shook hands, the impact made me look down involuntarily; it felt as if I'd taken a clenched fist.

Hugo, the man who had introduced us, noticed and laughed. 'Some hand, eh?'

Beto had been a bouncer at one of the *bayus* – a café with a juke-box and rooms in the back for the girls – that used to be located where the Bitirí now is. 'Imagine being grabbed and flung out by those hands!' said Hugo.

'All that is past,' Beto said, 'since Fidel put on the cassock.' He pointed to Hugo and the jeep driver for Public Health, and added, 'These are his acolytes.'

A girl came out on the porch of the house next door and Hugo called, 'Looking for El Resbaloso?' El Resbaloso – The Slippery One – had become notorious in the last two weeks; in several neighbourhoods of Mayarí women had reported a Peeping Tom at their windows, and he had already acquired the name of El Resbaloso.

Beto did not believe in El Resbaloso. 'It all started with a woman who made a date with a man to come to her bedroom after the lights were out in her house. But that night one of her daughters decided she wanted to sleep with her mother, and she raised a hullaballoo when the man came swinging in.' Beto threw out his arms like a high-jump man; he acted out every part in his story. 'The poor man was caught and let go when the mother confirmed he was an invited guest, not a house-breaker. But did that stop the story that had already got started? No! There was another woman who had bought one of those domesticated collective-farm chickens which she corralled in her living-room at night with chairs. Well, that chicken saw a roach on the wall and pecked at it – *tam, tam* – and out came the woman screaming, El Resbaloso, El Resbaloso! There is no stopping the story now.'

While Beto talked, Hugo kidded the girl next door. He put his middle finger to one cheek and then stroked his cheek with it. The girl laughed and went inside, and I asked Hugo just what the gesture meant. Hugo asked Beto to show me the middle finger of his right hand and Beto obliged. 'It is a de-flowering instrument and she knew I was referring to Beto's famous finger,' Hugo said.

'That one!' Beto said. 'Her flooring is already cracked.'

The trip to Cueto was called off, and I went back to the

Bitirí early. There was time to get a drink at the bar before it closed; the girls were clearing the tables and there was no one at the bar but Marta, a pretty black girl who worked at the cash register for the dining-room. Her mother had died just before I went to Guatemala and this was her first day back at work after a week's mourning. She was all in black and she didn't joke or tease me as she usually did. She leaned her head on one hand while she talked to Minín and occasionally wiped away fat tears with her other hand.

'My mother and I were like friends,' Marta said. 'I told her my most secret troubles, and when I think she is not there to talk to now when I go home . . .'

'Yes, yes,' Minín said and cried too.

'I cannot understand children who mistreat their mothers, I cannot. You do not think of your mother as someone you need until she is gone.'

'When you are sick,' Minín said, 'there is no one you want but her, no one.'

'My mama, my mama!' Marta said.

'If you could say that she is going to come back after a month, you could comfort yourself.' Minín shook her head. 'But that she is gone for good –'

'My grandmother complains that I do not love her,' Marta said. 'She says that I am not happy though she is in the house with me. But it is not that. I need my mama, she is Mama, that is all.'

'Yes, yes,' Minín agreed.

'Even if the house is full of people – there you are – it is not enough without her.'

When Marta left the Bitirí a half hour later with Amelia – they both lived in the 26 of July project beyond the hospital – she felt better enough to wave good-bye. I had forgotten about Basilio's party and I didn't hear any noise from my room. No one said anything in the morning, and I thought Margarita was acting subdued because Angela's being off made it necessary for her to work harder that day. Poor Granda looked so woebegone with his swollen and bandaged face that I did no more than tell him Margarita, who was to give him his penicillin injection, was in the linen room.

Before dinner, when Padrón came by for his shower, he told me that Angela was an almost classic case of rheumatoid arthritis, so much so that he had already prescribed aspirins and a steroid before the results of the necessary tests were in. 'She is a strange girl,' he said. 'I think she is a bit oversexed, and she is troubled too. Her husband got into a fight, she said, and he is in jail.'

'But they are separated,' I said. 'He lives in Guaro.'

'I guess she is worried that in jail he will not be able to help support their child, for I told her it might be necessary for her to find a job that will not require her working with water so much.'

During dessert, Granda came and sat with me. His bandage had been changed to a smaller one, and what it revealed of his face looked discoloured and even more swollen. Robertico Silvera, the young Army man, was seated with me, and he exclaimed at the sight of him. 'What happened?' he said.

'If the girl had been a beauty or if I had been sleeping with her, then maybe I could console myself. But she would be the last one I would pick – all skin and bones! And her husband came at me when I was not even looking.'

'What, what?' said Robertico. 'Start at the beginning!'

'Late last night I was at the reception desk,' Granda began again, 'and one of the compañeras came by and said would I walk her home because it was late. So I obliged –'

'Ahaa!' said Robertico.

'I told you she was no prize. I was only doing her a favour, just as I would do it for any compañera who came and asked me. It was not even on my mind. As we were getting near her home – on the other side of the Reforma Urbana – a man is coming toward us. I remember noticing that they seemed to know each other and so I was not on my guard. The next thing

I know he has hit me one tremendous blow without saying a word to me or to her!'

A construction man from Havana at our table said, 'He can go to court for that.'

'He will,' Granda said. 'There are charges against him and the case comes up in three weeks. They have to wait to see how my injury comes out. Meanwhile he is in jail. I did not even know she was married and he turns out to be her husband!'

'You know what I would have done?' Robertico said, quite serious, tracing a pattern on the table with his forefinger. 'I would have let him get away with it, I would not have taken him to the police. Not one word to them. Then when I next ran into him alone, I would have given him a good beating. Even if I had to use my gun. That is what I would have done.'

It did not occur to Robertico – or anyone else – that this was strange advice from a man in the uniform of the Revolutionary Army.

'I did not turn him in to the police,' said Granda, falling in with Robertico. 'After he hit me, I just lay on the ground trying to get my bearings and he ran off immediately. It happened that two men from Orden Pública were on the next corner – they saw the whole thing, and arrested him.'

'Oh, that is different,' Robertico said, and the construction man nodded.

'It happened I had my gun with me,' Granda admitted, 'for I was in Orden Pública in Santiago. He ran away so fast and I was stunned, but there was a second there when it crossed my mind I could reach for my gun and fire after him. I did not do it and I am glad. The police were there and they would have seen it. And what if I had hit him – it would have been worse! No one would have blamed me, of course, but I would have been in jail now and for a long time.' He turned to me. 'We are very hard on people who make free and easy with their guns.'

'You did right,' the construction man said. He was the oldest at the table and it seemed correct that Granda's exoneration should come from him. Then we all nodded and Granda felt better.

No one asked who the girl was. But I did ask about the trial and Granda promised to take me with him. Later, I decided the girl was Angela and that Granda's intentions – if they'd been at Basilio's party together – could not have been so pure. I was sure Angela would tell me the next morning, but she didn't show up, and Margarita did not volunteer any explanation and, strangely, did not complain about the extra work; I had to think up the excuse that Dr Padrón wanted Angela to rest as much as possible until the tests were done.

Angela did not come the next day either. 'Maybe she will not come any more for reasons of health,' I said.

'We shall see,' said Margarita mysteriously.

During the weeks before the trial came up – the wait was extended to four weeks although Granda's eye improved daily – it was a surprise to me that Margarita did not gossip about Angela. Dr Padrón said, 'There is hope for her character. It is a sign that Margarita feels some stirrings of a revolutionary conscience, for one should feel some responsibility for the behaviour of the compañeros at one's work centre.'

Not Amelia. 'That girl!' she exclaimed, and launched on a comparison of her own conduct with Angela's which very much amused old Mercedes, who was also listening: Amelia seemed to overlook the fact that Angela was good-looking and far from thirty-eight. 'She is one of those crazy women – telling people she has no husband and egging men on. Would I ask a man to walk me home if I was married and had a man waiting for me there? I have a fiancé and there is nothing between us, but when we marry do you think I will go around saying that I am not? I am friendly with the guests here. I say to you, Hello Jose, how are you? but I do not egg men on! There is simply something wrong with Angela's head.'

As soon as Amelia walked away, Mercedes expelled her breath in a way usual with her before she made a caustic comment. 'A fiancé! a fiancé! Young girls have fiancés, not old women of thirty-eight with children.'

But old Mercedes confirmed that Angela had lost her job. 'She had been warned once. There used to be a man who was staying in one of my rooms on the other side and Angela said he was in love with her. Then she said the Russians were. I used to tell her, Angela, you are married, it is not right you should go around saying, So-and-so is in love with me. Who ever heard of such a thing! Of course men will say they are in love with you, they will make a try and see if you fall, it is only logical. But she did not listen. You have to be very careful in government jobs.'

She thought it over and then told me about a man who had once stayed in the same room as I. Angela went out drinking with that man and did not come home until two in the morning. 'Her husband hit her when she got home and they spent a few days apart. But they were not separated. He came back and he lived with her as if he were the cock of the walk!' Mercedes expelled her breath in her special way to show what she thought of him.

'I used to try to advise Angela. I said to her, Do not say you have no family. You have your mother even if she lives in the country. What is greater in this world than a mother? Whom can you go to for better advice than your mother? Not to some girl like Margarita as she did – *there* is another one who as soon as a man addresses a word to her reports that he is in love with her! I have gone out without my husband, with my children or alone – there is nothing wrong in that. I have even gone to Havana and spent several days. Also to the Isle of Pines. And no man ever said a word to me. The respect one wants from others one first has to adorn oneself with.'

I ran into Angela with her baby on Leyte Vidal, and she told me she was feeling better. Dr Padrón's treatment had helped her, but she did not think she was coming back to the Bitirí because the work was bad for her rheumatism. The Federation of Women had promised her a job at the Círculo Infantil as soon as there was an opening. Meanwhile she was resting and getting better.

Across the street, after I left her, Chepi, the maintenance man for the new pizzeria, said, 'Ay, ay, Jose, I guess you miss your regular lay now that she is not at the Bitirí!'

'I am no young bull like you, Chepi,' I said. And he was, stocky and red-faced, with bright blue eyes that seemed to be asking the most important question of all each time he looked at a woman.

'That one gets on her back for everyone but her husband.'

'How do *you* know?' I joked.

He answered quite soberly. 'I laid her in one of the rooms of the Bitirí. They sent me there to fix the plumbing in one of the rooms and she came in to fix the bed. I told her not to change the linens yet and she said why not and I told her why. A skinny thing, no ass to bounce on, but she enjoyed me because she said they get guests at the Bitirí who do not get it up even when she touches them. Mine was standing in my pants as soon as I said the first word to her.'

I laughed, and he liked that. 'She asked me to come up to her house too,' he said. 'Imagine, I could have been in the same trouble as Granda. These muscles are not worth anything if they come upon you unawares.'

The last week before the trial came up I had to go to Havana for a couple of days, but I flew back and made it in time. At the Havana airport I saw some inexpensive souvenirs that I thought the girls of the Bitirí would appreciate and bought a bunch of them. At dinner that night I had just finished distributing them all when Marta dashed out of the kitchen expecting to get one. 'You false old man,' she said, in mock indignation. 'I shall never address a word to you again. I know why you did not think of me – it is because I am the ugliest and the blackest of all the girls!'

I had not seen her in such good spirits since her mother died, and I found out, after she returned to the kitchen, that she was one of the union delegates for the Bitirí. She was early for work the next day, and I called her over to where I sat in front of my room. 'I found out that you are a very serious girl, Marta,' I said.

'Do not let them tell you stories – I am a flirtatious little black girl,' she said; she used the word *sata*, which is stronger than flirtatious. 'But I am hard to catch.'

She sat down across from me and told me that besides being a union delegate she was in the militia, in her local Committee for the Defence of the Revolution, the Federation of Cuban Women, and the Young Communists; she was also counsellor for a group of thirty-one young Pioneers.

'That should not leave you much time for flirting with the boys,' I said.

'Oh, I am engaged,' she said. 'He is twenty-two, a militant in the Party, and he works in Los Pinares. He is a beautiful *jabao* – oh!' A *jabao* is a fair – sometimes blond – boy whose features and the texture of his hair are African. 'We were going to be married this month but we have put it off because ...' Her face got sad remembering her mother.

I asked her what she thought of Angela's case.

'I think the decision we came to was the best,' she said, taking for granted that I knew all. 'We went to the union and to the Party, and the Party told us that it was up to us collectively to decide what to do but not to just let it ride. So we got together with Angela and she accepted our decision – one year without being able to work at the Bitirí, and a review of her case in three months if she has not been able to find a job. Right now, the Federation is hoping to place her in the Círculo Infantil, and we hope that she can learn from what happened.

'We had to do something because otherwise this could happen again and another compañera could say, Well you excused Angela. In a small town such an incident can give the Bitirí a bad reputation when what we are trying to do is make it a model. Soon they would begin to say, Oh yes, the Bitirí girls, you know how they are.' Remembering she had told me she was sata, she laughed and shook her head.

'The fact is,' Marta continued, 'that Angela put her foot in it. For she went to the course in Holguín with the rest of us and she knows that under no circumstances can a girl enter a room with a guest, or a waitress have amorous relations or make a date with a guest. You know how it is even with a fiancé: you give him a kiss and then you cannot look him in the face for timidity and shame! How much worse is it for a girl to have sexual relations with a guest and then have to serve him in the dining-room! She had already committed a bad error in the dining-room where she started – she poured a glass from which a guest had already drunk back into the pitcher, and the guest reported her. True, she had taken the pitcher back to the kitchen and emptied it, but it was a mistake nevertheless.

'Then she really put her foot in it in the rooms. All this was discussed with her very discreetly, but it was necessary that she and the rest of us know that such behaviour cannot be allowed. For what do we want for the Bitirí? I want it to be known all over the island as a wonderful place to stay, where the compañeros are given the best service, so that Mayarí really deserves what the Revolution has done – that a small town like ours had such a beautiful work built for it, where there is always good food and every weekend a show.

'I was born in Mateos Sanchez on the other side of Chavaleta, which is on the other side of the river to the right of where Leyte Vidal ends. You know where that is? If you go left where Leyte Vidal ends then you are in El Naranjal. But this is out toward the country, and my mother always raised animals and grew vegetables to pay for the three of us. For my father divorced her when she was pregnant with my brother and I was only a few months old and my sister a little over a year old. Oh my father, he had twenty-two children with different women, seven by a woman he married later in Sagua de Tánamo, three by my mother and the rest – you know!

'I did not see my father after I was six until the triumph of the Revolution. And that was when I met some of my brothers from Sagua de Tánamo, for they had all been Rebels in the monte and they came down through Guanina. They were beautiful with long beards and I got to know them and love them. There are others I have not met yet and there is one in Baracoa that even my father has not seen. Some of my father's children are the same age – there are two the same age as my sister. I tell my father that I want to travel all around Oriente and get to know it well, but that I am afraid I shall fall in love and he will turn out to be my brother. He says I am very fresh and I tell him, That is the way I am!

'My mother was under age when he got her pregnant and that is why he married her, but after they were divorced my mother met a fine man and they married, and I have five brothers and sisters from that marriage. My stepfather is a Party militant, and I live with him and my little brothers and sisters. I had thought that when I married we would go to Havana to be near my older sister, but I feel responsible to my little brothers and sisters, so we cannot do that. I shall have to think about what I will do.

'My father is dark although he is the son of a Galician and a Jamaican woman, both of whom died when he was a boy. On my mother's side they were very light. I remember my Galician great-grandfather – he used to share his meals with me until one day I told him he always gave me the worst bits. I took after my father, black like him. When I was six, my sister and brother and I were sent to study each day with a woman in the neighbourhood we all called Aunt. They paid her fifteen cents a week and she taught us so well that when we started in the regular school in Mayarí we were put in the second grade. But it was not as nice there as it was with Aunt, because of the racial discrimination.

'Once I got involved in a schoolgirls' quarrel, you know how they are, she was even a friend of mine. But the teacher intervened and said to me, "I shit on you and your parents and on all the degenerate race of Negroes." I shall never forget those words. Sometimes my sister and I get together and talk and I say to her, Remember that teacher and those words she said? How different from the schools now where everyone gets the same attention, where all is brotherhood! My mother told me that before the Revolution they used to rope off a section of the Parque when they had an outdoor fiesta, so that the Negroes could dance on the other side of the rope. I do not remember because I was only eleven when the Revolution came.

'When the Revolution came, we were all able to go to school in Mayarí. For a year, only my sister used to go, because my mother could not get enough clothes together to send all three of us. Then came the alphabetization campaign – when the three of us were thirteen, fourteen and fifteen – and we were wild to go and teach the campesinos and we had to argue for days with my mother. But she gave in and we all went to Varadero for the course in how to teach the illiterates. It was my first time away from Mayarí and I shall never forget it. When we finished the course, we went to Havana for a day and I shall never forget that either.

'We selected Oriente as the place where we wanted to teach because we hoped to be near home, but we were sent to Palenque de Yateras, which is in the mountains in the Guantánamo area, and we had to travel five days from Guantánamo to reach it, the last three days on foot. There were thirty of us and we brought all the material we needed to teach the campesinos. Also, a lantern, boots, two uniforms and a hammock. The first night with the campesinos I fell out of the hammock four times and never learned how to sleep in it, for they took pity on me and gave me a bed to sleep in and one of them slept in the hammock.

'There were four persons in the family I stayed with who had signed up for alphabetization. They were semiliterates – that is, they did not really know how to read or write but they knew something – and I took on four more from another family that were really illiterate. The older people had a hard time learning and there was one sixty-year-old man who never did learn more than to write his name. But the twenty-five-year-olds and the children learned well, though there was one man who could never master *Reforma Agaria* – Agrarian Reform – he always said Renforma Jagraria. How we used to laugh about that!

'I stayed there eight months with only one trip back home in the whole time, and when we came back I finished Secundaria Básica – junior high school – and at night took stenography. Then I signed up for the teacher's course that takes five years. I went for a year at Minas de Frío and then for a year at Topes de Collante, and in both places I was the secretary of the Young Communists. But I got asthma at Topes and my mother began to get very worried. "I will die if you do not come back," she said. "You can study in Mayarí." So I came back and studied here and went to a Party political course in Moa and then got a job with the Party in Nicaro. Until they decided that I would be more needed here at the Bitirí. In Holguín I learned to be both a receptionist and a cashier, but I like being a cashier better.'

'Now that I know, Marta, that you are not sata,' I said to her, 'I am going to ask you a question that will embarrass you. If young people are in love, do you think it is all right for them to sleep together?'

Marta shook her head. 'In Cuba, no . . .'

'What about your own personal view?' I said.

'My own view is very much my own. It is my belief that a girl who loses herself with a man will no longer interest the man. It is not that I do not trust men, but that is the way I see that men are. I have discussed this with my girl friends, whom I like to advise. My mother always was good to me that way and I like to do the same. A man runs after a girl but if she gives in, he loses interest. Two people in love is something very special and it is up to the girl to act right. I hope for great happiness from my marriage. Maybe my sweetheart and I will break up, but we have the same interests – we are both revolutionaries – and we should be happy together.'

Marta thought over what she had said, and it did not seem

to satisfy her. I told her that a young man of thirty (it was Chepi) had told me there was more 'degradation' today, even without the brothels, because the girls were so free and easy.

'Young people today are not corrupted, they are not tempted into vice as in the old days,' Marta insisted. 'Of course, there will always be some who will be loose – they are wrongheaded. But if a girl does take that turn – well, there are wonderful schools they can be sent to, where they will come out serious, sincere persons who know the value of work and good behaviour. At the course in Holguín, we had one girl who departed from the proper behaviour. She had sexual relations that reflected on the group and set the wrong example, at the very start, of what we wanted the girls of the Bitirí to be like. We held a meeting, we also spoke to her parents, and we told her what we thought. She herself said she had been wrong, that she was sorry she had acted in a way to demoralize our group, and she said she thought she should no longer be part of it and resigned. It is not true, as they told you, that there is more degradation now, that girls sleep around freely. Young people now have wonderful opportunities, they have wonderful enthusiasm and they work together – you see how they go out to cut cane and study and work. Oh yes, the Revolution is beautiful!'

There was still one purplish-blue streak in Granda's eye the next morning when he and El Gallego came around to take me to the court building for Angela's husband's trial. Time and penicillin had cured the rest – even the talk. The court building was on Maceo, two blocks from the back entrance of the Bitirí, and on the way there we passed the girls who had made the nurse's aide course at the hospital; they walked in twos demurely down the sidewalk heading for the hospital. 'They are my little nuns,' Dr Padrón had said. 'One of the first things I told them was that dresses were to cover the knees. They are not at the hospital to inflame the patients!' I greeted Jaime Hernandez's daughter and she managed to look both proud and shy.

El Palacio de Justicia – some people still gave it that grandiloquent old name – was a disreputable hangover from bourgeois days: it did not resemble a palace and revolutionaries did not care much for the kind of justice it dispensed. 'What is the use of that kind of justice,' the Organizing Secretary of the Party said to me one day, 'where one man decides you are guilty or you are not? If they are not guilty, they should not be there, and if they have done something wrong, it should be their neighbours who judge them and talk it over with them. That is what the Popular Tribunals do. This way no one learns anything from one man sitting there and deciding about another one.' The organization of the Popular Tribunals had begun two years earlier, though in Mayarí they had yet to be put into operation, and the Palace of Justice had the condemned air of the barracones in Guatemala.

It was a one-storey, cement-block building squatting on a half block of Maceo, and after Hurricane Flora only the mud had been swept out of it. Or so it seemed. The broken windows remained broken and the others looked as if they had not been cleaned since. Most of the expanse of the building was taken up by a bare inner patio off which was the horizontal entrance hall and, to the sides, large open rooms with desks for the business of the court. One of the large rooms was the Municipal Court, one door of which led to the hall, another to the patio, and another to a large, open, dingy room where municipal birth, wedding and divorce records were kept by two or three clerks. At one end of the court-room was the raised bench at which the judge and secretary of the court sat, so that defendants, plaintiffs, witnesses standing in front of them were at eye level; the bench made a right-angle turn at each end and that is where the prosecuting and defence attorneys sat, or rather, were supposed to sit, for in the one hundred cases I saw, there were only two occasions when there was a defence attorney and none with a prosecutor. Each time I showed up, the secretary and the judge invited me to draw up a chair alongside them, a very unorthodox procedure for a bourgeois

court. There were several occasions when defendants and witnesses insisted on making some important point clear to me,
even when sentence had already been pronounced.

But on this first visit with Granda and El Gallego I found
myself approaching the court-room with drawn breath – a
residual awe that had nothing to do with what Mayarí's Municipal Court looked like. There were no guards at the double
doors; it was simply a thoroughfare into the large room below
the judge's bench, and all that faced you, as you walked in,
were slatted, movable wooden benches, worn and discoloured.
Against the walls towards the front several broken-down chairs
were placed because without the walls to support them they
would have fallen, and to the left as I walked in was a worn old
table; there was no use for any of these things: they were
placed there as in an attic, to be thrown out on a more energe-
tic day. On the table and some benches there were people sitting and chatting, smoking and crushing their butts on the
cement floor; later, when the court was in session, and the
room filled, some even sat gingerly on the decrepit chairs;
others leaned against the wall. One could not say that the court
was ever in session – not in the sense that the smoking and
coming-and-going and chatting died down – and on the two or
three occasions that the secretary called out, 'Silencio,
silencio,' less than half the audience responded to the command.

El Gallego knew some of the people there; I did too, and
those who didn't know me took me to be a compañero from
Santiago like Granda. I found myself sitting on the table (the
atmosphere was so relaxed) with a campesino named Conato
who told me he was a brother of Pancho Gonzalez, a man who
had been a comandante in the second front, and I understood
immediately this time that they were childhood buddies, hermanos de crianza. Conato too had been in the monte and until
four months ago he had been head of Orden Pública at Moa.
He was very glad that he had been transferred from Moa at
that time, for only twenty-three days later a group of his

friends, all with responsible positions like his and most of them veterans of the insurrection in the second front, were caught a couple of miles off shore in a good yacht with the best weapons on the first lap of a trip they hoped would take them to Venezuela to join the guerrillas.

'Twenty-three days earlier and I would have been with them,' Conato said. 'They had told me about it and I thought it was a good idea.'

'What happened to them?' I asked.

Conato gave a couple of shakes to his right hand with the fingers loose so that they made a snapping sound – an exclamatory Cuban gesture. 'Raul came down and gave them all a good talking-to and they are all in the U M A P now taking political courses!' The story had not been in the newspapers, but they all knew it and everyone laughed to hear it again.

Angela showed up soon, looking withdrawn and serious. She nodded to me and signalled to Granda. He went over to talk to her, but came away as soon as he could. She went out to the corridor, looking composed but occasionally chewing her nails. An assured young Negro of about thirty waved to El Gallego, and he led Granda and me to a small room behind the court-room where the Negro, named Roberto Milian, told us the judge would be there any second. Meanwhile he introduced us to Evelia Belet, a trim lady in her fifties who was the secretary of the court; like him she had worked there before the Revolution. There was only space in the room for two desks, both covered with papers, and battered bookcases filled with law reviews and reference books; but they had found room for a coffee pot and Evelia immediately gave us all some. Evelia said to Granda, 'The judge will want to know the condition of your eye.'

Into this crowded room whose door was never shut came the judge, with wet, extended hands, looking for a paper towel. He apologized for holding everyone up, but he had been cutting cane all morning and his hands had been black and sticky from the cane juice. He was in militia uniform, a short, serious man around fifty, diffident about his work but delighted with the way his cane cutting had improved that year. He was a judge of the higher court in Holguín but two weeks ago had been temporarily assigned to the Mayarí Municipal Court, and since, during the harvest, court was in session at most twice a week, he was spending all his time in the cane-fields.

He looked at the papers on Granda's case and asked if his eye was all right now. Roberto Milian grabbed a man standing outside, who was a local doctor, and got him to examine Granda's eye. It looked fine to him but this did not satisfy the judge; he asked Granda to get a letter from the doctor at the hospital who had been treating him stating that there were no complications. 'Otherwise, if there has been some damage, the case cannot be tried here.' Granda looked worried; he too was on a temporary assignment and did not want to spend another week in Mayarí. 'You go to the hospital now,' the judge said. 'Get the letter and come right back.'

El Gallego and Granda hurried off to the hospital. Evelia picked up a file of manilla folders, the cases for the day; Roberto Milian stuck a cigar in his mouth and said, 'I guess you can start now.' The judge said to me, 'All this is going to change, you know, with the Popular Tribunals. They are already working very well in several places.' He saw I was interested, and stopped a moment to explain briefly that each neighbourhood had selected judges from their area at an asamblea and that these judges were given special courses; they were not to become professionals, however, but to remain at their regular jobs and live in the neighbourhood where they acted as judges. 'The cases are held at times when all the neighbours can come and the object is not to punish or jail anyone, for we are going to do away with jails too,' the judge said. 'And the tribunals will be held in the neighbourhood, not at a formal court like this.'

I nodded, and the three of us walked into the court-room through a doorway behind the bench. Roberto Milian leaned against the doorway and kept an eye on things, but no one called the court to order or called for silence or stood up. An old man from Orden Pública leaned an arm on the bench from below; he was known to me as the Practical Geologist, for, as he explained, he had tracked every inch of northern Oriente since he was a boy and knew the terrain so well that Soviet geologists and men from Havana had used him as a guide in surveying the area. He usually brought defendants to court who had been in the police headquarters' cells awaiting trial; a two-year-old boy could have got away from him.

The innards of the easy-chairs at the bench had been sprung by Hurricane Flora, and Evelia brought her own cushion to place on hers, but the judge simply lowered himself into one whose springs formed a well-defined peak at the centre. Evelia picked up the first folder and read out the names on the cover; only one or two persons came forward, and Roberto Milian stepped away from the doorway to tell me that during the harvest people could delay responding to a trial summons until it was over. A dog came in from the patio, sniffed around, found the place uninteresting, and went out to the patio again.

Before El Gallego and Granda returned with the letter from the doctor, the judge heard about six cases, and in only one case was there a jail sentence. (In Municipal Court it could not be more than six months.) Only in the first case did Orden Pública send the arresting officer to court to testify; for most, the charges given in the folder, read aloud by Evelia, and the statements made by plaintiffs and witnesses at the time, were sufficient for the judge to begin questioning. The only formality followed was Evelia's directing the defendant to stand on the far right and the others in a row, elbow to elbow, to the left. There was no court stenographer, and no one raised his voice to make it easier for the audience to hear.

The first case involved two men and two young boys; they had killed a pig and one of the men and the two boys were leaving to deliver sections of it to clients when the police came up to the house. The man said they were innocent; the pig had been killed for family use and one of the men was simply a neighbour who was helping in the butchering. A woman got up from the crowd and approached the bench; the judge let her speak after he found out she was the mother-in-law of the defendant and the grandmother of the boys. She raised an arm and half turned to the court-room. 'In my house there has never been any traffic in pork!' she said in a shrill voice; they had not even meant to kill the pig: it had drowned in a puddle, so they had to quarter it. The arresting officer listened with a pained expression. 'My grandson was only taking some to a member of the family.' The judge looked at the older of the boys and the boy nodded; then at the other and he said, 'I only had a tiny piece of skin.' The judge fined the son-in-law $120, and they left satisfied to pay Roberto Milian the fine.

There were two cases of 'trafficking in agricultural products'. One was a sixteen-year-old campesino boy who transported corn for farmers to individual buyers in Levisa; he also worked on the family farm. He would carry a large load at a time, and he got picked up by the police on the law that more than twenty-five pounds being transported is evidence of black-market activity. The boy's mother stood by him in front of the bench; he was tall and manly and nodded as the judge explained to him that since he was a minor the law could not be applied to him, but that he could be sent away for rehabilitation. Evelia said, 'He is the oldest son and his mother is a widow.' The judge explained how important it was to the Revolution to stop black-market activities, and that he was inadvertently helping profiteers by taking the job as a delivery boy. 'You must have suspected that you were not doing right,' the judge said. 'I tell you what we shall do, we shall sentence you to one year of *reclusión en domicilio*.'

This meant, simply, that for a year he was to spend his time at home when he wasn't at school or working, but the phrase was so formal – the judge did say 'sentence' – that the campesino boy misunderstood. He did not walk away from the bench, as everyone did when sentence was given, but stood there unable to move with the shock. He was directly across from me and I saw his right cheek begin to tremble spasmodically; he brought up a hand to contain it, and then he could hold out no longer: the tears gushed out and his shoulders shook. Evelia yelled, 'Do not be foolish! It is nothing – this sentence is nothing at all!' And Roberto Milian jumped down from the doorway and said, 'You are not being sent anywhere. Come, come and sit down.' And he took him into the office and sat him down and gave him an aspirin and coffee as soon as he got his breath. When Roberto Milian again appeared in the doorway, the judge looked up at him and Roberto smiled and nodded: the boy was all right.

The other case of this type was an older man who had been picked up when he got off the bus on Leyte Vidal; he was carrying a package with thirty-eight pounds of garlic. He knew the law and he had only bought it for family use. 'Thirty-eight pounds?' said the judge. The man explained that he had actually bought only twenty-five pounds and that the rest had been given to him free because it was not in good condition. 'I shall have to apply law number 520,' said the judge, 'which allows of no extenuating circumstances and gives me no leeway in sentencing. One hundred and twenty days in jail.' The man walked away meekly and the Practical Geologist followed him with a sad expression.

Two campesino couples came up to the bench for the next case, the wife of the younger one with a baby in her arms. The younger couple had brought charges against the older for making their life miserable; the older husband had accosted the younger often, had once had to be subdued, and all sorts of calumnies had been spread about them. 'I am here to get them to stop,' the younger man said. The judge started to question the older man, but his wife, a thin, rachitic little woman, interrupted. 'It is all my fault,' she said. 'I thought my husband was interested in her. It is a foolishness of mine.' The judge frowned and asked the younger man, 'Do you think they can be good neighbours?' The young man said, 'That is all I

ask.' The judge turned to them all. 'Try to be good neighbours,' he said, and they walked away in a group at first, but
the younger man suddenly veered away and led his wife out a
side door.

The next was a group of five men from Guatemala whom
another, using marked bills given to him by Orden Pública,
accused of running a numbers game. All avowed that they
were innocent; one was a seller of government lottery tickets,
and he insisted the whole thing had been a misunderstanding
– they had thought the accuser was trying to buy a lottery
ticket. In one man's room a can full of slips of paper with
names and numbers had been found; he said he had only
recently rented the room and didn't know the can was hidden
there. 'Take paper and pencil,' the judge said. 'I am going to
dictate to you.' He had the slips of paper in front of him.

The man said, 'I cannot read or write.'

'Not even numbers?' the judge asked.

'Not even numbers,' the man said.

The witness against them spoke up. 'It is true that they took
the marked bills, but I must admit that none of them actually
did sell me a number.' He stopped and then started several
times until he remembered what he wanted to say. 'All of them
are working men, so perhaps I was wrong.'

'All of you work at the mill?' the judge asked, and as he
looked at each man, he nodded and the man nodded back.
'That speaks well for you.' Then he took a deep breath. 'You
know that our country has changed – none of us makes money
from the work of others any more. We are all working hard to
reach a level of production and abundance that will take us to
communism. Gambling is a vice of capitalism and it has no
place and no reason for being in Cuba. We have other things
to occupy us now.'

The man who had not been found with a marked bill and
against whom there was no other evidence was exonerated.
The others were fined $180 each. The exonerated man began
to talk, and one of the others elbowed him and said, 'Do not

talk any more!' But the judge asked and the man explained
that he wanted a religious medal that had been taken from
him when arrested. 'You will get that with your bail,' the judge
said, and they filed out of the court-room to the small office
to deal with Roberto Milian. Their wives and families and
friends followed them and sounds of relief and joy drifted into
the court-room.

I got off my perch and joined them.

'That Lopez is so stupid he got all mixed up,' said one man
before counting out an enormous bundle of fives and singles;
he was talking about the man who passed them the marked
bills but then spoke up on their behalf.

'No, no,' said a tall thin man, the only bachelor of the group.
'He got lost there for a while but he was all right.'

'You can thank him,' Roberto Milian said. 'I do not know if
you got him to tell it that way, but he certainly helped.'

None dared look at the others and all kept quiet. Then the
bachelor sighed. 'Never, never again,' he said. 'To get into all
this trouble for a bit of piggery.'

'Then you are satisfied with the sentence?' I said; amongst
them they were paying almost a thousand dollars.

'Oh yes!' said the bachelor.

He saw that I was thinking that they had all declared themselves innocent.

'Well, what can you do!' he said. 'So long as I can keep my
job, that is all I care about. Never again!'

When I got back to my place at the bench, El Gallego,
Granda, Angela and her husband were already standing waiting for Evelia to begin reading the statement taken by Orden
Pública the night of the arrest. Angela's husband was a tall,
slim young man with an open, confiding face, the effect of
large round eyes which he directed at the judge in a curious
and pleading stare. He was light-skinned like Angela but his
hair was thick and kinky: a jabao. He leaned both elbows
on the bench as if he needed to, and he saw no one but the
judge.

I remembered Amelia saying, 'Such a good, good boy. Already he has had to spend ten days in jail. What more trouble will that crazy girl bring him!'

Evelia read that for fear of El Resbaloso, Angela Peman, an employee of the Bitirí, had asked Granda, on temporary assignment there, to walk her home since it was a late hour, and on the way there her husband came up to Granda and gave him a *piñazo* that knocked him to the ground and caused him an injury. When she said El Resbaloso, there was laughter from the audience, but none for the vernacular of a blow with a fist – *un piñazo*, literally a pineapple blow.

'What is this El Resbaloso?' the judge asked. 'I am new here.'

Laughter again, and Roberto Milian explained that El Resbaloso – also called The Vampire, because he came out at night – was the name given to a Peeping Tom said to be bothering women in Mayarí. The judge smiled and it was reflected faintly on Angela's face. 'About this being afraid,' the judge said, looking at her, 'women are not very much afraid any more, you know.' Angela looked vaguely at some spot between the judge and Evelia.

'Do you have the letter from the doctor?' the judge asked, and Evelia handed it to him. He read it and returned it to her.

He turned to Granda, and Granda said, 'I was at the reception desk when the compañera came and asked me to escort her home because she was afraid. I felt obliged to comply, as I would have with any other compañera –'

El Gallego interrupted, 'We usually take the girls who work late home in a car.'

'But it was already gone,' said Granda, 'and that is why I accompanied her on foot. I did not know the compañera's name, nor whether she was single or married. That is all.'

The judge asked Angela if it had all been the way it had been told, and Angela shifted her position and nodded.

The judge finally turned to Angela's husband, and Angela's husband looked back with eyes that watered but would not form a tear. I looked at Granda and El Gallego and found myself part of a conspiracy that hoped the judge would ask no more questions: not learn about Basilio's party nor that Angela had not been working late at the Bitirí. For if the judge did not find out, then Angela's husband would not either.

'In cases where no permanent physical damage has been done, the law allows that consideration be given to other than the simple facts of the case,' the judge said to Angela's husband. Angela's husband stopped supporting himself against the bench, and nodded when the judge paused: he had not understood but he had heard the judge's tone.

'In your mind – am I right? – you believed that it was different from what has been said here,' the judge continued, 'although it all happened as has been explained. Am I right?'

Angela's husband did not answer; he seemed to waver.

The judge hurried on: 'So I will conclude that although there was no reason for what you did, you personally thought there was, and I dismiss the case.'

Angela's husband kept his eyes on the judge, hoping he would continue to reassure him. Then he slowly nodded, as if it had all become clear to him: when one was trustful, as he had been in court, things came out right; when one was not, as he had been on that dark street waiting for his wife, life was troublesome and miserable. He smiled at the judge and turned to follow Angela, who was already out of the court-room.

7. La Enfermedad

One of the times that Jorge, the young man who needed a pair of pants to ask for his girl's hand, came out of the wind-ups he practised in front of my room, his eyes fell on my feet, and he stepped back with surprise and admiration. I had put on leather thong sandals bought in Greenwich Village that I wore only around the Bitirí, and he had failed to notice them earlier because it was night-time when he arrived with his friends. 'My God, look at those sandals!' he said to them. 'Jose has *La Enfermedad!*' And we all laughed because La Enferme-dad – The Sickness – is an illness that attacks only young males.

The most common symptom of La Enfermedad is a pen-chant for tight pants; any of the clothes young men wear in Europe and the States, in fact, would qualify as *tremenda enfermedad*. 'If you dress well – that is enough,' I was in-formed by a fifteen-year-old who was in the first stage of the illness. 'They suspect you and DOP [Orden Pública] will pick you up. You look close, though, and you will see that they wear their uniforms real tight. But do not say it and do not say La Enfermedad in front of them – it is like criticizing them, you know what I mean. All the young people feel like me, Jose, they hate the UMAP. They want to dress well. Do you want to sell your sunglasses?'

The first stage of the illness is nonpolitical: the young man is mainly seized with longing for stylish things, most of which are unobtainable, and he spends much of his time trying to get them or talking about them. (The vision is somewhat behind the times; the ideal style is the Italian designers' of four years ago or early Pierre Cardin: they do not know Mod and it might shock them.) They are restless and unhappy that they cannot get such clothes and angry about the revolutionaries who frown on them. In the last stage of the illness, they are counter-revolutionaries; they despise everything about the Revolution and are only waiting to reach that magical age of twenty-seven when they can apply to leave the country.

Girls cannot catch La Enfermedad. Whatever a girl does to make herself noticeable and attractive is cause for approbation, sometimes expressed aloud as a *piropo* – 'Take me home with you, my dear!' – or silently with a complete parabola of the men's swivel eyes. I liked to think that I could spot a Party member in a group of men: he was the one whose eyes braked in mid-course when a pair of flowering thighs went by. A young, handsome Party member of the Committees for the Defence of the Revolution was explaining the mentality of La Enfermedad – 'Men with such values can be enticed into counter-revolutionary activity …' – when a good-looking blonde went by, and someone with us exclaimed, 'Look at that! Couldn't that entice you?' The Party member took a quick look, laughed, and said, 'I have been cured of that!' But obviously he approved of all the aids – the hair dye, the cinch-waist belt, the aggressive brassiere, the tight skirt – that tempted him to look. 'Aha, he is lighting a cigarette,' the other said. 'It makes him nervous!'

The fifteen-year-old with La Enfermedad wasn't recognizably hooked – he wore baggy pants, a nondescript shirt, ordinary shoes – and I met him at an unlikely place for someone with his interests. Perhaps not, for he had a consuming hunger for girls, and the occasion was the graduation of 250 girls at Los Pinares as 'lot leaders'. They had spent three months there learning tractor driving and practical techniques in horticulture in order to become foremen of the twelve thousand women already signed up to work in the mesa. Since it was also International Women's Day, a programme of speeches, songs, awards and a play was planned, and I caught a ride up to Los Pinares, a half-hour uphill drive from Mayarí, with some women of the Federation of Cuban Women. Towards the end of the programme it began to rain, and we got back in the jeep for cover; two boys got in back with me and one of them turned out – in time – to have La Enfermedad.

The boys horsed around, and I spent most of the time talking to the driver of the jeep and two of the women who sat in front. But before the boys left, I asked the one if he was attending the horticultural technology school at Los Pinares. The jeep driver turned around and with a sarcastic smile said, 'Not him, he is one of the frogs of the town.' It was a perfect name for him: he showed up everywhere during the six weeks left to me in Mayarí, and I got to calling him El Sapito, the little frog.

He was a familiar young man; he got on a first-name basis with you – without permission and no matter what your age – after one encounter, and was apt to stop you on Leyte Vidal with much fanfare to ask you to change a ten. It was obvious he did not need to change the ten; he just felt it was a debonair thing to do. He got to dropping by the Bitirí, whether he had seen me on the street or at El Parque, because it gave him status; he liked draping himself over a chair, one leg swinging from an arm of it, and asking for a cigarette, which he smoked with many gestures and then flicked away into the bushes with great élan.

But the first time I saw him after the ceremonies at Los Pinares, he told me quite soberly that he was leaving the next day for the Soils and Fertilizers School in the Sierra Maestra; he was taking a bus to Bayamo and from there walking or hitching his way up the mountains. Until a few days earlier he had been working as an apprentice at a garage near the Palace of Justice, but he had decided that being a mechanic did not appeal to him; he went to the Party and told them he wanted to go away to study. 'I do not know much about soils and fertilizers, but I can keep studying and working at it and then studying some more and get somewhere. Right?' At the moment he had just returned from Party headquarters, where he had shown them his sixth-grade diploma and a letter from his block's Committee for the Defence of the Revolution attesting to his good character. He shook hands when he went away, and I said to myself that no one could call him a frog of the town now; he was set and on his way.

Three days later he was back. The class he was to have joined had already left, as had many throughout the country, to work in the countryside for forty-five days. El Sapito was told to return on 1 May, and he had a six-weeks vacation, he said, before he got down to work. I asked him if he were going to cut cane around Mayarí or get involved in some other voluntary work. 'I might do that,' he said, but I could see it had never occurred to him. It was a Friday night and he had come to see the weekend show at the Bitirí. The chairs in front of my room were a good place to watch for friends arriving that he could join.

'Jose, are you sure you are an American?' he said. 'The first time I saw you I thought you were from one of the ships. I like to meet the sailors from the ships. Zing, as soon as I hear there is a ship at Guatemala or Nicaro I get on the bus and go there. A Greek once sold me a pair of sun-glasses for fifteen dollars and I sold them for thirty! Pretty good, eh?'

I nodded.

'How do you say, Give me a cigarette? How do you say socks? And condoms, how do you say condoms?' He practised each a couple of times. 'You do not have to teach me how to say Chiclets. Or Chesterfields or Lucky Strikes or Camels. But I like Chesters best. I have to get some Chiclets and Chesters. I am invited to a wedding and I want to have some to impress the girls. I want to walk in chewing a Chiclet – oh man! I hear there is going to be a ship at Guatemala soon.'

He sat up in the chair in order to reach into one pocket. He looked around and showed me a pack of condoms. 'They are Chinese. See the butterfly on the cover? We call them Butterflies. Not because of the picture, oh no. It is because they have a short life. If you have not done it for a couple of days, you can shoot right through them!'

You didn't have to answer El Sapito: he kept right on talking, assured you were interested.

'The Greeks have the most to sell,' El Sapito continued. 'They always want to get laid. They say, *Fuck-fuck signorina.* I take them to a couple of loose ones in Mayarí who do it for five dollars. They just do it on the side, you know. There are no more women of *la vida* and you do not want to do it with them. You get syphilis and your hair falls out and your teeth go bad. I go to a woman in Cueto. She gives it to me any time I want.

'This woman was a servant at a house on our block. I put in some time with her – you know, talking and convincing her I was all right. I knew she would do it because she was past her time – thirty years or more so she would not marry – and why should she not get what is coming to her? I told her I loved her and she let me. Now I go to Cueto every time I want it. Only it is not so convenient. I need to catch a girl right here. Right? Is it true that in the United Sates all the girls do it? Oh man, how I would like that! I would wear myself out.

'I had a girl lived right next door. She still does, but it is all over. Not because of me – I still want to. It was last year. I was fourteen and she was eighteen, so one day when there was no one in our houses – I have been watching for the chance – I asked her over. I have something to tell you, I said. I was shaking I was so nervous. I told her, Oh I want you to know that although I am only fourteen I have been watching you and I love you so much I do not know what to do. I was looking down when I said this. Seeing I love you so much maybe we can make love? And she said, Look, if you do not tell anyone then maybe we can do it. But she would not do it then because it was too dangerous.

'So one night we met at the Secundaria Básica, the new school across the field from the Reforma Urbana. It is dark there at night like the mouth of a wolf. No one comes by. Why would they? She did it for the first time. I told her, Get on four points. I saw that position on one of the postcards I have. A good thing I remembered, because she said, How are we going to do it? She did not want to lie down and get dirty. I said, From behind, get on four points. So she got on four points and I lifted her dress. There was such a spout of blood I thought she had been injured. I got scared I would be jailed or something. Then I remembered that she was eighteen and I was fourteen, so they could not do anything to me. What a relief!

'That was the only time I did it with her. I do not know why but she got angry with me. She started saying *usted* to me. As if I was some stranger she did not know well. Then she stopped talking to me altogether. She had become engaged to a fellow in Guaro. You know, I do not think the poor fellow is passing it to her yet. He is going to have to marry her to get what I got. But you know how women are. I worked a couple of weeks for the cigarette distributorship and she wanted to get Aromas, the mild cigarette. So she spoke to my sister for me to get her some. But not to me. I got them for her.

'I do not have a girl now, except that woman in Cueto. There is no time. But maybe up in the Sierra I will get a girl. Not maybe, sure. You pick one out and work on it and you got her. I also want to get a pair of sun-glasses and a pair of sandals. You cannot get them just like that. You have to get a prescription. Oh man, sun-glasses! That is something with *el feeling* – sun-glasses! That is an American word, *feeling*, right, Jose? I would like to have one of those Italian suits. Real tight, oh what a feeling! But I could not wear it, of course. In Havana maybe. But here in Mayarí the DOP picks you up right away. Sun-glasses and sandals okay, but no tight clothes. Not me.

'You know, Jose, I once got picked up by the DOP. Not once, twice. They keep an eye on you when they see you with a foreign sailor. They saw me. I bought some Chiclets and Chesters, for the next day I was going to an engagement party. I went to the party and I passed out some Chiclets. The girls got the feeling and then I thought I would pass out a couple of Chesters. I reach in my pocket and all I have is Aromas. That is not too bad but I want to make a big impression. I went home to get the Chesters, but I did not get there because the D O P picked me up and searched me. All they found was the Aromas. What luck!

'The next time I brought it on myself. But I did it for the feeling. I bought a pack from a sailor and at the cafeteria I took one and leaned against the wall like this and I smoked the Chester like this, letting the smoke right out. You can smell those American cigarettes in a room full of people smoking. They are very special, they have feeling. So they took me to D O P headquarters and they made me take off all my clothes. But all, and they asked me where I got the Chesters and I told them I bought them. They looked at me and said, Do you have more? I said no. Okay, they said, you can go home. They kept the Chesters. That is all they did.

'How much did you pay for those shoes?' El Sapito asked.

They were Hush Puppies. 'Twelve dollars,' I said.

'You can sell them for a hundred,' he assured me. 'You should sell the sun-glasses. You can get thirty like I did.'

I saw him on Leyte Vidal two days later. He had borrowed a bicycle and was riding around on it looking as if he had the feeling. He called me over and took a piece of paper from his pocket. It was a prescription for sun-glasses. 'I had to lie a little,' he said. 'I said I drove a motorbike for the Army. Now I have to go to Holguín to buy them. They do not have the kind I want here.'

'I guess Cubans like sun-glasses so much,' I said, 'because the sun is so bright here.'

'Oh no, it is for the feeling,' he said. 'Say, Jose, did I tell you I danced with one of those girls that night at the Bitirí? There was a bunch having a party for one getting married, remember? They were most of them gusanas from Holguín and one went out on the dance floor with me. I got up real close. I hold my left hand in hers this way, I pull it all the way back and she has to get close to me. I put a real shine on it and she acted as if she did not notice it. Then she said I should visit her in Holguín. Her father would be glad to receive me since I am a nice boy. Wait until I get the sun-glasses and then show up at her house. She is going to notice it then!'

Chepi, the maintenance man, came out of the pizzeria to talk to me, and he simply stared at El Sapito as if saying, I know kids' stories are mostly lies, and El Sapito found a reason to leave. On Sunday, Chepi said, the pizzeria would open, a reminder that we had a date to eat there on the inauguration. 'There is not much else they can fuck up,' he said; the opening had been long delayed. 'But they may find something.'

Rose-bushes and shrubbery had been planted a week ago in the beds along the sidewalk, and round metal tables set into the terrazzo floor of the open dining-room. Over each table brilliantly coloured umbrellas – yellow, blue, green – blossomed; they were in the shape of inverted tulips, and yielded slightly, femininely, to the breeze: a modern setting from which to look, with one's back to Leyte Vidal, at my favourite view from Mayarí, the valley with the winding river and the horses and cattle grazing. On Sunday, the waitresses wore wine-coloured uniforms with white cuffs and collars, and they moved among the tables, as the moment drew near, as if enchanted, readjusting the black wire chairs and the settings to their sense of perfection. On the other side of the ropes stretched at waist height along the sidewalk, the crowd watched and talked.

The sun waned, the mountains in the distance turned blue and purple, then black; and the crowd in the street grew. After the first hour, I signalled to Granda, who was watching the girls get the dining-room ready, and told him when he approached that I hoped he would have a table for me and my friends. Granda told me not to worry, they would have a table for me. I was glad he didn't ask me how many we were, for I didn't know. Chepi knew everybody and a whole new crowd I had not met came over to talk while we were outside the ropes.

The waiting made Chepi impatient: it was one of those in-
efficiencies he could not bear.

He became ironic, then sarcastic. He laughed at himself for
having given up being an independent mechanic, hiring himself out for a job at a time, and having taken a regular job with
the pizzeria. 'Working for INIT is a *jamón* – a ham – an
easy job,' he said with disgust. 'I think I am going to marry in
another month. She is a girl of poor family, but a good girl.
That is a problem now, too, getting married. I like to dominate
my wife and that is not so easy any more. Nothing is so easy
any more. You see, they will not get one fucking pizza served
tonight.'

He was one of three sons of a Spaniard – Chepi did not
know what part of Spain his old man had come from – who
had worked hard and established two stores in Mayarí. His
brothers all went to schools and did well. 'But I was dumb, I
still am dumb,' he said. 'God, I am so dumb.' He left school,
worked around the court-house for a while, then left for
Nicaro and did 'brute's work' clearing out swampy areas; but
by 1957 he had done several different types of work around the
plant, been a garrotero lending money out at high interest,
owned his own car, and saved ten thousand dollars. 'Then I got
a fistula on my backside and I went to Havana to get it cured.
There was no hospital here then.'

He got the fistula cured, but he did not come back to
Mayarí because he had been a little too active in the Movement and his mother told him it was dangerous to come back.
'Do not think I was a big revolutionary like everyone tells you
now that I was,' Chepi said. 'One reason I did not leave
Havana was that I was leading *la dulce vida*. I had found a
house full of little girls. They ran around in little panties, for
they were smooth above, nothing to show there. The first time
I went I had not had a woman for five months because of the
fistula and I was surprised to be given a little girl. I thought I
would never stop fucking. I went back every day.'

But Chepi did not have La Enfermedad. He had not bought

a new pair of pants in a couple of years, but he did not care. He told it to you – as he avowed that no one could beat the United States in a war – because these were facts and he had respect for facts. 'And what government of Cuba has done as much for the country as the present one? None. The public works! The planting and the modernization! And they are honest – not one takes a penny for himself!' It was while he was saying this that he and I both noticed that Victor Bermudez, the head of DOP, was staring at our table, trying to get my attention; Chepi blushed and then waved at Bermudez. Bermudez only nodded at him but beckoned to me. He wanted me only. As I went towards him, I knew – for I had seen Bermudez earlier, before he caught my eye, gazing at the others at my table with a serious, appraising look – that he was not happy about the company I was in.

But Bermudez seemed only to want to show me the inside of the kitchen. He took me around proudly with Granda and the regional head of INIT. There were walk-in refrigerators, many work surfaces, built-in ovens, two stoves: they were not making the mistake of the Bitirí, with its tiny kitchen and cramped space. We drank a glass of Spanish sherry in the kitchen and wished the pizzeria success. Yet when I went back, I looked at the collection of young men at my table and wondered why Bermudez had been disappointed with the company I kept on so gala a night for the Revolution in Mayarí. There were Jorge, and Eider Cesar, the sports teacher, and El Chino, the electrician, and Hugo Ramirez, the young barber, all with varying degrees of devotion to the Revolution but none a counter-revolutionary.

There was one I didn't know and hadn't seen around Leyte Vidal till that night. The others didn't seem to know him well, but he introduced himself and said I was to call him El Rubio. When we broke up around midnight, he said he lived in the Reforma Urbana and would walk my way. The narrow sidewalk along Maceo made it necessary to walk close and then I could smell his cologne. I had not seen him in Mayarí because until two or three days ago he had been in Havana, where he had had a temporary job as a male nurse in a hospital. 'But I could not keep the job,' he said. I volunteered that I knew the government was now filling jobs that were not physically demanding only with women. He nodded reluctantly. 'I have a month of doing nothing before I go to my next job, which is in agricultural production in Las Villas. A hard job.'

When we got to the Bitirí, I realized that he had walked past the block where he should have turned off. He had been telling me, at my request, how they got water up to the third floor of the Reforma Urbana – a tedious process with a pail on a rope – and he was too polite, I thought, to tell me I was taking him past his home. But his face lit up as the orchestra in the dining-room began playing for the last show of the evening, and he said, 'If you are not going to retire, I should be pleased to keep you company.' I said I was only going to sit in front of my room and smoke a cigarette. He took that as an invitation and joined me. I was to smoke several more cigarettes before he finally left.

'Aaah, listen to that music,' he said. 'I have spent the last three days in my room, not going out, just listening to my radio. I have a radio but I would like to have a transistor. I like to lie in bed and put on the dim light in my room and listen to music. What else is there to do? I used to have a lot more things in my room. I had red damask curtains and I hung them over the wall behind the bed, but one has to sell those things to get other things. Or I spend the day desiccating insects, I like to do that too. I do them for the schools here, for their science classes. I inject them with formaldehyde and they are desiccated in a day or two. One day this week that is all I did.

'I have a lock on my room, I like privacy. I live with my mother and my sister and my niece and they do not come into my room. I have had a lot of adventures but now I can spend hours in my room just listening to the radio. I am trying to take myself in hand. I have a fiancée in Havana and I have a lot of things to think about. I went out tonight because it is Sunday, and I am glad I did because I met you. It is interesting to meet people from other countries. You used to meet them in Havana. How I would like to travel! That is what I think I would like to do now – get a job on a merchant ship and travel. I think I would like to go to the United States. Not to stay there but to go on to places in Europe I have heard about. Like Greece.

'One of my sisters lives in your country. She went there right after the Revolution to join my father. He has been there a long time. They live in Brooklyn, New Jersey. Do you know that place? I have asked them to send me a phonograph. I have records of feeling music but I cannot play them. And rock-and-roll. The Beatles. Do you know them? They are very hard to get here. Like everything. I am going to spend two years at *cara al campo* – face to the country, that is what they call work in agricultural production. I do not like it but I have to do it.

'I can do anything. I was fourteen when I first went to Havana alone. Now I am twenty-two. That was not the first time. I went the first time with my mother and my sister because my sister had to go to a hospital there. I was twelve but I got to like Havana, and when we came back and I had a quarrel with my family, I took off for Havana alone. I already had friends there. I got a job in the mornings, another in the afternoons and evenings. And one on Saturdays. And I went to parties. Do you like parties? I like to do everything because I do not like to have people tell me stories – I like to be the one to tell the stories. Oh, I had a very good time in Havana.

'I like adventures. That is why I want to get a job on a ship that will take me to the places I want to see. In 1958 when the Rebels were winning more and more I started back to Mayarí, but at Camagüey they were not letting buses go on to Oriente. I got stuck there for a whole month. I slept in the bus station the first night. And when I ran out of money, people gave me things to eat. Some nights I would sleep in someone's home or in a hotel or on a bench. I got to know many people in Camagüey and I had many adventures. I was never so happy in my life, it was so free and easy and friendly. You have to be careful about friends, though. That is one good piece of advice my mother gave me.

'Is he a friend of yours?' El Rubio said in a low voice, and looked towards the dining-room. El Sapito was skipping across the lawn towards us. El Rubio frowned.

'Oh Jose, I got a prescription for sandals!' El Sapito said. Then recognized El Rubio: 'Jose is a friend of mine. I did not know you knew him.'

El Rubio smiled tolerantly.

'Where did you get your sandals?' El Sapito asked him.

'From a Greek for five dollars.' Then he turned to me: 'They only cost about a dollar and a half in his country. I got them so cheap from him because he was drunk, or they would have cost more.'

'I am going to get mine in Holguín,' El Sapito said and took out his two prescriptions. 'When I get my sun-glasses. Have you got a cigarette on you?'

El Sapito sat on the arm of the other's chair, not noticing El Rubio's chagrin. 'I been dancing again. Close up. This one fitted right in.' He got up and began to move around to the hot music from the dining-room. 'I have to learn more steps.'

El Rubio got up. 'I can only dance well on the loose. When I am up against a girl only one thing responds. The other day I was with one who was too short and it pressed against her belly. So when they played a bolero I had the excuse to bend my knees and crouch and get it in the right place!'

El Sapito grabbed himself. 'I have to go right back. It will end soon and I have to get her out on the floor one more time.' He started off and then turned around. 'I see you later, Jose. El Rubio is a good friend of mine.'

'He is just a neighbour,' El Rubio said. 'I do not tell him

much. He talks too much. Not like the friends I had in Havana when I was his age. We did what we wanted and our mothers did not find out. He is the way I was before I ran away to Havana, trying to get girls and going to the country for animals when you could not get a girl. I used to take a rope with me and go for a walk in the country. I kept the rope inside my shirt so no one would guess. I tied the rope around their necks – goats or calves – and pulled them down. Their heads bent down towards their bellies from my pulling and they spread their back legs and I would mount them! Oh, the things I did as a boy!

'It is not so good, don't you agree, that there are no more women of la vida. Now men have to masturbate and that is weakening. You have to make such a mental effort. And then we do not get the proper food to be able to respond. Of course, not when you are young like my neighbour there. But he does not know what he is missing with this Revolution.

'In Havana I used to go to the *fiestas de percheros* – the clothes-hanger parties – when I was younger than he. A friend took me. He had been to them before and he invited me. No, you did not pay any money. It was a party at someone's house and you just got together for fun. We went in and everyone got introduced to each other if they did not know each other from before. Then you had a drink and there was a little talk and joking. Then you got given a clothes hanger. Everyone got one – it was to hang your clothes on. I whispered to my friend to tell me what to do and he said, "Take your clothes off and hang them up."

'But the lights were all on and I said I would keep my shorts on. My friend said, "Do not be a fool, take them all off." I did, but I was greatly embarrassed and my insect would not stand up. I kept my hands in front of me and sat in a chair apart. Then a girl came over laughing and took my hands away and touched it with her hands. She leaned over a little and put one of her breasts in my mouth. I liked that, I must admit. While I was doing it, a fag came over and kneeled on the floor and sucked me. I kept my mouth on that breast and my hand on her other one. I got so drunk that night I had to chew a lot of Chiclets so that my mother would not suspect when I got home. But I had to get up from bed and throw up and my mother half suspected it was not just indigestion.

'I went to a lot of clothes-hanger parties after that. Sometimes two perverted women would lie on a mattress while the rest of us watched them. Then someone would turn off all the lights and we would each grab a girl and have a wonderful time all night. If we were broke, we went to the Parque Central or the Prado and walked until some homosexual talked to us. They would pay me five or ten dollars to play with me and nothing said later. I do not like those fags who act like girls in the street and talk to you like you are their fiancé. There was an old American with a young wife, he used to ask me to their room to watch me lie with his wife while he masturbated. Then we went out together and everything was perfectly normal. I respected him a lot.

'None of that is possible any more, because the UMAP took all those people if they had not already left. Anyway, I am taking myself in hand. I have a fiancée and her parents approve of me. Now all I would like to do is travel, for I did everything there was to do in Havana in those days. Except for one thing. I did not get to go to that theatre in old Havana with the shows and movies.

'I could not get in because I was too young. I was fourteen and my ambition was to be like El Chocolate, who used to appear there. He was the highlight of the show. So I borrowed a gun and went up to the box office and asked for a ticket, and the man looked at me and said I was too young. I told him I was in the police and told him I had a gun to prove it. But I did not know there was a real policeman there until this man started to walk towards me. I ran and ran and ran and did not fall into their hands.

'I never got to see El Chocolate but I knew what he did in the show. He was famous. He had women – and men – waiting

216 In the Fist of the Revolution

for him every night. The cream of the cream of society wanted him. They paid anything to get him to go out with them, and I saw him come out of the theatre several times. He was a nice chocolate colour. Even all over, they tell me, for he appeared completely naked on the stage. They pulled the curtain back and there he was sitting on the middle of the stage. Half turned, he was, to the audience, so that his long insect was in full view. People took opera glasses to see it well.

'He was sitting like this – the left leg extended so that it did not obstruct the view. Then the right leg was drawn up, so that he could lean his right elbow on it like this. His right hand supported his chin and he was looking down at his insect all the time. He never moved – that was his act. He never changed position. Every time the curtain was pulled back he was sitting on the stage in that position. Like this . . . see?'

'You mean like The Thinker?' I said.

'Yes, you could say he was like a man thinking. He had to do a lot of thinking. Or whatever he did. That was his secret and I wanted to see it and figure out how he did it. He sat there thinking, and without moving, without any girl showing up on stage or anything – just maybe some woman in the audience yelling, Oh Chocolate, give it to me! – his insect began to get bigger slowly and stood up by itself. Slowly – that was the thing. Very slowly with perfect control it went up and stood at attention. It stayed like that while the people yelled, and without twitching a muscle he would shoot off. Zing, zing, it shot off. Then slowly, slowly it came down and lay on his leg and got softer and smaller the way it was when he began. Then the curtain closed. Every night he did that act and I never got to see it.

'Here he comes again,' El Rubio said.

The music had ended and people started to leave. El Sapito was very excited. An English ship, he heard, was coming to Nicaro next day, and he had forgotten how to say the English words he'd asked me about. When he and El Rubio left together, they were both repeating 'I want to buy some socks' over and over and stumbling over the word 'socks'; 'esaxs' was the closest they could get.

At the opening of the pizzeria, the regional head of I N I T had told our waitress that no bill was to be presented to our table, and a second round of beer was also served us on the house. It made me feel I had to patronize the place, and I was back at lunchtime the next day. This time I sat at the counter, a long winding one, only a few steps away from the open dining-room and the lovely view. A slim, light-skinned Negro in a bus driver's uniform came towards me, his face happy with recognition, and when he got to me and took the seat next to mine, I told him I had met so many people last night that I had almost forgotten this was where I met him.

He smiled. 'It was last night that you forgot where you met me. You came to Mayarí in the bus I drive from Nicaro, remember?'

I said of course, but I did not remember that short trip. I had driven to Nicaro with Soní and two days later returned on a local bus.

The pizzeria was getting jammed for lunch. The counter was soon filled and people stood at a take-out corner in a bunch; the dining-room tables were starting to fill up. A group of people from the Federation of Cuban Women and the Committees for the Defence of the Revolution sat at a long one, and they waved to me and asked me to join them, but I had already been talking to the bus driver for a while and did not think it polite to leave him. The waitresses kept running in and out of the kitchen, working at the counter, opening and closing the counter refrigerators; but seldom serving anyone; the bus driver began to heckle them. It turned out the one he kidded most – a lovely girl with green eyes – was his young cousin. She was white but that no longer surprised me, just as it would not have occurred to the bus driver to explain.

He did not have an Oriente accent and he was in his thirties, and that was sufficient explanation for the fact that he realized the service was unskilled. I didn't take his criticisms to be more than pleasantries and a way of keeping the conversation going, for his tone was lighthearted and he never stopped smiling. And I was not particularly interested in him: he had only come to live in Mayarí after the Revolution. Not even when he told me his name was Bill and took out his bus driver's identification card and showed me it was his legal name.

'An American name, right?' he said.

'Yes,' I said.

He looked pleased and smiled at me as if we now really had something in common.

'I like peace and quiet – that is why I settled down in Mayarí,' Bill said. 'Also, I married a Mayarí girl.'

Casually, I asked him if he had been a Rebel in the second front. 'No,' he said. 'In the Escambray.'

'The Revolutionary Directorate?'

He nodded and smiled slowly and became interesting.

'And you live here because of the peace and quiet?'

He shrugged. 'I am neutral.'

Despite its name, the Revolutionary Directorate was made up of liberal enemies of the Batista régime, and it was composed mainly of Havana students whose base of operations was in the Escambray mountains of Las Villas province. Fidelistas tell you that they lived off the peasants and never engaged Batista's army in any battle; they did not fight until Camilo Cienfuegos and Che Guevera reached the Escambray in the last months and forced them to join the ranks of the 26 of July Movement. Were it not for them, revolutionaries say, there would have been no counter-revolutionary bands in the Escambray later, for the peasants had such bad experiences with them that they did not trust the revolutionary government. With the exception of Fauré Chomón, the Directorate's leaders did not follow Castro's direction, the most famous of the early defectors being Hubert Matos, who was jailed in 1959.

When I said that he must know Chomón, now a member of the Central Committee of the Party and Minister of Transport, Bill nodded and smiled, managing an ironic look that showed he did not think well of Chomón. 'I had the rank of lieutenant,' he said, and lowered his voice to add, 'and served under Hubert Matos.'

'What was he like?' I asked.

'A brilliant man, a man of enormous knowledge,' he said, in a normal voice because he was not mentioning his name. 'A pure revolutionary.'

I nodded.

'Camilo was like that too – a pure revolutionary.'

'But it was Camilo who arrested Matos,' I said.

Whenever I was to ask, during the time we spent together, for an explanation that required more than a simple expression of opinion, he would shrug, as he did now for the first time, and say, 'It is a long process, too long to explain now.' This time he looked around to indicate we were in a public place. 'Please keep smiling and talking as if we are saying nothing out of the ordinary,' he added.

'If you like,' I said, grinning falsely. 'But do you think anyone cares?'

'No doubt I was seen talking to you last night on the sidewalk and reported. We met by accident today, but there are people here from the security police. Our every expression is being watched. Those people who greeted you from that table, of course ... that fellow in the orange beret is supposedly a stove repairman but in reality he is a member of the Ministry of the Interior. I have counted at least five already. And of course all the girls who work here are integrated – they will report any conversation they overhear.'

'What about your young cousin?' I asked.

'No, she is an innocent,' he said. 'She is a good girl. But the others got the jobs because they are integrated.'

'Would you lose your job?' I asked.

He shook his head. 'There have been two or three attempts to get me out of my job. It is a good one, three hundred dollars a month. But I am neutral. I go to work, then home, stay out of political discussions and mind my own business. So they leave me alone.'

My eyes strayed over his shoulders and I saw a leader of the Committees smiling broadly at me from their table. At any other time his smile would not have seemed sinister; now it did. I waved at him, and turned back to Bill and smiled as if Bill had just told me a joke.

Bill was saying, 'I have always loved freedom, I have always believed in God, and I was always a revolutionary, so it is best for me to keep quiet, for you do not know – I told you my young cousin is a good girl. She is. But now you cannot trust your own brother. Sons have turned in their fathers!'

Jorge slapped me on the shoulder, and Bill smiled at him. But when Jorge walked on, Bill said, 'He is another who is in all the organizations. Possibly in the Ministry of the Interior.'

I did not tell him that Jorge might easily come down with an attack of La Enfermedad. His mistake made me take his conspiratorial manner less seriously. Of course, it did not demolish his argument, but it took the force out of it and made me feel less worried for him. We were interrupted several times at the counter by people we knew, and Bill said nothing but pleasantries to them, continuing to smile, and gesturing in the same way he had with me, so that an onlooker would have no sense that the tone of the conversation had changed with the arrival of the third person.

I suggested we go when we had finished our pizzas, and he said he would walk me down Leyte Vidal. I waved at the table with the Committees leaders and the Federation women, and Bill warned me not to look back when we got to the sidewalk. A jeep with a driver from the municipal administration slowed down and the driver greeted him. Bill answered gaily and crossed over to talk to him. A Federation woman I knew sat next to the driver, so I too stepped over. In time to notice that Bill, while talking to the driver, kept a hand on the woman's knee. She frowned and slapped it, but it did not put him out of humour.

Walking along Leyte Vidal, I asked him if the Revolution's course was one he had foreseen. 'Never, never,' he said. 'It is not at all what we wanted. Not what Camilo wanted either. There was not a drop of communism in Camilo.'

I reminded him that Camilo's parents had been active supporters of the Spanish Republic, had remained with the Revolution after Camilo's death, that his brother, Osmany, was a leader. And he shrugged and indicated again that the explanation was too much to go into. He said that Osmany was a 'captain of something', unaware that he was the head of the Solidarity with Other Nations organization, an important post in Havana.

Unaccountably, he admired Che Guevara enormously. 'An extraordinary man. A great fighter. He is a real revolutionary.' And he smiled and almost laughed when he said it, knowing that it was a kind of dereliction of his to feel this way about Che. He also thought the public works were wonderful things the Revolution had done and continued to do. Much of his conversation covered the same ground that disgustados in Mayarí and Guatemala had gone over with me: the hardships of rationing, the unjust treatment of people who apply to leave, the pressure to join revolutionary organizations, the necessity to appear integrated if one is to work, study or get any consideration at all. He even got carried away and said things I knew not to be true.

But there was never in his complaints any overtone of frustrated personal greed. He was a political liberal, a sophisticated man, and he was also simply a nicer person than most disgustados. He spoke about the state of the nation, not personal grievances. 'I never imagined that this was where the Revolution would take us,' he said. 'After all, when you think about it, what was wrong with Batista's régime was the killings. There were too many killings. Take away that and life then was much better.

'People know that, too,' Bill continued. 'No more than forty per cent of this Army supports the Revolution right now.'

But he did not think another revolution was possible. 'It is the fault of the Cuban people themselves. They allow themselves to be held back by small, material considerations. Things that never influenced real revolutionaries. If they act, if they speak out, will their scholarship child be thrown out of school, or will they lose the house they are on the list for, or their job? That is what is on their minds. When thirteen of us were picked out of a theatre in Havana and thrown into jail – some for six months in the dungeons – we thought only of life or death. And as soon as they allowed us into the jailyard we devised a way of escaping. Six of us died in the attempt. ... So what if one has a job, so what if we have money – it is worthless to buy anything, for food, clothing, shoes are not to be had, nor peace of mind.'

We had turned off Leyte Vidal and stopped on the corner of Céspedes, for Bill was headed home to El Naranjal. This speech depressed him, and he stopped a moment and the two of us were quiet on that sunny street, silent with the siesta. What, I wondered, had kept him from exile? His intelligent, realistic view of the possible? Being American I had noticed he was a Negro – or rather, made note of it – when he told me the green-eyed girl was his cousin; but I had been in Cuba so long that I did not think of his negritude in any other way – as the cause, I decided now, why he was not in the States but in this remote section of Oriente, content to come home and live quietly.

Bill sighed. 'See that man on the corner waiting for the bus for El Cocal? He has been waiting a year to leave. Both he and his wife have no work. He makes shoes at home now, out of whatever materials he can find – old inner tubes, rope, canvas. They are badly made shoes. They are made with desperation. But we buy them – we do not know if it is legal, if it is a crime to buy them, and we do not care – for he is a good man and he needs help.'

The man made a slight movement and brought his feet together, as if standing at attention for our inspection. There were two bundles at his feet. He was plump and tall but pale and worn too, and his eyes opened with fear and pleading. I felt that only because Bill was at my side had he not broken into a run.

At that moment a jeep turned our corner and braked. Soní was driving it alone, and he stopped to ask me if I wanted a ride to the Bitirí. I said I could walk, that if I knew him he'd be going out of his way to do me a favour. Bill came up behind me and said, 'Go with him, man, the sun is too hot to walk.'

As I walked in front of the jeep to get in beside Soní, Bill greeted Soní and I looked quickly to see their encounter. Soní half turned his face and said, 'How are you?' There was no sweetness in his voice, he was cutting Bill off, and the smile on Bill's face remained on it by an effort of will.

We drove to the Bitirí without mentioning Bill. Soní and I were old friends now and he simply gave me a look that said, I'm sure you know what kind of character you've been with, so don't expect me to tell you. The boys of the Administración had told him to remind me that, in a week, I was to go to Tirso, where they all expected to be cutting cane during the Playa Girón fortnight, a promise I had made. 'You know who will be in Birán five minutes away, also cutting cane?' Soní asked; I knew but he told me anyway, for it made him so happy: 'Fidel and the whole Central Committee!'

I did not see Bill again — except once when he honked to me from his bus — but there was no escaping El Sapito and El Rubio. It was a symptom of their illness that they had to ask me to describe — item by item — what young people wore in New York, what it was like to hear the Beatles at Shea Stadium, how much a second-hand car cost. Just to be in my company made day-dreaming easier. 'Oh Jose, what a feeling it is to talk to you!' El Sapito often said, and El Rubio would agree.

When they weren't exclaiming about things American, they were complaining about Cuba. El Sapito was very open about himself; it did not matter to him who might be with me. But

El Rubio only criticized the Revolution if El Sapito was the only one with me, and even with El Sapito he did not talk about himself. Little by little I learned his plans: to leave when he was twenty-seven. He had already made two attempts.

The first time was during Camarioca, as the Cubans say. Camarioca was the little fishing and yachting town where Castro invited exiles to come and pick up their relatives. For a short period boats of all sizes came there from the States and waited for their cargo, until the daily flights were negotiated with the State Department. Some Cubans headed for Camarioca and waited for the relatives they knew were coming to get them, but most waited at home until they received notice that there was a boat at Camarioca that had claimed them. The Cuban authorities speeded their clearance, fed them at Camarioca, even drove them there when they were claimed.

El Rubio had no relative to claim him, nor knew of anyone there. But he hoped, if he got to Camarioca, to bribe or plead with someone. He sold his mattress, also the red damask draperies. 'You had to be very careful. The head of the Committee at the Reforma Urbana had the nerve to advise me. He said that I should not have sold the mattress, that if I hoped to leave Cuba I would not get cleared unless I left all my possessions, and the mattress was one. I told him I had simply given my mattress to my sister. What makes you think that I plan to leave Cuba? I said. I also sold some clothes – that is why I do not have any now – but when I got the money together, they closed up Camarioca.'

'But how could you have got away?' I asked.

'There are ways. You know, there was a man who went up to a man who came with a boat, and acted as if he were embracing him like a cousin, but meanwhile he held a knife to his ribs and said, My name is so-and-so, claim me or I shall kill you! He got away like that. If I had been there, I would have looked around. I would have found someone from the old days in Havana.'

A few months ago, El Rubio confessed one day when he was

very dispirited, he had sent in an application to leave via Varadero. His father and sister in Brooklyn had not claimed him but he hoped to get them to do so. No answer came from Havana, and then when he was there working at the hospital he called them on the phone. 'I waited and waited while they looked up my application. Finally the girl came back to the phone and told me that I would have to wait until I was twenty-seven!'

El Rubio expected me to be indignant too, forgetting that he had told me he had been excused from military duty because he was his mother's only support. But the fact was she lived with his sister, and he not only did not support her but lived off them. As the time got closer for him to report at his job in Las Villas, his denunciations of the Revolution became less realistic and his depression increased, so that he showed up less often at the Bitirí.

The last time he and El Sapito visited me together, I had already heard their litany of complaints many times. This time they told me about injustices done to others. 'See that doctor?' El Rubio said about a member of the hospital staff. 'He became very aroused the other day in front of everyone because of the number of consultations they are forced to have. I think he has been reported.' He did not know I knew the doctor, an ardent revolutionary, and I did not tell him. I simply nodded, as I did at all their stories.

Then El Sapito began another one about two young men from Holguín who left for Miami in an amphibious Cadillac.

That made me sit up. 'An amphibious Cadillac?'

'Yes, I heard something about that,' El Rubio said, but he looked unsure.

'They had a Cadillac and at night they would take it to the beach and practise with it. People thought they were crazy – driving a car into the water! But they were fixing it all the time and each time they put it into the water they looked for leaks they had to fix. Finally one night it was fine and they took off! The shore guards fired and fired at them but they did not hit them. When they got Up North, you know what happened? The Cadillac company gave each of them a new Cadillac!'

'A new Cadillac – oh!' said El Rubio. 'I can see myself in New York driving a new Cadillac ...'

I began to laugh, and El Sapito said, 'What is the matter, Jose, you do not think it can be done?'

I shook my head.

'But I heard that they told the whole story over the Miami radio and the two fellows were right there,' El Sapito explained.

I shook my head again. El Rubio looked from El Sapito to me, reluctant to drop his dream of a new Cadillac. Then he said, 'Maybe it is not possible ...'

It was mid-April and the Playa Girón fortnight was beginning. To celebrate the anniversary of the victory of the Bay of Pigs many enterprises close down – schools too – and an attempt is made to recruit everyone for work in the countryside; it is the best time for cutting cane, for in May the rains begin. In the pause that followed El Sapito's unfortunate story, there was suddenly a great deal of noise from the street leading out of Mayarí. A line of open trucks filled with young people went by; they wore straw hats and waved them at anyone that would look; they also sang songs. In a minute they were gone, leaving us quiet again.

The next day El Sapito came up to the Bitirí on the borrowed bicycle. 'I am leaving, Jose,' he said. 'Someone from my school came to get me. They are all at a collective fertilizing the cane-fields that have been cut.' He was flushed and also stunned. 'They say they have a very good time there. They work and study and every night they sing songs ... you know.'

I was talking to Marta and I saw her smile when he told what had happened. 'Good,' I said, and went inside and brought him a pair of stretch socks that would fit him.

They made him very happy; he lost the unsure look he had

about what was in store for him. From the bicycle, he held out a hand and said, 'I do not know when I will see you again.'

As soon as he was far enough away, Marta said, 'I guarantee you he will be a different person.'

El Rubio did not come back to the Bitirí and I did not see him on Leyte Vidal. One day, when I thought he had already left for his job in agricultural production, he came up to my room again. He had figured I should be leaving in a day or two and he was right. 'Do you think it would be possible for you to send me a phonograph when you get back?' he asked.

I told him that only medicines could be sent from the States. 'When are you going to Las Villas?' I asked.

He looked vague. 'There is no hurry,' he said. 'One of these days.' He stroked his beard; he had not shaved in many days. 'I cannot find a razor blade. I apologize for visiting you this way.'

I went inside and brought him a blade.

'Let me pay you for it,' he said but made no motion to do so.

'Well, good luck,' I said, for I had already told him I had an appointment.

'Listen, if you are going to stop in Madrid,' he said, 'perhaps from there you could send a phonograph ...'

8. A Little Story about Hortencio

One morning during my first month in Mayarí I stood in one of the wide doorways of El Parque Cafeteria, smoking and savouring the coffee just strained, and listening to the 'Eleven O'clock Novel' on Radio Rebelde; the loudspeakers in the little triangular plaza were turned on loud that day and I had no trouble hearing the two fruity male voices that opened that morning's episode. A man was discussing the slave women with his nephew; the nephew had just returned to the plantation after some years in the capital, and the uncle, his voice heavy with cynicism, gave him advice that he apparently didn't need.

These little black girls are worthless once they pass fif-teen —

Of course, because they pass from hand to hand!

They both chuckled at this, but the uncle's laugh was lusciously evil; you knew the nephew was still redeemable.

Enjoy the girl, entertain yourself for a while, but do not get involved ...

My father left me two carriages ... one hundred slaves to look after my slightest need ...

Again the uncle chuckled.

I am still young ...

I realized I was still smiling when I saw a young man at the first table, just inside the door, smiling back. He wore a straw hat, the brim curled up along the sides, short boots, work pants, and a denim shirt: a handsome young cowboy. He had just been served eggs, french-fries, a bottle of beer, and he asked me to join him, holding the waiter to get my order. I said no, but he insisted on getting me beer. He asked my pardon for beginning before my beer arrived, and immediately punctured the yolk of an egg with a piece of bread; he leaned his head forward a little and put it all into his mouth, licking his finger-tips in the same motion; he swallowed, took a sip of beer, and told me he was an *economista* – an accountant – at Los Pinares.

I was surprised, for I had taken him to be a campesino – perhaps a champion cane-cutter on a day off in town – and he noticed and held up a hand and swallowed again. 'But that is not what I really am. It is not my vocation. I want to devote myself to literature ... to drama.' He gestured in the direction of the loudspeakers broadcasting the 'Eleven O'clock Novel'. 'But not like that. It is a bit romantic. Though things like that happen in life. Still, it is not a direct impression of life. That is what I want to write. It is the kind of poetry I write. Life as it is lived – life here in the country. Even the first poem I wrote – when I was thirteen – was like that. Though I knew nothing then about the technique of poetry.'

His name was Pepe Delgado, and he was twenty-three. He was excitable, he gestured, he had the high voice and the sweet accent of the Oriente country people: not at all the Western cowboy he'd looked like at first. 'In another month, I go to Santiago for an interview. The Cultural people arranged it, for I have been after them many times. I have written plays for them. We put one on at Los Pinares. I must study literature. I must get to Havana.

'You understand that, don't you?' he said. 'You are from Havana.' When I told him about me, he could not contain his excitement. He had wiped his plate with a piece of bread and he put it down, then picked it up again and once more put it down; he did not want to fill his mouth when there were so many things he had to say. 'You are a writer!' he finally exclaimed. 'This is the first time I have met a writer. Dancers, actors, yes, at Nicaro, but never a writer!

'You can advise me. What should I do? You write poetry, of course. I do not write prose, it does not interest me, and I do not care for novels. I want to write about life as it is lived. But I already told you about that. Well, well, well!'

He sat back and looked at me a moment. 'And to think I just happened to come down from Los Pinares today and did not go home but came to El Parque. I am catching a bus, that is why I am eating here. Not a bus, a taxi. I would like you to read some of my poems. I have kept them all. The poems, the theatre pieces, songs too, and oh yes, *pensamientos* – thoughts that occur to me. I have kept them all, except the poems I wrote to girls at school on the occasion of their birthdays and saint's days. They kept those, so I do not have them. And to the girls I fell in love with – I fell in love a lot of times!

'When the ballet came to Nicaro, I spoke to Alicia Alonso. I am very forward, I went to talk to her. When she heard some of my poems, she said, You must come to Havana and study. That is what the interview is about, whether they will give me a scholarship to go to Havana to study literature. Do you think I need to study? Anyway, in Havana I will be with people who understand what I do and then I can be published. The same thing happened with a man – he was not from here – who heard a song for which I wrote the lyrics – I also helped compose the music. He said, You must go to Havana.

'I once showed my poems to the Regional de Cultura and they said, If you had a baccalaureate degree, these poems could be published. Leave them here and we shall see. But I said, No, I want to have them with me because I like to read them over and change them. Is that the right thing to do? I like to write a poem and put it aside and let it ripen. Is that right?'

I nodded.

'Writers like to do that, do they?' he said, and moved in his chair with the excitement. 'Then I am acting like other writers? Oh what a good thing to hear!'

I asked him if he remembered the first poem he wrote.

He nodded with enthusiasm. 'I was thirteen, but I cannot forget it, for it was my first poem and I was under the influence of strong emotions. It was about Hortencio, my father.

My father was a very big influence with me. I always worried
about how he would feel, and I used to wait for him when he
came home from work. Especially on pay-days. He worked in
Nicaro and we lived in Felton and he used to drink a lot. I
worried that he might have spent all his money. Do you want
to hear the poem?'

I said yes, and he suddenly became ashamed that he might
be overheard. He looked around and then spoke in a low voice.
'The title is "Hortencio",' he said, then recited the poem; his
voice got stronger toward the end, and when he finished, he
wrote the poem down for me.

It was a short poem:

> *Hortencio*
> *sale desde Nicaro*
> *como un disparo*
> *que sale*
> *de una manigua*
> *rodeada de tibisí,*
> *y yo esperándolo*
> *aquí*
> *con el corazón*
> *en la mano –*
> *temiendo que le*
> *meta*
> *al Bacardí*
> *Sano*
> *Sabroso*
> *y Cubano.*
>
> (Hortencio
> leaves from Nicaro
> like a shot
> fired
> from an overgrown stretch of weeds
> hedged by *tibisí* trees,
> and I waiting for him
> here

with my heart
in hand –
fearing he will
go
for Bacardí
Healthful
Savoury
and Cuban.)

The last three lines were an advertising slogan that the Bacardí company used years ago, and Pepe smiled as he recited them, charmed at the ingenious boy he had been. Aware, I thought, of the irony that even as an anxious boy he had sensed, in using the advertising slogan, that there was delight in the rum that was his father's curse. He then wrote down the poem and added at the end: 'Poem by Jose Delgado Gomez. Written at thirteen years of age when he lived on the swampy shore of Felton in Oriente.'

He said, 'You notice it almost has metre. I do not like metre any more. It is something I have put aside, because it is something that is not right for the thoughts and impressions one has. You understand what I mean? I do not know if I translate it well – I use the word translate to mean to tear out of myself, to reach down profoundly inside me.'

I nodded, wishing he would talk about his father.

'In order to have metre in a poem you are forced to change or cut off what you had thought of, and it ends by killing your inspiration. I prefer free verse. What do you think?'

I said that sounded very sensible.

'Another thing I do not like to do is to address myself directly to a hero. To the Apóstol Martí, for example. Or to any living man. To name him or write directly about him. I like to write about people, yes, like the heroes of the Revolution, but without saying their names, so that people get the feeling anyway. As if they were not warned, as if we were looking at him out of the corners of our eyes.'

After he wrote that first poem, he began to put all his

thoughts down on paper. He loved notebooks, particularly lined notebooks; he felt that if he filled them in it would be like making his own books. 'I had one notebook I liked very much and I used to go to the fields behind our house, lay a big cardboard on the ground, and lie on it face down and write. My sister found the notebook and she announced to everyone, Look how he says that Mother did this and Father did that! I was ashamed and I could not bear that they had all read it and misunderstood it.'

I asked him how he had become an accountant – meaning that it was surprising, given his literary interests – and he told me he had been very lucky, for his family was very poor. He had four aunts who lived in Santiago, and he went to live with them when he was a boy and thus was able to go to junior high school and take a business course. 'I was living with them when my father Hortencio died but I came back here after I got divorced.'

'You were married?' I said; he seemed so young.

'I am twenty-three,' he said. 'I have a six-year-old son.'

'What happened?' I asked.

'Oh, another woman,' he said.

'What happened to her?'

'That was over a long time ago.' Then he smiled. 'Women ...' He shook his head. 'But I do not let them distract me. When I got off the bus from Los Pinares, I ran into a girl. You know, one I know will do it. She wanted to meet me to-night, but I said no. I have an errand to do now in the middle of the day. But I did not want to meet her. I know how to control myself. I want to spend the rest of the day and the evening writing. That is what I want to do – to translate all these feelings I get inside me!'

It was two months before I saw Pepe Delgado again. He was standing on Leyte Vidal talking to Robertico Silvera, the Army man. At least I thought it was he, although he looked slighter, less dashing, until I got up to them and saw it was not Pepe. When Robertico introduced us, the fellow said, 'Osvaldo

Delgado, another friend.' Brothers, no doubt, but I said nothing about it. It was Robertico who interested me at the moment.

'Well?' I said to him.

'Just yesterday I was by the Bitirí and you were not there,' he said.

I laughed.

'I swear!' he said, and then laughed too.

'What about last week's appointment?' I asked.

Robertico slapped himself on the forehead. 'You will have to forgive me, Jose, I was in the south doing work.'

Osvaldo was interested. 'What kind of work, Robertico?'

'I will tell you what kind of work,' I said to Osvaldo. 'He was dashing from one place to another in jeeps and trucks – running them into ditches, overturning them, crashing them into –'

'Oh Jose, Jose, you have been in Mayarí too long!' Robertico protested.

'What about Teresita?' I taunted him. 'Is her father going to give his approval?'

Robertico jumped up and down, slapped himself a few times. 'Oh my God, oh my God! How did you find out about that?'

During my first week in Mayarí I had considered myself fortunate to have run into Robertico, because I had learned that he appeared in the photograph – very popular in Cuba in 1960 – of the nationalization of the United Fruit Company's Central Preston (now Guatemala). It is a superb photograph: a line of men, mostly on horseback, jubilantly advancing on the road along the railroad track into Guatemala; they are wearing cowboy straw hats, holding their rifles high, waving the Cuban flag; all of them fierce and happy. At the centre rode Comandante Nuñez Jimenez, a geologist who is now the head of the Academy of Sciences but was then in charge of INRA (the Agrarian Reform Institute); to his left rode Robertico, who could not have been more than thirteen or fourteen then. An historic occasion. I hoped Robertico would sit down with me and tell me about it.

He never did. We met everywhere, had lunch and dinner together, chatted, gossiped, philosophized, but it was never properly an interview. The only thing I would not do with him was get into a car he drove or on the back seat of his motor bike. He was reckless. At that moment his right leg was bandaged under his uniform; he'd got a burn by scraping it against a parked car when he made a tight turn with his motor bike. Rather, the Army's motor bike. He had ruined two of his father's cars, and Hugo Ramirez told me that Robertico had said, when Hugo asked him why he was not more careful with his father's car, 'It is no more than the old man deserves – he is a counter-revolutionary!'

Robertico had already explained to me that the only people in his family he liked were the aunt married to Chanda, the man who ran the cafeteria in Guatemala, and Chanda himself. 'They are the only ones with the Revolution,' he said. 'I was for it since the age of ten and I used to get it from my old man!' In the first year of the Revolution, when the age of recruits was not looked into too closely, he joined the Army and had been in it ever since. At seventeen he married a girl from Cueto, and one of the times I saw him on Leyte Vidal he had his two-year-old-daughter, a beautiful child who inherited his big eyes, with him. He didn't seem to know what to do with her: he couldn't gossip or tell her jokes.

'Maybe you had better get your divorce before you go ask for Teresita's hand,' I said.

'I have it, I have it,' he said, and threw up his hands as if he were being held up. 'We went to sign it the other day.'

'So what does her father object to then?' I asked.

'Listen, I am not going into that with you,' Robertico said, and doubled up with delight about the whole turn the conversation had taken. 'For all I know you are not a serious writer like you say and you will be telling the imperialists all about me!'

Osvaldo turned to me. 'You are a writer?'

'Look at him,' said Robertico. 'Why do you think he is so interested in gossip?'

'I want to talk to you, with your permission,' Osvaldo said. 'I have interests along those lines —'

'That is right, talk to him,' Robertico said. 'I have an appointment and I am already late.'

'I do not know if you have an appointment,' I said, 'but I am sure you are late.'

'We will get together, you will see,' Robertico said. 'I am coming by the Bitirí this week. Count on it.'

Osvaldo was glad to see him go, for he was anxious to talk to me about writing. He began to make short, nervous gestures that were like his brother Pepe's, and to tell me how he had been writing for several years now. He worked as a solderer in a machine shop in Mayarí, and he had volunteered to go cane cutting for the whole Playa Girón fortnight; they were leaving the next afternoon. That was why he had a notebook with him that he usually kept at work for moments during the lunch break or any time when there wasn't work to keep him occupied. It contained the second section of a novel he was writing. 'I have already written fourteen novels that way,' he said.

'Wonderful,' I said.

'I would like your advice,' he said. 'For example, there is a word on the last page of this notebook that I would like your opinion on . . .'

I asked him if he would like me to read the story.

'Would you do that?' He put the notebook in my hand immediately. 'With your permission, I shall come to see you tonight. You see, we leave tomorrow . . .'

I said that would be fine, and he got so excited that he began several statements and then broke them off by saying, 'But I shall see you tonight, I shall wait until then.' When I moved away from him, he stopped to remind me about the last page of the story. 'There is that word that bothers me. I shall want your opinion on it. It is the word egoist, please remember.'

The notebook he gave me was worn and moist with use. It contained algebraic problems, notes about various metals, and, on the back of those pages, the story he was writing. This section, though it covered dramatic events and years elapsed between the first and second scene, was short and did not quite fill the notebook. In the first scene the young hero takes a girl of the town to a hotel and, although she is a virgin, convinces her to let him have his way with her; at the last moment, he has to force his entrance into her and the experience is not good for her. She never sees him again, but three or four years later, when he is a successful artist, he receives a visit from her father who brings him a little girl who is his daughter. The old man sits the girl on the chaise where only a short time ago the hero had been making love to a beautiful model and tells him, 'You are an egoist and do not think of others, but now you shall have to take care of this child!'

When Osvaldo showed up at the Bitirí that evening, I asked him how old he was, and he said twenty. 'Well, you see, it is because of your age that the story is both good and bad,' I said. 'The first scene of the girl being both seduced and forced is good, I dare say because these are emotions you have felt' – I was being delicate about it – 'and you have been able to project them into another character who is more or less your age. Right? But the second part is another matter – here is a man unexpectedly being confronted with a child who is his. Under rather unusual circumstances too, by the irate father of the girl. If you had lived such an experience, you would have been able to make it real, the way you did the sex scene.'

Osvaldo was so happy to be discussing his work that he nodded and nodded, to encourage me to go on. 'I see what you mean,' he said. 'I should have done both scenes the way they happened, in other words. Yes, yes, that is right!'

'I meant you should not have tried to do the second scene,' I explained. 'Not just yet, in any case.'

'I see, I see,' he said.

'It is a rather complex situation,' I said. 'Think of what a man must feel suddenly to be faced with a child of his own. To be asked, without preparation for what it entails, to *be* a father. All this is still beyond your experience . . .'

Osvaldo smiled shamefacedly, and I hurried to put him at his ease. 'That does not mean you should not be daring in your conceptions,' I said. 'A writer must not lose that quality, to take a situation to the very limits of probability, not just stay safely within what we all know.'

I stopped because Osvaldo still had the shamefaced look.

'It is partly autobiographical,' he said. He shrugged. 'Of course, I did not become a famous artist and have a studio and models and all that. But it did happen. Let me tell you the story. When I was eighteen I was working in Banes as a teacher and I went around with this nice girl. She *was* a nice girl but I was desperate, because a teacher should not be going around with all sorts of girls. So I talked her into going to a hotel with me and when she changed her mind I had to use – well, not force, but all the force of my personality. She was a virgin, so she half enjoyed it and half not. As in the story.'

'Yes,' I said.

'Then a few months ago I was in Banes for the day. I had not seen the girl since almost that day, for she repented of our relationship and I was a little ashamed myself, to tell you the truth. I was drinking coffee at a café by myself and there was this older man there who I thought kept looking at me. But he left, and I remember thinking he must have thought I was someone else, for I certainly did not know him. When I left, he introduced himself to me on the sidewalk. He told me I had ruined his family, a good family, and he insisted on my going home with him.'

'And you did?'

'He was a good man. The girl had been a virgin. He did not tell me why he was taking me home with him. I thought he wanted me to see his daughter and I thought it was the least

I could do. But when we got to the house he told me his daughter was not in Banes; she was away studying to be a teacher. The first thing I saw inside the house was a little girl playing with a toy, and the man said to me, "That is your child." I picked her up. Except for her mother's blonde hair, she looked like me. My heart was grabbed by a mixture of strong and conflicting emotions.

'Then the old man softened towards me and his wife came out and served me coffee and they talked to me. I did not say anything at first. I said to myself that they were being nice to me because they wanted me to marry their daughter. I kept thinking about all this and watching the little girl playing. Finally I told them I had to get back to Mayarí but that I would be thinking about what they had told me.'

When he finished, Osvaldo leaned back on the high-backed chair and sighed. 'It was a hard experience,' he said, relieved. 'I could not face it. That is why I could not write it. But now I shall rewrite the story and tell it the way it was!'

I was grabbed by a mixture of conflicting emotions, and did not give him further advice.

'About that word – egoist,' said Osvaldo. 'What do you make of it?'

I told him an egoist is someone who in all situations thinks of himself first.

'But isn't everyone like that?'

I laughed.

'At work, when I take out my notebook during a break and sit aside to write, they say, "Look at him, he is an egoist!"'

He thought that over a moment. 'I like to write about conversations and encounters I have had, to extract the drama from them and bring it into relief. Sometimes I write a story like that for a girl and it pleases her, it always does. It makes me feel good – that I have been able to bring out what I have inside me and another person can have that experience.

'Sometimes I sit down to write something, I may even have

an inspiration, and then nothing happens or it comes out badly. I reach the point – I tell you frankly – that tears come to my eyes. I need to go away and study and learn much more. I went to the Cultural and asked them to send me to a literary school like Pepe –'

'Like Pepe?' I said.

'Oh yes, he got a scholarship for seven years. In a month or two he goes to Santiago and then to Havana. But they told me I would have to wait. It is not possible now. It is all right with me because the more I live the more I have to write. Now when we go to cut cane we will read things to each other in the evenings, poems, songs, things like that. Though I do not *see* poetry. That is why I do not talk to Pepe about writing – I just do not see poetry, so why discourage him?

'If I am an egoist, why is it that I enjoy being with others like at the cane cutting? You know what were the happiest years of my life? The three years I spent in Matanzas going to school. I had two wonderful friends. I wrote a story about that called "We Inseparable Three" and it is the only story I do not have. I left it back there. All the others I have kept.'

'Was that before or after your father Hortencio died?' I asked.

'After,' he said, and looked at me closely. 'You do not know that Hortencio did not die a natural death?'

He saw I did not know and I saw him consider whether to tell me or not. I seldom urged anyone in Mayarí to tell me something; it had to come willingly or not at all: I had a theory that this was the way important things got said. But to Osvaldo I said, 'Tell me about it.'

Osvaldo put his elbows on the arms of his chair, clasped his hands, leaned forward, and began.

'It was in May 1959. The Revolution had triumphed and we were still living in the house on the shore at Felton. In the evening Hortencio liked to sit in the doorway and look toward the water across the high grass and watch the sun set. There were no houses near us, it was in the country, and he could look directly into the sun. That evening he was doing just that, all by himself, for he had been angry with me and he also had other things on his mind.

'There were four of us only at home that day. My mother was in Santiago because one of her sisters was sick, and Pepe was there going to school. I was twelve and going to the new school, and there was my younger brother who was just a little kid. I do not know where he was in the house. My sister Margarita was in the bedroom lying down, for she had been sick in the hospital and she was still not entirely well. I was twelve, as I said, and innocent about what had happened to her. I did not learn about it until later and then it was because I overheard adults talking. No one told me directly.

'I knew Margarita was married, that I knew. She was married to a Rebel, a fellow from around our way who had been in the monte, and she had become pregnant. That I did not know – that she had become pregnant. The Rebel did not want her to be pregnant, he did not want children, and he became enraged with her when she still had the foetus in her womb. He gave her such a strong beating that it killed the foetus and she had to be taken to the hospital, where they performed a Caesarean operation on her. The Rebel warned Hortencio that he was to do nothing about what had happened. "If you tell anyone," he told him, "I shall kill you."

'But Hortencio went to Orden Pública and told them what the Rebel had done to Margarita, and they picked up the Rebel and questioned him for three days. Then they let him go. That evening it was three days since Margarita had come home and she was still not well. She was not healed. And Hortencio sat in the doorway looking at the sun, as I said, and brooding about what the Rebel had done to his daughter. He was looking at the water. You could see it smooth from our house and across the inlet to the isthmus.

'Behind him was the living-room and on the other side of a

curtain that my mother had put up was the dining-room. I was sitting there working on my mathematics homework and I had drawn the curtain, though that made the room dark and I had to turn on the bulb over the table, because I was angry with my father. He had said to me, "You are going to work out that problem and I am going to sit here until you do, and I am willing to sit until morning." Hortencio always took a personal interest in our studying. That is why he was willing to send Pepe to Santiago to my mother's sisters – so that he would get the advantage of an education.

'After I learned about what had happened between Margarita and the Rebel, I tried to think of what Hortencio was brooding about in the doorway that evening. Perhaps the Rebel had fallen in love with another woman and that is why he did not want a child with Margarita. Perhaps this was what the motive of the Rebel was, for he was a good fellow – he came from our part of the country, we knew him, and he had fought for the Revolution. Perhaps he did not want a child because a child forges a union between a man and a woman and makes a separation more difficult.

'The sun had just set and I heard some shots. So quick one after another that I thought it was a machine gun. At first I thought it was some stray member of Batista's army, for in the early days of 1959 there were still some hiding out in the woods, and my family had helped the Rebels and hidden some of them, so they would know we were not friendly. I put out the light as soon as I thought this, and waited. I heard more shots and then I pulled back the curtain. There was Hortencio on the floor. He said to me, "Flee, my son, they want to kill you!"

'I did not know what to think and then Margarita, who had seen the Rebel from the bedroom, screamed, "Run, run!" I turned and ran through the living-room and the Rebel fired and hit the piece of furniture where my mother stood the china up so that it would look pretty. I heard the crash of china and kept running through the back of the house. All this time I did not see the Rebel, and I ran across the yard heading for the pole fence that Hortencio had put up to corral the two cows. I heard my sister yell and again he fired. I had my hand on a pole to slip between them and felt the bullet hit the pole right above my hand.

'Later I had to take the police from Orden Pública to these places and show them where the bullets had hit, so that they would know that the Rebel had fired at me too. It is remarkable how everything that happens at such a moment remains so clearly in your mind. Past the fence, I took a short cut to the water through the grass and trees that the Rebel could not know about. And so did my sister. Out there was a little boat with an outboard motor that belonged to us. I used to go out in it with Hortencio to fish or just for the pleasure of it.

'It was not working right. As a matter of fact, Hortencio had said that when I finished the mathematics problem we would go out to the boat and try to fix it. The difficulty was in starting it up. It would falter and not catch when you pulled the rope to start the engine running. I knew this and knew that the noise it would make would give us away to the Rebel, so we walked into the water full of reeds and pulled the boat out a little way before I got inside it to start it. Margarita had pulled three stitches of her operation, but she stood waist high in the water holding the boat.

'I prayed the motor would start the first time I pulled the rope. I put it on high speed because it caught better that way and I pulled. It sputtered and did not catch. I pulled again and again it did not catch. When I wound the rope for the third time I think I was crying, and that time it caught. But those two false starts had given us away and the Rebel had come to the shore. The sun had set and it had been getting dark fast, but there was still enough light for him to see our silhouette and he fired and fired. He did not hit Margarita or me but he hit the boat, and as we went across the little inlet to reach Felton water began to come into the boat. We got out as soon as we could and we walked in the dark across farms and knocked on doors until we found someone who told us where the telephone office at Felton was. It was closed, but someone went to get the man to open it and we called Orden Pública.

'When someone from Orden Pública came, we started back to where the boat was and a block away we saw the Rebel. He was walking to the telephone office to turn himself in. I shall never forget that terrible night nor the terrible anxiety I felt crossing the inlet in the boat. It was in the boat that I remembered my little brother. Until then I had not thought of him and now there was nothing we could do. When we got back to the house that night, Hortencio was dead on the living-room floor and my little brother was under the house where he had hid the whole time. Nothing had happened to him!

'We made fifteen trips to Holguín for the trial. I never saw the trial nor heard the testimony of other people. Nor saw the Rebel again. They took me into a room and there I told my story. Finally, the trial was over and they gave the Rebel thirty-six years for what he did.'

'Do you think the Rebel was insane?' I asked Osvaldo.

He shook his head. 'The judge said he was not. That is why they sent him to jail. But you know, he was a good man. We know his family, we still do, and we have not let what he did make a difference in our feelings.'

A few days later I saw Pepe, the Poet, in Los Pinares. It was lunchtime and he had taken his tray away from the dining-room and sat under a tree. There were several girls there too and he was joking and flirting with them. When he saw me, he got up and left them.

'I got the scholarship!' he said, and told me more or less what Osvaldo had. 'Another month and I am through here.'

I congratulated him and we shook hands.

'I have been thinking about our meeting,' he said. 'If you are going to write a book about Mayarí, would you write about me and even perhaps publish the poem I wrote down for you?'

'That is an idea,' I said.

'I have thought about it several times and I sometimes conclude that you will do it. Why not? After all, it is real life.'

9. Machismo

During my first week in Mayarí, I was indefatigable, by Cuban standards, in my attempts to make appointments with organization leaders, old residents, professionals – the kind of people who could give me a sense of the structure of the town and also a bit of its history – and I paddled with insufficient regard for the hot sun up Maceo, across Leyte Vidal, down Céspedes several times each day. Directions I received seemed vague, for no one ever named the streets, and the results of my errands were frequently marginal to my purposes or totally unexpected. I met Mella Sorel that way. His father, Mario Sorel, I had been told, had taught a couple of generations in Mayarí and was probably the only expert on its history. As I approached for the third time his old, large wooden home next to the Frank Pais Elementary School, on an unpaved block below Céspedes, Mella came out determinedly, as if on an errand; he was a short, compact, virile mulatto in his late twenties. He was on an errand – a couple of last-minute arrangements before he took the early afternoon bus for Santiago – but he put all that off as soon as I introduced myself.

Not that he could take me to his father – the old man was in Santiago where he was teaching history at the Preuniversitaria (the high school) – but he hoped to introduce me to another Mayarí citizen, a lawyer, who had done as much research as his father. We went to the man's home, then to Administración, where his wife thought he might be, to a couple of places on Leyte Vidal, and finally, to the Regional de Cultura facing the triangular park. On the ground-floor lobby of the Regional was an exhibit of the classwork of one of the Worker-Peasant Evening Schools, and I noticed a grammar textbook open to a page that illustrated the use of the subjunctive with a passage from John Steinbeck's *The Grapes of Wrath*; a box on the same page gave biographical notes on Steinbeck, written before he became known as a supporter of the Vietnam war. One of the young men from Regional whom I had met on its steps the first day came over, looked at the text with me, and said, '*Would* that Steinbeck had not grown old and conservative!'

Mella and I were thirsty, our man was not to be found, so we crossed the park and went into the El Parque Cafeteria for beer; we sat at one of the tables halfway between the view to the street, where the presence of taxis and their drivers kept the scene lively, and the view out the large back windows to the peaceful valley and the Mayarí River. A year earlier beer had been scarce for a while, but no longer, and we sat there and drank a couple of bottles each during the two hours that Mella had before he was to make his bus. He was, in fact, going to Santiago to take his father his files on the repercussions in the Mayarí area to the calls for independence at the end of the last century. Research on a national level was being done on that period and Mella's father wanted to contribute what he had on the subject. In December Sorel had won a prize for his contribution to the *Granma* contest (the *Granma* is the official newspaper of the Cuban Communist Party) with a monograph on the participation of Negroes in the army of the War of Independence. He estimated that sixty per cent – at the very least – were Negroes.

By the time our first beer was served, I felt free to ask him why he had been named Mella. (Julio Antonio Mella was one of the founders of the Cuban Communist Party; he fled to Mexico when Machado, a president as hated as Batista, established his dictatorship in the twenties, but was assassinated there, allegedly by agents of Machado.) Was his father a Communist?

Mella shook his head but the question pleased him. 'This name of mine is the cause of many stories – it has long given me trouble, but no more,' he said, and poured his beer with great precision. 'My father was not a Communist but he was a man of left-wing ideas, and because he admired Mella he tried to name me after him. The civil authorities did not let him, on the excuse that it was a surname and not a proper Christian name. Just an excuse, for I am sure you have noticed that we Cubans are always inventing new Christian names. Nevertheless, that is what I was always called whether it was my legal name or not. Once when I was still a boy two men broke into our house and were later caught. Because I had seen them I appeared at their trial to identify them. During the questioning, my father referred to me as Mella, and the judge said, "What did you call him?" My father repeated it and the judge said, "Then you are a Communist! Why did you give him that name?" "Because I wanted to," my father said. The judge was very indignant and told my father, "Do not forget you are speaking to the court!" From then on my name used to worry me a lot.'

Unlike Despaigne, the gardener at the Bitirí, Mella knew his surname was French. His great-great-grandmother was the concubine, as he explained, of a French coffee-plantation owner. 'He passed on his name to all his bastards,' Mella said and smiled, as if he could well understand his lusty great-great-grandfather.

'Like everyone else, I was in the clandestine movement during the insurrection. During the last year in Santiago where I was going to school. The only thing unusual that happened to me – and that kind of thing could happen to anybody, so you could say it is representative –' He nodded his head, to show that he was aware he was talking to a writer, who would, naturally, only be interested in the typical, not the personal. 'I got into trouble with one of the local police – we called them *casquitos* to distinguish them from the Army conscripts – because he and I were always having personal troubles, mostly arising from his political posture. At a cafe on Leyte Vidal one afternoon he took out his pistol and pointed it at my Adam's apple and said he was going to kill me. I knew he was a coward and said, "You are not going to kill me." He talked and talked – while I kept quiet – but did nothing. My father went to the police station when a neighbour told him, and thought he had cleared up the whole thing.

'But at two in the morning that night there was a knocking on the door and I escaped out the back. I went to Santiago in a friend's car and from there to Havana, where I sought the protection of an uncle who was a colonel in the Army medical corps. I got a safe-conduct letter from him to return to Santiago, and that was all. When the Revolution triumphed, I walked to Mayarí and as soon as I got here I went to the police station and we went to get the casquito. He had not tried to flee with the ones who headed for Guatemala and we found him at home. He was given thirty years, not for his bullying but because it was discovered that he had murdered a campesino.'

After the Revolution, Mella had thought he could best serve by becoming a technician. He applied to study abroad and he was sent to Hungary, where he spent almost three years. When he returned, he brought a Hungarian wife, already pregnant.

'She lives here in Mayarí?' I asked.

He nodded with pride. 'She loves our food, our climate. She has had no trouble adjusting to any of those things.'

When he returned, he was given a job at a tyre factory in Havana. They were not happy there, especially after the baby was born, because they couldn't find adequate housing; also, the scarcity of raw-materials made him not too useful at the factory. He finally asked to be allowed to quit his job and come to Mayarí to teach. At first he taught first grade, but now he was teaching history at the junior high school and also at the night schools for adults. He seemed settled and happy, except for the fact that he felt that, as with his three sisters, his taking up teaching history was 'an imitation' of his father's career. 'I guess I want to keep on studying.'

This information about himself was incidental to our long

talk. What interested Mella most was to talk about the politics of the Revolution, and he was articulate and forceful on the subject. Finally, I asked him if he was a member of the Party.

'No,' he said and shook his head. He drew his glass across the wet rings on the table for emphasis. 'And I do not think I should be.'

Curiously, this was the first time he struck what I thought was a genuinely personal note, so that there was tension in his voice and he looked at me with his head held back as if making a bold confession.

'In my judgement, I should not be a militant, and if I am asked I shall decline. There was a hint of it once – you know, if I wanted to take on tasks to prepare myself for it – but I got out of it. You see, I was already formed by the time the Revolution triumphed, by a kind of *petit bourgeois* life. I am full of vices.'

'Vices?' I said.

He nodded. 'For one thing, I like to sit and chat and pass the time as we are doing now,' he said, confessing first to what was easiest. He looked down at the table without talking for a moment. 'I like beer.' Another pause. 'I like to sleep with women other than my wife – and I believe that a Communist should be an Immaculate!'

'An Immaculate?' I said.

'Yes, yes. Members of the Party do not sleep with other women just because the opportunity presents itself. If they do, they do it so hidden, so carefully – well, in such a way you could not call it screwing around. Perhaps in time I shall rid myself of all my vices, but now I should not be considered a candidate for the Party.'

I told him that I had the impression, though it was only my first week there, that girls now had a more liberal attitude towards sex. He stopped smiling, and I explained that I meant that where love was involved they might not now wait for marriage.

Throughout the last part of my speech he began to shake his

head. 'Have you been talking to the girls of the Bitirí?' he said and then smiled again. 'They are not representative, not at all. No decent girl will sleep with a man before marriage. But the girls at the Bitirí are girls who are serving men all day long – what can that lead to? There are rooms right there, the men are from out of town, so they end up being light about sex.

'Of course, it is because of the way we Cuban men are that girls have to be careful. I say so because of myself. When I go to Cueto, the fact that I am married does not act as a brake on my having another woman who is willing. All this drives my wife wild, though Cuban women are resigned to this behaviour from their husbands. They do not like it, they are simply resigned. But not my wife, she is terribly jealous. I say to her, "But you are European, there they are much more liberal." "Do not speak to me about Europe," she says, "I do not want to hear about that."'

Mella knew it was not right to believe as he did that men could sleep with all the women they want and still have the wife remain faithful, but he felt he was making an important concession by insisting that the husband must respect the home by allowing no scandal to touch it because of his behaviour. 'I know that in Europe they are more advanced. Women are more liberated. And in Cuba, as they gain more economic independence, they are going to demand more and more faithfulness from the husband. But it is no use arguing about all this in the abstract. The thing women must do is create the conditions, get jobs and become independent. My wife teaches, right now she is in Havana taking a special short course for physical education teachers, and that is the way it is going to happen.'

No doubt because of the turn the conversation with Mella took I walked, after I left him, into the headquarters for the Federation of Cuban Women. Four regional leaders were having a meeting in the back office but interrupted it to talk to me. It was being chaired by Elvira Prieto, a handsome mulatto, and she seemed an example of the kind of woman Mella said would create independence for women. 'What can we do for you?' she said eagerly.

'Give me a biography of yourself,' I said to her, and they all laughed because they did not think I meant it. Elvira had a heartier laugh than the rest, 'I mean it,' I added.

'Very well,' said Elvira. 'I come from the peasantry. I worked as a domestic at six dollars a month and I did everything there was to be done in that house from six in the morning to nine at night. Some of that family left the country, the others may have by now – but I do not know because they do not interest me. I had only gone through the second grade when the Revolution triumphed, and I immediately set out to organize the domestic workers so that the new law raising our salaries to twenty-five dollars would take effect. Then in 1960 I quit that job – I had decided I would never again be a domestic – and I went home to Victoria de la Tunas and began organizing the Federation without pay.

'The Federation sent me to Havana to school and after six months I came out at a fourth-grade rating. I continued to organize for the Federation without pay. I got a meal here and there and kept going, for domestic work was the only kind I knew and I was not going back to that. By 1963 I was a full-time worker in the Federation and I have remained so ever since. I also belong to the militia.

'In January of last year I was sent to a Party school in Santiago and there I got through the sixth grade. We studied political science, history, grammar and literature. I went from it right into the mobilization that came when one of our soldiers was killed at Guantánamo and we mobilized the entire country to show we were prepared for whatever the provocation signified. We got military instructions daily, and we also had school classes when we were not at our posts. I had a chance to examine and I got an eighth-grade rating.

'I have been married two years. My husband was at Guantánamo during the alert and since I had been in Santiago at school just before that, we did not see each other for four months. Now he is at Banes and we see each other once a week. It has to be, it is no sacrifice. When I returned to Tunas after the mobilization, the Federation assigned me to this region. My ambition is to see our work succeed, to see the end of socialism and the coming of communism.'

'There is one more thing she is not talking about,' said one of the other women.

'All right,' Elvira said, making an exception though she did not know me well. 'It is my great ambition to be a militant of the Party. There is no greater thing that one can be. But for that I have to do a lot of work – a lot of work for me to do.'

When I turned to each of the other three women there, I found that all were in the Party, though Elvira, it then came out, was Secretary of the Region. I did not ask for an explanation, but one volunteered. 'The Party looks for the best person for each job and Elvira is the best person.'

'I take it that the Federation works to get equal rights for women,' I said.

One or two started to agree, but stopped and looked puzzled. 'Oh no,' Elvira said. 'There is no work to be done about that. Those rights have been won.'

'The Federation works to get participation by women in bettering the nation,' said the delegate from El Cocal.

At first, the Federation's problem was to get women to join the organization itself. Cuban women never had organizations of their own before, other than ladies' auxiliaries at the churches. To join an organization was a new idea, at least for working-class and campesino women. The Federation's work has been to alphabetize, train women for new jobs, help set up kindergartens for working mothers, recruit for work in special projects.

'We have the responsibility for recruiting the women for Los Pinares,' Elvira said.

I knew twelve thousand were needed within two months, and I asked if that had presented a great problem. They burst into laughter. 'Yes, yes!' one said. 'But not what you would imagine. We have had to screen the applicants very carefully – there are many more than are needed – because some of the compañeras already have jobs where it would be a problem to replace them. Such enthusiasm! We have to explain very carefully to those being turned down, so they will not be discouraged.'

That night when I told Dr Morales, the surgeon from Havana, and Dr Padrón, the director of the hospital, about Mella's views, Morales grimaced disapprovingly. 'He is one of the dinosaurs,' he said.

'Barbaric,' said Dr Padrón; then he opened his eyes wide. 'I know who *she* is! She is the girl with the maya stockings – she has a lot of cachet!'

Forgetting his mien of a second earlier, Morales said with all the innuendo he could muster, 'Ahaa! Is she one of your patients?'

'I saw her on Leyte Vidal, doctor,' Padrón replied, but she was to become his patient, and the circumstances were unusual.

I met Ilona Sorel about a month later, on my second visit to the Frank Pais school near her home, and she was chic, but on that day the teachers had all dressed up for the show the children were putting on. She was wearing her string mesh stockings and the other teachers, with whom she was popular, kept pointing them out and threatening to take a trip to Havana to buy a pair for themselves. The seven teachers of the school were of all ages – a couple, like Ilona, were in their twenties, others were middle-aged, and at least one was sixty – but they all turned into giggling girls about the stockings.

They were, however, a serious group of teachers. I had gone into Frank Pais school one day, after noticing on the several occasions I had passed it that the name painted large on a stucco outside wall included the adjective 'experimental'; and I learned that it had also won the designation as a model school for its excellent record, and the year before had been selected the 'vanguard' of all the model schools in northern Oriente. Its students were not specially selected from the neighbourhood it served – the only control over students that distinguished it from other grammar schools was that each class was restricted to children of the same age – but its teachers received special courses and, probably, greater supervision. During the two summer months that the school was closed, the teachers spent one taking special teaching courses.

The principal of the school, a middle-aged Negro woman, felt so sure of her teachers that she walked me without warning into each of the class-rooms. Since each room gave on to a covered walk, our entrance was no surprise after the first two visits. In any case, each visit was an interruption: we stood at the front of the class and watched while some lesson capable of being observed – that is, no quiet reading or writing at their desks – was given. As we entered each class-room, the students all got up and recited a greeting in unison.

'We are a model school,' recited the kindergarteners, 'and we are working hard to keep Frank Pais a model and vanguard school this Year of Heroic Vietnam!'

Almost every class's greetings included something about Vietnam, and the fifth grade praised the friendship between Cuba and the Soviet Union. I asked the principal if these slogans were set ones for all schools, and she exclaimed, 'Oh no, what is the point of that? They are made up by the teacher and the students.'

Although Frank Pais was built soon after the Revolution, it had to begin from scratch after Hurricane Flora. All their books and materials had been destroyed, and they still suffered from many lacks. 'That is why the teachers deserve so much praise,' the principal said. 'They make up their own teaching aids.' And she pointed out that the cardboard squares the third-grade teacher had just distributed for a lesson in short division had been made entirely by her; on one side was the problem, on the other the answer.

There were seven classes in the school and 211 students. Classes began at eight and recessed at noon; the students returned at two and remained until four thirty. Remedial work was done with little groups in the early evening. There was a 'science corner' in each room, exhibits of class-room work on the walls, and each room had a neat, disciplined air. Any new teaching technique that worked with the model schools was then passed on to all other schools throughout the nation. They believed very much in planning and did not think any teacher should improvise in the class-room at all, but should have every day's work worked out in advance. 'Though learning by rote is something we think is outmoded,' the principal said.

Perhaps the one innovation they most liked was the manner of teaching reading and writing. This was done in the first grade by a progressive method that has not worked as well in the States. The children progress through a rather clever text-book in which they work through groups of sounds that alone or in combination make up words, so that at the year's end they have learned to read and to write in block letters. No attempt is made to memorize lists of words or to memorize spelling. Perhaps the reason for their success is the unvarying relationship in Spanish between sound and written symbol.

The teachers invited me back for 'ceremonies' to be given in April just before the two-week recess for Playa Girón. Grammar-school children did not, of course, go to the country-side to work during those two weeks, but in conjunction with the Regional de Cultura the schools organized *el plan de la calle* – street projects – where entertainment and games were held for the children. In Mayarí, the street beyond the Regional de Cultura was roped off for them. They also paid visits to the cane-fields and sugar mills: now that the revolutionary government has learned that the production of sugar is Cuba's natural and most lucrative role – not the imposition of an imperialist power – the details of the process are exhaustively and lovingly given in newspapers, books and films.

I could not avoid a second visit to Frank Pais because the children often stopped me in the street as the day approached to remind me, and it was then I met Ilona Sorel. She had black hair, worn in a page-boy style, very fair skin and large, round green eyes, and was so naturally appealing that the children and the other teachers made their voices go soft when they spoke to her. There was no opportunity to talk, for the school had no auditorium – 'We need one very badly, very badly,' said the principal – and we were all milling in the front yard to watch the show which would be held in the wide passage in front of the principal's office. Ilona had already heard about me and had discussed with Mella whether she should give me her brother's address in Cleveland; Mella had advised against it, but she gave it to me when I agreed there should be no trouble in my writing him when I returned and enclosing a photograph of her.

'He is my only brother and we shall never be able to see one another again,' she said, and her eyes got tearful. 'He cannot write to me because maybe it would get him in trouble in your country, and last year when I was visiting my parents in Hungary, he called on the telephone. The only time I had talked to him in years, and something happened and we were cut off!'

Her brother had escaped from Hungary during the 1956 uprising and had been living in the States since. Ilona said he missed home very much but could not come back. I told her many had, and that I understood the Hungarian government accepted them without prejudice. She nodded and then shook her head. 'But not he,' she said. 'He cannot come back. He was in the army and those who were in the army are not forgiven.'

I did not know what to say to console her.

'But he was only seventeen when he ran away – he did not know what he was doing!' she said. 'He is sorry, but it is too late.'

She had to go off then to take care of her little boy, Mellita, who had fallen on the cement walk; he was a chunky three-year-old and would not cry. In any case, he was so popular that several others reached him before Ilona and soothed him.

And finally, the show began. It was the usual school show — slow, endless, full of crises that were unforeseen, and a total delight to students, parents, and teachers whose students did well. There was a skit about the guerrillas in the Sierra Maestra, a puppet show about Vietnam guerrillas routing a company of North Americans, but the rest was songs, a scene from an old-fashioned operetta, poetry recitations. Ilona's students did some gymnastics to music and one short, athletic ballet piece.

She apologized a great deal for it because it had to be done out on the cement walk and the phonograph was too far away to be properly heard. But she praised the students. The students, however, praised *her* and so did the parents and the teachers. Everything ended in a burst of good feeling and much talk around a table set up for the adults, who were served cake and soda. I did not get to talk to Ilona again, but before I left I approached her and said I would like to visit one night and talk to her and Mella together. It pleased her, but she called me back and said, 'Perhaps you should not tell Mella I gave you my brother's address?' This was the only sign there was trouble between them, but I did not suspect it then.

It was two weeks before I ran into Mella and made an appointment to see them. I would be leaving in a week, and it still seemed a good idea to me to have a picture of an international young couple whose marriage and life together in Mayarí was a kind of happy product of socialism. The afternoon of the evening I was to see them I walked by the Frank País school just as it let out, and one of the teachers called me in; they were having a little party for the kindergarten teacher to celebrate her forty years as teacher in Mayarí. We sat in the principal's office and ate cake and drank a sweet Spanish wine. A young soldier was there, too, for each school besides having a representative from each mass organization on its council, also had a kind of circulating godfather from the Army at each of its functions. Ilona came in with Mellita and said she could only stay a moment. She was going to deliver Mellita to a friend and then turn in at the hospital.

'He can stay with me,' said one of the young teachers.

Ilona explained that her in-laws would be coming to Mayarí from Santiago that evening to take care of him for the few days she would be in the hospital. She was tearful, and when Mellita walked out of the room for a moment, admitted she was a little frightened. 'But it is nothing, nothing at all,' she said when asked, and told me that Mella would see me alone or together with her after she was dismissed from the hospital.

There was a pause when she left. 'You can imagine how she feels,' said one teacher. 'Her mother is so far away. Not like us when we get sick.'

They discussed that a moment and planned to visit her and take care of Mellita as often as possible. 'But her in-laws will be here,' someone said, and one of the teachers replied, in a neutral voice, 'Yes, they will.' 'And Mella,' someone added, and the teacher simply grimaced this time.

. 'Well, well, congratulations to Hilda!' exclaimed an older teacher to break the pall that had fallen on the group. 'I think the presence of men should not deter us from following our usual practice at festivities like this.'

'What is that?' I asked.

'It is our custom after the cake and wine have been served to sit like this and tell stories,' she explained. 'Not as strong as the stories you men tell when you are together, but enough to entertain us.' And one by one each told a mildly off-colour story that sent Hilda, the old kindergarten teacher, into shrieks of laughter. Until the one who had started them suddenly covered her mouth and exclaimed, 'Oh my! I forgot the compañero is a writer and he will go off and present an awful picture of us!'

I promised I would never tell, and Hilda said with assurance, 'Of course, of course.' Being in her sixties, she knew about old-fashioned gallantry.

When Dr Padrón came to the Bitirí for his shower that

day, I asked him about Ilona Sorel. He did not know; another doctor must have signed her in. I knew he would be making a tour of the wards that evening or, at the latest, the next day; but we missed each other the next day, and Ilona had been in the hospital two days before I learned from him what her illness was. She was running a low-grade fever, suffered pains and chills, and was also very anxious. Dr Padrón paused a moment after telling me this, and then added, 'She is two months pregnant and has been trying to abort.'

'She is unhappy,' I said.

Padrón nodded. 'She is very worried that her husband will find out what she has been doing. A friend has helped her with injections, she says, but all that has happened is that she has an infection. She desperately wants to lose the pregnancy just because, as you say, she is unhappy. It is not our job to give her an abortion. You know we are rather relaxed about it. We have to report abortions to Orden Pública, and they come and question the women, only to find out if there is someone who makes an illegal profession of giving abortions. But in her case – well, all that we can do is treat the infection.'

On his second trip through the ward after Ilona was signed in, she made an effort to appeal to him. 'I had to dissemble, for what she was urging on me was an abortion. I simply kept saying to her not to worry, we would cure her, that her case was a simple infection and so on. I acted as if her worry was that she was ill. Of course, you know, I believe that this infection is a sign that something has gone wrong with the pregnancy, and she will, as a result, lose the foetus, but it is something I will not predict and cannot tell her.'

I told Padrón that my plan to interview her had been disrupted by her illness, and that I hoped it would be all right if I visited her at the hospital.

'You want to see her together with her husband as you had planned?' Padrón asked, suddenly very formal with me.

'Of course not!' I said. 'Can I see her any time?'

'Her husband is there every time I walk through the lobby,

asking me how soon he can take her home,' Padrón said, with a smile. 'He seems very concerned.'

After a little more of this teasing, Padrón promised to ask her if she would see me, and to allow her to talk to me outside the ward. 'Well?' I said to him the next day, for I had only a couple of days left in Mayarí.

Padrón smiled at me, then said, 'She seems very anxious to talk to you. She was overjoyed that you asked. She has had no fever today, so she should soon be leaving us.'

I could not see her that evening – Padrón did not want her walking out of the ward to the unprotected balconies connecting the wings of the hospital, the only place we could have a private conversation – and the next day would be my last full day in Mayarí. For a moment I thought of giving up the idea of seeing Ilona again, because I had just learned that the Methodist minister had been sent home from the UMAP and I wanted to make sure I caught him on the last day I had. But Padrón promised me that if I arrived at ten in the morning she could come out immediately, and there would be a full hour before the visitors arrived.

At ten the next morning, Padrón dragged a couple of chairs out to the second-floor balcony, to an alcove where we could be by ourselves; it overlooked the grounds that Padrón, in the two and a half months since I first saw them, had had enlarged and replanted; in the distance were royal palms and the green, rolling countryside. Ilona came out in a long silk robe, extended a hand and gave me a pitiful smile.

'Oh compañero,' she said, 'it is so kind of you to come, so kind. No one knows it, but I telephoned you at the Bitirí the first day I was here. You were not there and I could not leave a message – it might not have seemed right. I have been long enough in Cuba to know how such a thing can be cause for gossip. So you see how lucky I felt when Dr Padrón told me yesterday that you wanted to speak to me. For *I* want to speak to *you*, to ask you to help me. I know of no one else who can. And now it is perhaps too late. . . .

'I am going to be dismissed today. At one in the afternoon when my husband comes for me. I want you to help me before he comes. I know that you are a good friend of Dr Padrón. He is so serious. . . . I have tried to speak to him. I see that you do not know and therefore he must not have understood me. I am pregnant and I want to have an abortion – it is as simple as that and I am ashamed to tell you.

'But they are dismissing me today. See, see how my hand is wet when I touch my forehead? I have fever right now. An abortion is the only way I can make something of my marriage. If I have another child now, there will be no way out of my situation with Mella, no way except to return to my country. Mella wants me to have the child. He wants it because it would definitely chain me to the house, and there is so much work for me already that I do not know how I would survive. And I do not want to give it up, I do not want to break up this marriage. He says if I leave him, he will kill me. If I go to Hungary, he will follow me there and kill me. If I do not have the child now, there is a chance that things will get better between us, that he will change. But not if I have the child.

'When I was in Havana for the course, I went to my embassy and I told them there about my problems. "Leave him," they said, "many of the other girls who married Cubans who were with him in Hungary have gone back" – and for unimportant little reasons, that they did not like the food, they were homesick, nothing like mine. I came to Cuba already pregnant with Mellita and I have had so many troubles ever since.

'No, as soon as we married in Hungary, he changed. It was only before we married that he was sweet and affectionate with me. Then – though customs are so different in Hungary – he began to subject me to his view of what a wife should be. I am not allowed to go out of the house – only when I go next door to the school to teach – except with women friends. I have been in Mayarí two years and I have been to the movies three times, twice to the Bitirí and once to the Club Praga. Always with Mella, of course. And nowhere else. Do you know what a Hungarian feels about the ocean? We have no shore and we love to bathe on a beach. Here I am in Cuba and I have never gone swimming because I am not allowed to wear a bathing-suit. Other men would be looking at me!

'I do not just teach at the school, I do all the work in the house. I clean house, wash clothes, cook, take care of the baby. And I dread it when my in-laws are there because I have to work for them too. You understand I am not *fina* – not delicate – I like work. I was always taught at home to take care of my own things, to help clean the house, all that – I do not want servants. But Mella does nothing and the salary I get for teaching, Mella collects it and drinks it all.

'You know what is the truth about him? – he is lazy. He just teaches, that is all. He was thrown out of the militia and he spends all his time drinking or with other women. If I cross him in anything, he beats me or he treats me so badly that I prefer to do what he says. I have no one with me – just my son and he is too young – and I must have affection. I cannot bear to live in a house with an angry man who does not speak to me because I did some little thing he did not like. So I do not fight back.

'You remember the performance my students put on at school? Well, during Playa Girón there was a morning at the Cultural when all the schools participated and those dances were listed on the programme for the last act. When I saw it would be after lunch before they went on, I ran back home and prepared Mella's lunch, left him a note, dressed Mellita again and went back to the Cultural. Mella came home and then to the Cultural. He grabbed me by the arm and forced me to come home to serve him the food. I was so ashamed in front of everyone! The food was all prepared, he had only to warm it, but that is not proper for a man to do.

'He says he is a revolutionary, but I do not believe a person is a revolutionary because of what he says but because of the way he acts. I wanted to join the militia but he did not let me – "You in the militia to stand guard with a rifle and let all the

264 In the Fist of the Revolution

men see you!" I cannot join the Federation of Women or any other organization because I must stay home. When a woman friend comes to the house, he acts so rude that they never come back.

'I do not know how I am going to have this baby, for I am terrified at home now. I get sick, the way I never did with the first, and if he should learn that a friend gave me an injection, he would kill me. Just as he says that he would kill me if I go to Hungary. He never comes home before two in the morning and I am in terror of the rats. Twice they have bitten Mellita and I have brought him to the hospital.

'I know I am married to an exaggerated case, but his point of view is very Cuban. The position of Cuban women is terrible – if you knew how different it is at home! There men and women are equals. They can be friends. Of course, there are some things men can do better and they earn more in those jobs, but I am not talking about that. I was a chemical technician in industry – I did hard work, physical work. I like that, I am not delicate. I studied ballet for six years and languages too. I had hoped to study French and English in the evening, but there is no place in Mayarí. I took a course in Cuban history and I did not have to take the final examination, for I was not trying to qualify for grading as Cubans do to have a school record. Although my Spanish is not very good, I came out first in the class.

'I think Cuban men are this way because of customs. It is going to change with the Revolution. You understand, I am not unhappy with the Revolution. Oh no, I am in perfect agreement. But although I have much hope for the young people going away to live-in schools, I think it may only be their children who will be different. It will take fifty years.

'I know Mella has a psychological problem. He is, as the Cubans say, *un abusador* – a bully. But although they do not act the way he does, Cuban men generally believe the way he does. Oh, the ideas they have about what makes a man a man! A man who helps in the house – he must be *that way*! Effemi-

nate. Something it would not occur to us to think in Hungary.
I have thought very much about what makes Mella this way
– and I know he is actually better already, for although he
treats me the way he does he *has* changed a little bit – and I
have come to the conclusion that it all comes down to the
colour of his skin. Imagine, something I do not care one bit
about! I think sometimes he wants everyone to know that it is
nothing to him that his wife is white. As if he were saying,
"See, I can treat her any way I want and still have as many
other women as I desire."

'Oh, it is eleven o'clock!' Ilona exclaimed. 'No, it is all
right. Today he comes at one to take me away. But there is so
little time. I could talk to you for ever but I must let you go.
I appeal to you – would you speak to Dr Padrón?'

It was terrible to listen to her story with interest but to feel
her appeal as an embarrassment. I nodded.

'I mean right now,' she said. 'So he can do something before Mella comes. So he will not take me away, for the regular doctor has already signed me out.' She put her hand to her
forehead again and it once more came away wet. 'I think I
have the fever again.'

We got up and she suddenly became more formal, as if
ashamed that she had been importunate. Her eyes became sad
with the thought that I was a stranger and that either I would
not talk to Padrón or my mission would fail.

I told her I was leaving the next day and that I would probably not see her again. It was then I remembered that a Hungarian agricultural technician had just checked into the Bitirí,
and I told her that she had a compatriot she could look forward
to meeting.

'Is he young?' she asked.

'Yes.'

'Oh, what a pity!' she said, losing interest. 'Why could it
not have been an old man? Then there might have been a
chance to meet him. But a young man – Mella will not allow
him in the house.'

I walked down the stairs, wondering how I would put the whole thing to Padrón, and when I passed the reception desk on the way to his office, I saw Mella. He greeted me first and shifted Mellita to his other arm to shake my hand.

'What are you doing here?' I asked. 'I hope everything is all right.'

He was grateful for my interest. 'My wife had a little touch of fever,' he said. 'Nothing at all – right, Mellita? And we are here to take her home.' He smiled. 'Everything is all right, but we missed her.'

In Padrón's office, I quickly told him what she hoped he would do for her. Padrón only said, 'Did you see him outside?'

I nodded.

Padrón half veiled his eyes and studied me for a moment. Then Oquendo, the administrator, came into the office, and Padrón got up to leave with him. To me Padrón said, 'We shall see what I can do.'

At six that afternoon I saw Padrón again at the Bitirí. I was waiting in front of my room to be sure to catch him when he came for his shower. Margarita had yelled at least a half hour earlier that the water was on, and I hated to detain him.

'I am turning into your assistant,' Padrón said. 'I went up to the ward to see her and told her that the matter she had wanted to talk to me about was something that she should have come to my office to discuss. She was disappointed, I could see, but I told her that I was available for her at any time. I also informed her husband downstairs that she still had a little fever and that it might be best if she stayed on another day. But he was very insistent and he took her away.'

'And that is all?' I said.

'No, no,' he said with a show of patience. 'I discussed in front of him that I was concerned with her state of health and I asked that she come to my consultation in two days. I made that a definite appointment. They agreed that she would come.'

I was relieved and Padrón saw it. 'But do not imagine there is going to be an abortion,' he said. 'For that they would both have to be in agreement. If it were a request of her own alone – I don't know, her embassy would probably have to be brought into it. But I tell you, there is something wrong there.' And Padrón pointed to his belly. 'She is going to lose it.'

'Then nothing is settled,' I said.

Padrón sighed. 'Well, Jose, God knows there is something she can do!' he said almost angrily. 'She can divorce him and he will have to take it. All that about killing her is a lot of nonsense. She puts up with him because she wants to. Love, if you want to call it that. In case you have not noticed it, there has been a Revolution here and women do not have to put up with that kind of treatment.'

He calmed down immediately and said with his usual sobriety, 'And now I am going to take a shower.'

On the bus from Havana to Mayarí I had first heard – with surprise and, perhaps, a little alarm – the opinion that most ordinary Cubans held about the U M A P, the work-prison camps that had been in existence for about a year and a half. 'It is good for them to work,' a man in the dark bus had said about UMAP internees, and gone back to sleep. So did everyone else: the subject was exhausted that quickly and only I, a frustrated eavesdropper, was left awake to worry some significance out of the two or three sentences and one complacent giggle that had followed the departure from the bus of a woman who had been to Santa Clara to visit a son in the UMAP camp there. How could these people, whom I had got to like during the long day's ride, be so unfeeling about the injustices of the UMAP?

In Havana, the intellectuals I met condemned it. The Artists and Writers Union was on record about the group of artists that had been scheduled to be sent to a camp. Castro himself had denounced what he had seen as concentration camps, and some intellectuals promised me – as if passing on a promise they had received from him – that the UMAP would be disbanded that year. The Ministry of Foreign Affairs functionaries had given me copies of the two articles that Graham Greene had written for English newspapers after his tour of Cuba in the fall, and one of them dealt with the UMAP. (The copies the Ministry gave me were Spanish translations of the originals, and they had not excised Greene's unfavourable comments.) He had been pleased that the Artists and Writers Union had prevented their colleagues' arrest, but he was dismayed by the existence of the UMAP: the Revolution can survive, he said, any political or economic error but not a moral one, and the UMAP was a moral error that must be corrected.

I was out for the evening with a Ministry functionary the day I read Greene's articles, and I asked him, in the informal atmosphere that being out on the town created, what he thought of Greene's condemnation of the UMAP. It embarrassed him. 'I do not think that Greene was entirely well informed about the UMAP,' he said. 'I do admit, however, that the camps were not well run, that they were run in such a way, as a matter of fact, that they would not have rehabilitated or reformed anyone. Some of the people in charge were in need of reform themselves, and that is what happened – *they* ended up in the UMAP!'

These Military Units for Aid to Production were begun to take care of young men of military age whose incorporation into the Army for military training was considered unfeasible. Young men known to avoid work and study were candidates; so were known counter-revolutionaries; and also immoralists, a category that included homosexuals. How the recruitment worked was difficult to define: some were unexpectedly picked up and shipped to a camp, others were notified to report, and others were called in and warned and given a chance to defend themselves. Who denounced them? The secret police, their colleagues at their study or work centre, and mainly, the local Committees for the Defence of the Revolution.

It should have been predictable that the recruits would not, in practice, be limited to young men of military age, that the categories of qualification would be blurred, and that their internment would not be educational but brutally punitive. This was all I knew about the UMAP; I did not make a study of it – I was loath to. At first, I did not bring up the subject in Mayarí; it did not seem to impinge on the life of the town: the nearest camp was halfway across the island; about a dozen men was the most that had been taken from the town, another six from Guatemala.

The first to mention it was Nelson Consuegra, a young campesino who, during my second day in Mayarí, walked across the street with a friendly smile to greet me. Not because I was a foreigner – he was not aware of that – but because I had nodded to him. He was a marvel of openness and trust and we sat together for a while and talked. He was out of the Army a few months although he was only eighteen: he had been allowed to join it when he was thirteen because he knew Comandante Pancho Gonzalez. I was to run into Nelson every few days, and it became a joke between us that he was always changing jobs or finding an opportunity to be off from the one he had. But he loved the Revolution, he told me, and would have remained in the Army except for the fact that he did not like Army life; it was too confining.

'I was offered a chance to become a sergeant before I left,' he said. 'My salary would have gone up from $20 a month to $110, but I did not want to serve in an UMAP camp out in Camagüey. A place full of marijuana smokers and men who want to be treated like women. Imagine, they complained if they were treated like men and even painted themselves up like girls!' Nelson shook his head. 'Not for me.'

I asked him if there had been any men from Mayarí who were sent to the UMAP.

'I do not think so,' he said. 'Oh yes, there was the fellow who worked in the funeral parlour. He was caught being speared and you know what he said? He said, "Do not desist now that I am caught!" He was the only one.'

'What about the one spearing him?' I asked.

'Oh no,' Nelson said. Nelson did not pursue complex ideas, but most Cubans would have taken for granted, as he did, that the partner was not a homosexual.

Mella Sorel, a few days later, explaining the enormous rehabilitation job the Revolution had to undertake, brought up the UMAP, and let me know that there had been several cases in Mayarí. He knew a forty-year-old man who didn't like to work and had several mistresses; he had been returned from the UMAP because his wife and four children suffered a great deal from his absence. 'He had always managed to find food for them – badly, but it amounted to some kind of support,'

Mella said. 'Well, they gave him a chance and sent him back with a letter to Micons to give him work. That man has turned over a new leaf completely.'

I asked him if attempting to reform homosexuals was not foolhardy.

'I am afraid I am very intransigent about that,' Mella said, not angrily but with a smile – everything about homosexuals struck him as funny. 'A man is biologically born a man, so why can he not function as a man? What is to keep him from it but vice? Artists, especially dancers, almost have to be homosexuals, I understand that, but why cannot they keep it to themselves? One night at the Bitirí, two dancers from Havana sat at my table and the first thing I know I hear one say, "Oh I have my eye on that young barber on Leyte Vidal!" Anyway, what do homosexuals do for production? – they become shop assistants and interior decorators!'

The only others in Mayarí who brought up the UMAP on their own were the boys with La Enfermedad. One day El Rubio and El Sapito, going over their litany of complaints, hit upon it, and El Rubio spoke with more compassion than I had thought him capable of feeling for someone other than himself. 'Listen, once in Las Villas, near El Ciego de Avila, I saw something so terrible about the UMAP that no one can deny, for I saw it with my own eyes and I would tell them so. Right in front of us on the road was a truck-load of UMAP men in their blue uniforms. Some were seated inside with their backs to the side of the truck and others at the end with their legs dangling down. They were homosexuals. They were in the UMAP because they were men who cannot, like other people, do things without publicity. For I tell you that some people have the sense to go into a room and do what they want, entertain whom they want – a man or a woman – but when they go out in the street there is an end to it. But there are those who need publicity – who would do it even out in the street. Well, that is the type those unfortunates in the UMAP were –'

'Oh, that UMAP is *de alma*,' said El Sapito. 'The work is from sun-up to sun-down and the *jame* – the grub – is little.' He made a circle by joining a forefinger and thumb. 'Little like this!'

El Rubio continued: 'Well, one of those sitting at the back suddenly jumped down and ran past the truck carrying them and threw himself in front of it. He wanted to kill himself. That is how desperate he was, and no one can deny it, for I was one of the ones who took him to the hospital at El Ciego de Avila. He was fortunate – he tore up an eyebrow, scraped his face and lost a four-tooth plate. He was out of his mind with desperation!'

One Saturday night El Sapito came to the Bitirí with three friends, boys in high school, and between shows they visited me at my room. Dr Padrón was seated outside with me, and he listened in silence to their story about a friend of theirs in Mayarí who was taken to the UMAP although his schoolwork was good and the principal of the school interceded for him. They were seated in the park across from him the night the police picked him up, and they all ran home. 'He was just a fellow who loved fiestas and was always getting parties together, and if you asked him to go cut cane he would say frankly that he would not because he did not like the Revolution. Some people said he was like that, but he was not, for he was my friend and I knew he was not.'

'Not like Badín at El Parque Cafeteria whom they also took,' El Sapito said. 'There was no question about Badín – all Mayarí had had him. But you know, Badín was a lot of fun. He could not talk to you without touching you, but he was amusing, he made you laugh.'

When the boys left, I argued with Padrón about the UMAP. It was the first time, and it hurt him to hear me criticize it; he knew that people picked up by the UMAP were at best apathetic and apolitical and he could not feel sorry for them. Especially since the criticism had come from young men who were so alienated from the Revolution. 'Can't you tell that the young man who goes to school in Holguín is a candidate for exile?' he said to me. 'He could be there on scholarship, he says, but he prefers to stay at a pension and pay all that money because he does not want to live with the other students and be subject to their discipline. He does not belong to any student organization, he does not do volunteer work – he is just nothing. If he does not make the university because his fellow students decide he is a counter-revolutionary who will leave as soon as he gets the chance, it is no more than he deserves!'

'You notice they admit that from what their friend in the U M A P tells them, things have got better in the U M A P,' Padrón continued. 'Well, do not believe them that people just got picked up like that. I am sure every case was gone into carefully. Of course, the men who run the U M A P are illiterates who could not make distinctions – there is a difference between an artist and other men. Writers, for example, are people who seem to waste time and they need to do as they please in order to produce. A man from Havana is not a campesino, and these illiterates do not know that.'

I became aroused, probably because I had not had my say in a long time. 'Padrón, every human being is inviolable. He must be left alone if he wants to be that way. If he has not broken one of your laws, you have no right to pick him up and send him to what is a prison – no matter what you call it – and reform him according to your lights.'

Padrón slapped his knee for emphasis. 'Jose, you must speak to Fidel. He will be able to explain to you!'

I said I had heard that Fidel did not approve of the U M A P.

Padrón opened his eyes wide to show he was hurt. 'Fidel may not like the U M A P, but he has not stopped it. Remember that, he has not stopped it. The men who want it may be illiterates but they fought in the Sierra, which you and I did not – lieutenants and comandantes and a whole hierarchy of heroes who are untouchable and have earned the right to be. That is why Fidel has not stopped it!'

It was disconcerting: our first deeply felt disagreement. I did not feel I had the right to continue it, and we were quiet for a while. But Padrón was a generous man, and in a moment volunteered, 'I too do not like the UMAP.' He said it just to make me feel better.

This argument was one I should have had with the Committees for the Defence of the Revolution, but since I suspected they played so large a part in the recruitment for the UMAP and since an organization devoted to propaganda work at the block level recalled to me only the ugliest antecedents, I kept putting off seeing its leaders. Two months went by and I still hadn't turned into its headquarters on Leyte Vidal. My fears that if I allowed the Havana Ministry to send news ahead of my visit I would be besieged with guides and eager propagandists turned out to be unfounded. Two weeks after I was in Mayarí everyone knew who I was, but no functionaries ever sought me out. Neither did the CDRs.

I knew that the regional head of the CDRs was the brother of Armín Vasquez, the night-watchman at the Bitirí who had been the first person to welcome me to Mayarí in the middle of the night, and that, finally, made it easier for me to take the stairs leading down to the basement headquarters of the CDRs. Argelio Vasquez had the same grey-green eyes as his brother and seemed as innocent of guile, but, as Armín had said, he was full of the kind of energy that had made him, though younger, the one to inspire others besides Armín. He was busy but he promised to come see me at the Bitirí, and he showed up for lunch a couple of days later with a young man, Adonis Gorra, who was the head of the CDRs for Mayarí.

It was Adonis who interrupted Argelio, when we were seated outside my room, to point out the blonde walking by and asked if she could not corrupt him. Adonis was not a member of the Party; Argelio was.

'I know a lot about you from Armín,' I said to Argelio, 'but I do not know what led you to take to the monte.'

'I shall tell you,' Argelio said. 'I have never told this before. This is the first time I am saying it but not the first time I have thought about it. It was a spirit of rebelliousness in me. I think I always noticed the misfortunes of others, the men without work, my own father who had not had a job since 1952, and it bothered me. There was my father, he had always been interested in international affairs. He had talked to me about the French and Russian revolutions. Things like that had built up this spirit of rebelliousness in me. It was not anger with the police – I had never had any trouble with the casquitos, none at all.

'In 1960, maybe as late as 1961, I still said, however, that I was not interested in politics. It was true, politics was not for me. In 1959 I was in the Army, then I was in the police, and then I went to work at the sawmill in productive labour. It was there I began to change. I began to see things as a worker and to understand the process of the Revolution. Before that I would have given my life for the Revolution, but now I began to change with it.

'You can see that I was not interested in politics at the start because I was not in the ORI or the PURS [two phases the official party went through before it became the Communist Party] and only became a Party member after it was completely reorganized. I was a union leader at the sawmill, and it was the workers there who proposed me for the Party and then it was the Party that assigned me to the CDRs. And here I am.'

'Were you surprised,' I asked, 'when the Revolution became so closely allied with the Soviet Union?'

'No, you see my father, although he belonged to the Auténtico Party, had always admired the Soviet Union and he passed on that feeling to me. My father had some friends who were Communists, but I never thought about communism, or rather, thought about it in a very disoriented way. There were three or four Communists I saw around Mayarí, men whose clothes were ragged, whose shoes were torn, and who were always out of a job and in bad straits. If that is what communism is, I told myself, it is not much to boast about. I did not make the connexion that they did not have a job because they were Communists and discriminated against.

'And there was something else that was also true about Communists. You joined the Communist Party in those days because you chose to. There were some who were opportunists, some who joined because a friend talked them into it – though there were and still are old Communists who have remained true. But now it is different – and it is not because Fidel was saying it the other night that I say it now – it is your attitude which determines your being chosen to join the Party. It is the work you do. Every true revolutionary, as Fidel said, becomes a Communist, but it is by their activity that they are Communists, not by what they say.

'The CDRs began when Fidel returned from the United Nations in New York and a couple of petards were exploded at a meeting. We are going to clean them out, Fidel said, block by block, for it was clear what the counter-revolution hoped to do. So it was the CDRs' job to be vigilant and to report all suspicious activities on their block. And people were eager. The day after Fidel made the suggestion in his speech, whole blocks spontaneously got together to do the job. Do not look sceptical – it was spontaneous. That is the marvellous thing about this Revolution.

'So vigilance was the first task of the CDRs, and members were set to watch the activities of people on their block, particularly of people known not to sympathize with the Revolution. The information was passed up to the municipal level and they turned it over to the security police. The CDR never did and does not take investigation into its own hands. If the police, from more than one source, had reason to worry about reports that some unsympathetic person had come home at an unusual hour carrying a strange package, then they investigated. Those were days when the danger of invasion and counter-revolution was very real, and the job was given to the people and they were eager.

'Now vigilance is only one of seventeen fronts on which the C D Rs work – education, public health, civic improvement, culture, housing, political education, state property –'

'State property?' I said. 'What is that?'

'Well, when a Cuban applies to leave for Up North, a functionary from Emigration comes to his house with a member of the Committee from his block. They make a list of the property in the house which the state will take over when the petitioner leaves the country, for he is allowed neither to sell nor to give away anything he owns but certain prescribed amounts of clothing and two hundred dollars worth of jewellery. Why should we allow him to leave under a smoke screen of confusion? Why should he suddenly be able to play the role of generous benefactor? And people say, "Oh, the good one has gone!" When he is neither good nor generous.

'Say that the petitioner has sold something of value during the previous year. "Well," says the member of the Committee, "and where is that radio you used to have? Or the TV set?" Things like that. We do not always make him replace it. We say, "Listen, we are interested in your leaving as soon as possible, so if you will pay us the money you got for the article in question, we will give you a receipt and there will be no problem." When the petitioner leaves, the C D R takes over all electrical equipment except the refrigerator, and these the C D R rations out to people who have put in for them and most need them. The other organisms then take over the house and furniture, and when the worker comes in to whom the house has been assigned, he gets whatever is in it that he needs and pays for it on time, on the basis of what he earns. But very cheap – a chair like this for a dollar or so. Other furniture he does not want is taken to the warehouse, and the C D R rations it to whoever applies.'

'You know, it is my theory that we here in Mayarí have

had an experience of what I call *comunismo analfabeto* – illiterate communism!' Adonis Gorra said. 'It happened during Hurricane Flora, and the C D Rs showed how they could function in such a society. For if real communism requires abundance and a high standard of living, then those days during Hurricane Flora when the C D Rs rationed everything that came in by block and by family size, free to everyone, when people here and from near-by cities came to work for nothing – those days when money came to have no value, because even cigarettes were free and could not be bought, and work was voluntary and freely given – were days of illiterate communism!'

There was an inspired, reflective smile on Argelio's face, and he looked at me to see what I thought of Gorra's speech.

I asked them both if they had any criticism of the Revolution and Argelio leaned forward and clasped his hands. 'You tell me what you do not like about the Revolution,' he said. 'That question means to me that *you* have a criticism. Right?'

I said it was their opinions that interested me. 'Besides, you Cubans are always trying to interview me when it should be the other way round.'

'It is only right that we should have a dialogue,' Argelio said. 'What is your criticism?'

'Very well, I do not like the U M A P,' I said, and Argelio immediately got a very serious look and leaned back in his chair. I told him what Graham Greene had said in his article, and added that I realized that the motives for setting up the U M A P were laudable, were even of a moral nature. Yet setting up work-prison camps was an injustice to start with and could only become worse because of the opportunity it gave people throughout the country to work out their intolerances.

'Do you realize what the old society left us?' Argelio said. 'You surely know Havana was one of the most vice-ridden cities of the world. Should people be allowed to live off vice, to be idle when others produce for them –'

'I know, I know,' I said. 'I agree that a parasite is immoral and an attempt should be made to reform him. But you cannot do it right, you cannot do it at all if you do so forcibly.'

'What would you have us do?' Argelio asked.

'You have criminal laws,' I said. 'When a man breaks one of your laws, you have the right then to jail him and attempt to rehabilitate him. But you should not pick up someone just like that, because you or his neighbours do not like the way he acts, and force him to conform to what you think is right.'

Argelio looked at me a moment. 'You are saying that we should do nothing, that we should let human beings rot,' he said. 'That is immoral. For there is one thing the Revolution cannot do, it is to do nothing. Given these people, you know that if they are allowed to continue they will eventually take to robberies, violence, even counter-revolution – and all to feed their vices, marijuana, gambling, men. Is it not better to take them now and rehabilitate them than to have to shoot them later? I exaggerate, but only to show you that the Revolution cannot do nothing.'

It was then that Gorra interrupted to point out the blonde walking by, as much because he admired her walk as to keep our discussion from being too heated. But Argelio continued, 'You should know the success the UMAP has had, the re-habilitated men it has returned to production and to their families after a short time.'

Somewhat superciliously, I said, 'Homosexuals too?'

'Yes and no,' Argelio said, refusing to take it as a taunt. 'Yes, they can be changed. Take the fellow who worked at El Parque Cafeteria. He was taking men to the rooms upstairs, making them right behind the counter even. He was a scandal in Mayarí. Why, he would run up to a man walking with his fiancée on his arm and greet him, "My love, my little daddy, I want you for my own!" And you should have seen him when he came home for Christmas – what a different style of man he was! Of course, I know he will take his taste with him to his grave, but the change cannot be denied. He is a decent man now.

'Only ten to twelve men in Mayarí were sent to the UMAP. They were men whose attitudes had been discussed with them. Some took a different attitude, accepted a job, but eventually slid back and at their work centres made light of the work done. And those with whom there had been no preliminary discussion were called only after a most thorough investigation had been made. There was never any doubt as to their being *lumpen* types.'

'I know what bothers Yglesias,' Gorra said. 'He thinks we are encouraging stool pigeons, that the CDRs are a spying organization. Right? It is true that many of our committees consider that just about everything is their business. You will see them criticizing someone for not taking care of the yard or sidewalk. Or a woman asking another at a meeting why she is not a good or friendly neighbour. For my part, I like that.'

Then Gorra smiled. 'But of course you must know that I am the stool pigeon of Mayarí – that is what they said on the Miami radio! I did not hear it, but one of the girls at the office did. I tell you what – please come to a little fiesta a committee in El Naranjal is having tonight. It is part of a campaign we are having to revitalize the CDRs, to increase membership and all that. Come tonight.'

El Naranjal is the last neighbourhood on the way to Guatemala and the new highway that leads to Nicaro, and it begins on the other side of the bridge at the end of Céspedes, a scraggly neighbourhood I passed when I descended Loma Rebelde away from the main part of Mayarí. The block holding the fiesta was one immediately on the other side of the bridge, and most of the houses on it faced a little arroyo with a thin stream above which the small bridge towered. As the jingle about Mayarí said, El Naranjal had no orange grove, and it was only a five-block walk from the CDR headquarters on Leyte Vidal. Argelio had to be in Moa, so Gorra and I and a man named Zayas, who was a provincial leader of the CDRs, walked over in the dark.

'You understand, this is nothing special,' Gorra warned me, 'we do not even know exactly what is planned. They have been carrying on a campaign to increase membership and have got almost everyone to sign up, so on their own they decided to have a fiesta and invited people from a block in Guaro with whom they are emulating and asked for someone from the Provincial – that is why Zayas is here. Also, they do not know you are coming. Though of course, you are welcome and they will be pleased.'

Even in the dark you could tell that the unpaved street had been levelled and swept. The few fences were all white-washed, and at a height over the arroyo whitewashed stones were arranged on the ground to say, *Long Live Heroic Vietnam!* There were also placards on fences saluting the VII Harvest of the People and, again, Vietnam. The yard between two clapboard houses was decorated for the fiesta: lines were strung from one house to the other and white paper streamers hung from them; to make it an enclosure tall palm-leaves were set thickly around the fence and the houses. Strings of light bulbs lit the yard. At the far end, kitchen tables were set for the speakers; on the canvas and palm leaves behind the table was a sign saying *El Comité Manuel Ascunce Domenech.* Domenech was a young literacy teacher killed by counter-revolutionaries during the alphabetization campaign of 1961.

It was nine o'clock but the meeting had not yet begun. There were about one hundred people in the yard, most of whom had brought chairs from their own homes, and more out on the street. We walked through them towards the table, and I was the one all eyes followed – not with awe but with the open curiosity of Cubans. Miriam from the Bitirí was there and she called to me – 'Jose!' – and I blew her a kiss and the girls with her all shrieked and she covered her face with her hands. Every face was happy with the expectancy of a good time, and you had to yell to be heard by the person next to you. We were all waiting for the contingent from Guaro.

When they arrived, someone yelled at them, 'You have lost the emulation – you came late!' There was to be much bantering, challenging, bragging between the Guaro group and the people from El Naranjal. One of the men from Guaro would have a place on the programme to criticize the report of the Naranjal Committee and to boast of their own block's work. Adonis Gorra explained, 'Everything tonight has been and will be the work and inspiration of the Naranjal people, all on their own with no help from us. The only thing you could call a set-up is this emulation with Guaro. But everyone knows it – it adds a little piquancy to the work.'

We all stood for the playing of the national anthem – a thumpity-thump-thump piece like all national anthems – that I recalled with nostalgia because my Cuban grandfather sang it often for me. It was played by a rumba combo – trumpet, drums and maracas – and the maracas were silent, since it would have been frivolous to accompany the national anthem with maracas; but the sweet trumpet and the drums could not help falling into a rumba beat. No one sang the lyrics and the night knew its only moments of quiet while the trumpet played. An old, white-haired Negro in the first row kept one hand over his heart.

The chairman was a middle-aged man from the block with whom I'd only had a chance to shake hands because he was busy getting his agenda straight. Like most Cubans, he was master, when he got up to speak, of rhetorical flourishes, but he only indulged them at the opening when describing the occasion and welcoming the audience and speakers. To my surprise I heard him introduce me to the audience. 'He is a North American writer who is here to tell the truth about socialist Cuba!' he added, and there was so much applause that Zayas, sitting next to me, suggested I stand. I did, and it seemed to me that everyone cheered.

From then on, until Zayas spoke, the meeting was all business. The report emphasized accomplishment and the Guaro delegate would interrupt with taunts. When the chairman came to the section on education and said this was 'a weak front', the Guaro delegate said they needed to do a poll. The chairman and others answered that they had already done a poll of all adults as part of the campaign to get everyone up to the sixth-grade level. 'What do you say to that?' someone yelled at the Guaro delegate. He shrugged and said, 'I was not the one who took exception. It was that Negro there!' They laughed at him for being cowardly and shifting responsibility for his original taunt. The key to the laughter was that, not the word Negro: as Soní had told me, Negro is a purely descriptive term in Cuba when it is not an endearment.

Before the final speech, new members received their membership books, and since the Playa Girón fortnight was to begin in a couple of days, a call was made for volunteers to spend those two weeks in the cane-fields. At first only one young man got up. The Guaro people announced their block had recruited five. There was embarrassed laughter while the young man stood alone. Then two more came up and stood with him, and the Guaro people laughed and one said, 'We are sending big men!' One after another they came until there were eight, and the women screamed and the trumpet player blasted away.

It was near eleven when Zayas got up to make the final speech. A long speech remarkable for two reasons: that he spoke quietly, in a neighbourly fashion, and that the yard now completely jammed was not restive to get on to the singing and dancing. Zayas went over point by point the work the C D R s can do, making them feel that their block and their town was in their hands to elevate and make beautiful. 'It is true that we have difficulties in accomplishing all these things because of the blockade,' he said towards the end, embarking for the first time on a political point, 'but think of our Vietnamese compañeros under a rain of bombs!'

Someone yelled, '*Viva Vietnam!*'

Zayas said, 'I do not want us to forget the North American people. Especially those young men who are sent to Vietnam at the point of a gun. The North American people are not to be blamed for what their government is doing. The world owes much to them. If they have a great nation it is because their people have struggled to make it so. Think particularly of the North American Negroes who suffer great oppression and mistreatment. We have no quarrel with them.'

He took a deep breath and leaned forward to speak with all his force. 'But think of the Vietnamese people! Think of what the Yankees are doing to them! They do not just suffer – they fight and they are winning. They fight for their country and not at the point of a gun –'

At the other end of the table I saw Gorra raise a fist and yell, 'Down with the Yankees!'

From all over the yard they answered him: 'Down with the Yankees!'

I could not see and I could not hear for the rush of blood to my head. It was a terrible moment to live through. No one was looking at me, no-one was thinking of me, I was not singled out; but I felt ill-used and angry. I think always in words and in my head a reply began: *Do you not know that Yankee is an honourable term? Do you not know that Yankee is an honourable term?* Over and over, never getting on to the next groove. I could not fault the comparison Zayas was making between the Vietnamese and my countrymen, and I ended by concentrating all my thoughts on keeping a composed look, knowing when Zayas had ended only by the tremendous burst of applause and the cries of '*Viva Vietnam!*'

Zayas came back to the chair next to mine. He was perspiring, his face was flushed, and there was a smile of pleasure on his face that his speech had reached the compañeros of El Naranjal. He looked at me, remembered who I was, and twice slapped my knee. 'Remember that we are brothers,' he said.

From the kitchen window of the house nearest to us came the first round of drinks: rum, coconut juice with little slivers of coconut meat floating in it. The mike was taken to the middle of the yard and the combo began playing accompaniment to a series of amateur performers from the neighbourhood. The chairman of the meeting came over to say goodbye; he worked on the midnight shift at Nicaro and had to run to get there on time. When he walked away, I said to Gorra, 'You mean he is just a worker, not an official?'

Gorra was puzzled by my question. 'He works in the factory but he is an officer of the C D R here. He is also a leader in his union. He belongs to the militia. I tell you something else: his father was a sergeant in the Batista police, a brutal man who is now serving a jail sentence.'

'And he got voted into his position in the C D R?' I asked. 'Do his neighbours here know about his father?'

Gorra slapped me on the shoulder; he thought I was kidding. 'We know everything about each other.'

They did not let us talk any more: the combo had begun playing dance music, and Gorra and Zayas were snatched away. Not away, but right where they were standing, they began to dance; the whole yard was a dance floor. 'Come,' a young woman said to me. I said I did not rumba. 'He has rejected me!' she yelled to the others, and I got up and did my best. I held my hands in front of me and made fists of them as if I were handling maracas. 'You have it!' the woman said, and we both laughed. I could see the whole yard; it was a jiggling, jumping, writhing, laughing mass. Old people, children, everyone danced. Even Pachucha, the mentally retarded newsboy who worked Leyte Vidal, had found a girl. Some girl near me pushed at my waist, and said, 'Now more with the hips!' and sang to the music of the soaring trumpet, '*Amor, amor, amor!*'

The next day at lunch at the Bitirí, Victoria said, 'I hear you are not a bad rumba dancer for a beginner.'

'Beginner?' I said. 'I am an expert!'

'Ay, ay, ay,' Victoria said. 'You are getting worse than

the Cubans.' And Alicia, who was nearby, called, 'Jose has been dancing the rumba?' Victoria answered, 'With Clara's mother over at El Naranjal.'

'My God,' I said. 'My life is an open book.'

'What have you got to be ashamed of?' Victoria answered. 'Clara's mother is a handsome woman.'

During Playa Girón I had to go to Havana for a couple of days. It was empty, but I saw some of my friends who were either ill or were performing or had plays in rehearsal. I told them that ordinary folk out in Mayarí supported the UMAP that they were so opposed to. 'It is only right that they should,' one said, and nodded several times. 'That is the way it should be, but I tell you' – and he paused as if to let me know that he had this from Fidel himself – 'that when this harvest is over, so is the UMAP.' He struck his hands together as if wiping them clean. 'Those under twenty-seven will complete their military service in the Army.'

At the end of the Playa Girón fortnight, the sports centre on Leyte Vidal was open again, and I ran into Alcides Salazar from Guatemala, who was coming over every afternoon to train for the nation-wide wrestling matches to begin in May. 'All the UMAP men from Guatemala who are over twenty-seven are back,' he said. 'The ones who had jobs are back at them.'

'Are they considered reformed?' I asked.

'They said everyone over twenty-seven was sent back, reformed or not. They said they told them that all of them had some fault of character which got them into the UMAP but that the Revolution had made a mistake in trying to reform them this way.' Alcides made a sceptical grimace and smirked. 'Do you believe that? I do not believe it the way they told it. The Revolution cannot make mistakes with types like that!'

Two days later I found out almost – but not quite – by chance that the Methodist minister had also been returned from the UMAP. I had neglected to visit the Methodist church, one of the better structures on Leyte Vidal, and was reminded of it at the Municipal Court when I heard a case involving Jehovah's Witnesses. I mentioned my failure to see the Methodists to someone working at the court, and he told me that it might be a good idea to go now because the minister was back from the UMAP. 'He is a nice person,' he added.

We agreed that genuinely religious persons always are. Like the three Jehovah's Witnesses who had shown up in court. A campesino had brought charges against one because he had, he said, been coming to his home to proselytize, though he had already warned him off once. The judge looked at the other two who had come up to the bench and asked who they were. 'Brothers,' one said, and the judge said, 'But your names are different?' The same young man replied, 'We are brothers in the faith.'

Quietly, with great serenity, the defendant explained that he had been to his neighbour's home but not to proselytize. The man's wife and some others were there but not the man himself, so the accuser could not be a good witness as to whether he had been preaching.

'You are a farmer?' the judge asked.

The defendant nodded.

'Do you make a living from your religion?' the judge asked.

'No, I do not. Never have I received a salary for preaching. It is something that comes from the heart.' He paused and added as serenely, 'Whoever says I get a salary is Satan.'

'Satan?' said the judge; it seemed to me he became angry because he appreciated that they were honest men and could not bear that they should also be superstitious. 'There *are* real Satans in this world. Do you think it is Satan who makes war and drops those bombs in Vietnam?'

The defendant listened with great care, trying to discriminate in the light of his beliefs, and he nodded with the hesitance of a man who is afraid his beliefs have been vulgarized.

'There is nothing wrong with having religious beliefs of any kind,' the judge said. 'Nothing at all, so long as you do not disturb or harm your neighbours. But I want you to understand that there are religious leaders – including some of your faith – who do draw a salary and they draw it from the CIA. There are people in this world who are the representatives not of Satan but of the CIA.'

The defendant, who was an old man, listened with wide-open, liquid eyes and said nothing.

'The greatest representative of Satan in this world,' the judge said, 'is the President of the United States!'

The old man explained again that he had come to his beliefs on his own. 'I gathered them from a great book – the Bible.'

The judge nodded; he agreed it was a great book. 'It has been said of you that you receive other books from abroad and that you distribute them?' The old man shook his head. 'Do you get any counter-revolutionary books?'

The young man who had called the old man his brother said, 'Whoever circulates counter-revolutionary books is not my brother.'

'It is foolishness,' the old man said, 'to force people to believe in my faith – it must come from the heart and willingly. Do you not agree?'

The judge nodded, and the campesino who had brought the others to court did also. 'You are farmers and workers,' the judge said. 'Your interest lies in seeing Cuba get ahead. But you must know that the President of the United States – that Satan, as you call him – does pay salaries.'

The campesino cleared his throat and got the judge's attention. 'I do not want them preaching in my home,' he said. 'But they are hard-working people. They are farmers too, and to my knowledge they do not receive any money for their religion and do not exploit anyone.'

'You are farmers, you are workers, you have no interest in Satans and the CIA,' the judge said. 'I dismiss the case.'

Not until the afternoon of the day I spoke to Ilona Sorel at the hospital – my last full day in Mayarí – did I get to see the minister. A reluctance on my part due, perhaps, to my having belonged during adolescence to the Epworth League of the Southern Methodist Church, and to having still, at this late date, undecided feelings about the experience. Not about the religion – that was not for me – but about those kind ministers and deaconesses who had chosen to become missionaries in a Latin community of the South – others in as remote places as China – while at their elbows the Negroes lived in semi-slavery. The stucco church and the large stucco rectory, looking so much better than all the homes around it on Leyte Vidal, reminded me of the handsome brick mission-house in my shabby home town.

The minister's wife came to the door, and asked me in. She was a slim, good-looking woman with quiet, middle-class manners, and she apologized for the toys her baby daughter had scattered in the living-room. I explained who I was, and she remained friendly and polite, but maintained a reserve quite different from a campesino, working-class or integrated woman. She excused herself as soon as the minister appeared; he was about thirty, vigorous-looking and fair, with large, candid blue eyes. He smiled often, in a way that courageous people have in a bad situation, and he was both direct and wary of me: he was not, like other disgustados, going to unburden himself of all his complaints simply because I was American.

First he took me across to show me the church. It was clean, well painted and in good repair inside, but he pointed to the ceiling and said that it still had some watermarks that seeped through the paint, evidence of the damage Hurricane Flora had done. 'After the hurricane the authorities took over the church and quartered people in it. People used to cook in it, and when we got it back a year ago it was in bad condition.' Behind the church was a walk with two or three rooms off it which were locked. A plaque in the wall commemorated two physicians who had given free medical consultations there.

'Hundreds of people were treated here,' he said, and

added, when I told him that Columbie, the barber, had praised the Methodist Church to the disparagement of the Catholic for such work, 'Our church has always been very interested in social services.'

When we were seated inside, I said, 'What chances do you think that your church has of surviving in this "violent" revolution –how are you going to get along with it and develop in the circumstances of such a thoroughgoing revolution?'

He simply stared at me, and when I repeated the question in another form, he said, 'That is the kind of political question I would rather not discuss.' He had explained earlier that he would not talk politics, but in time he made himself quite clear on this and other political matters.

'Let me explain that I am very sympathetic to this Revolution,' I said. 'That does not mean that I am uncritical of it. There are things I do not like. For example, the UMAP. I know that you have just returned from it.'

He watched me very closely while I talked, no doubt to see if I were dissembling, and he slowly loosened up. But he remembered always that I had said I sympathized with the Revolution and his replies most often had the tone of a debate.

Three years earlier the church authorities had assigned him to Mayarí. He was born and reared in Holguín, so the area was not alien to him, but because the church had been taken over to house victims of the hurricane, he had held services in the rectory. 'I was arrested by Orden Pública for this. I was held incommunicado for three days and under arrest for seven more until my trial. I was absolved, however, and I continued to hold services in the house right here.'

He kept in touch with church officials in Havana and Santiago, and approximately one week after a Havana church official assured him on the phone that there would be no more interference (according to negotiations he had held with government people), the minister got picked up for the UMAP without warning. 'I was never given any reason for my arrest but my religious beliefs,' he told me, as if challenging me. 'And that is something I am willing to swear to in writing.'

I asked him if it was Victor Bermudez who had him arrested; Bermudez was the present head of Orden Pública and a man I admired. 'It was another man who gave the order,' he replied. I asked him if he would permit me to inquire about this with Bermudez – for I considered it an injustice that I would like to see Bermudez explain or, possibly, make some amends for – but the minister asked me not to. 'I was in the UMAP sixteen months, from the very start of the camps until now,' he said, not asking for pity but making a case for my book.

The rehabilitation of the inmates had simply consisted of one hour of political orientation each day. The rest of the time they worked in the fields. All types – addicts, homosexuals, pimps, ministers – were thrown together. 'In my group I saw an undecided man become a confirmed homosexual by his association with an overt homosexual. I did not mind that we were thrown in together with all the others, for I believe that it is more likely that a bit of us rubbed off on them than of them on us.'

A typical campesino came in at that moment. He spoke with the sweet, high, lilting accent of the Oriental, and made a date with the minister for the evening. 'I want you to meet another of our faith – he is a lay preacher from El Guayabo. He was in the UMAP with me and has also just been released.'

I got up to shake hands, and the lay preacher and the minister both smiled at me to show their cheerfulness. There was no warmth in it. The lay preacher no more than nodded at the other's comments, and did not make it an occasion, as other Cubans would have, to tell his story, to philosophize, to make a new friend. He left briskly, and the minister followed him with a benign, admiring gaze. I was reminded of another Methodist minister who, when I had finished making a speech to the Epworth League, had said, 'Isn't Jose just fine?' and had himself been unaware, though I was not, that the completion of that praise was 'for a Latin'.

I told the minister what I had heard in Havana about the future of the UMAP and its partial confirmation in the release of the men from Guatemala. He admitted that all over twenty-seven were released when he was, but he said he was given no reason. 'But it was not disbanded. You go to Camagüey, for there is nothing like seeing for yourself. Perhaps the form of it has been changed, but the fact of it remains. Whether it will be done away with after the harvest? – well, the future will tell.'

When I asked, the minister listed the things he thought good that the Revolution had done. 'The attention to education, the hospitals, the public projects like roads ...' What else would he like to see the Revolution develop? 'More individual freedom,' he said, and shook his head as if this were just an academic discussion.

'Perhaps the lack of it is part of the system, perhaps that is what it is,' he said, glad of the opportunity to phrase it this way when I said that some revolutionaries (Party men) had frankly characterized the system as a dictatorship of workers and peasants. 'But we shall see, the future will tell.'

I said some people thought that the unfriendly presence and pressure of the United States so near by was the explanation for some of the strictness and vigilance. 'Well, perhaps, but how do you explain the lack of it in Czechoslovakia and those countries so far from the United States?' I said I thought it was the inheritance of Stalin. 'Perhaps it is in the system itself ... we shall see.'

For the first time, he expanded on his point of view. The Church, he said, does not ask a man's political beliefs. The congregation in Mayarí included revolutionaries and he saw nothing anomalous in that, nor even something which should concern him as a minister. 'We hope and preach that men will live at *las alturas de Jesús Cristo* – the heights of Jesus Christ. For the Church to take a public stand on the Revolution would be incompatible with our teachings, you must agree.'

I did not say to him that his Church, like all others, has

taken political stands innumerable times, that what it calls taking a political stand is speaking in favour of socialism. Instead, I asked, 'Since you say that it is not anomalous for a Methodist to be a revolutionary, do you think that you would have been picked up for the UMAP if you had been openly for the Revolution – belonged to revolutionary organizations, done voluntary work, been, as it is called, integrated?'

He did not like the debating-point I had scored – he even recognized it by his smile as that – but he was an honest man and said that he would probably not have been detained.

I told him then that in Mexico City, while waiting at the Cuban Consulate for my visa, I had talked to three American ministers waiting for theirs. They did not like the Revolution but had told me that the government had not confiscated their churches or property, that in every case where some had been put to use by the government they had always been returned when requested. The three ministers were hoping to get to Havana in time for a gathering of Protestant clergymen, and although I did not look into it when I arrived, I did remember seeing news of it in the papers, including the ordaining of a young woman who had just finished the course at the Protestant seminary in Las Villas. He listened to all that with interest, and told me that in El Naranjal there was one small meeting-hall which had not been returned to them but was used as living-quarters by a family.

We had been talking for almost two hours, and I finally asked him if he planned to go into exile. 'That is another matter for the future,' he said. 'We shall see.'

'Have you applied to leave?' I asked.

He shook his head. He considered that a personal matter and one which would require a personal decision. I said that even if one put aside the economic and political significance of such a decision there still remained an ideological one – 'Doesn't the question of abandoning your flock enter into it?'

He nodded unperturbed. 'That is one of the personal

considerations,' he said. 'That is why I said it is a personal de-cision.'

At that moment, his reasoning sounded confused; later it did not. But he meant that statement as his *envoi* and I got up. Just inside the screened porch door, I said that it seemed to me that he and the Communists were not being – well, realistic, if they thought individuals could keep their religious and poli-tical beliefs separate, that each of them represented ideologies that inevitably sought to claim the whole person. 'One or the other will prevail,' I said. 'Your outlook is not good.'

He flinched, then looked brave. '*Eso es el fín – que se logre!* he said. 'That is the end – let it come to pass!'

'Good luck,' I said, and held out a hand he was not eager to shake.

Out on Leyte Vidal I was angry with myself that I had wished him luck. The minister was the one person I had met in Mayarí to whom the Revolution had done a gratuitous in-justice, one that revolutionary necessity could not explain or justify; he had spent sixteen months in the UMAP away from his newborn first child. . . . It was a thought I did not finish, for I turned into Maximo Gomez and saw Sarmiento, the mayor, standing against a pole on the corner across from the Administración. Along that once dusty sidewalk the ground had been broken and rows of shrubs planted: one of the civic improvement tasks undertaken by the Administra-ción and mass organizations for May Day.

'With all the work there is to do, what are you standing there for?' I asked, and realized by a motion he made that he was listening to the radio broadcast from a small loudspeaker on top of the pole. A pop song was being played whose open-ing lyrics were: *If my fingers were pens, I would write I Love You in blood* . . .

'I ran out a moment to hear this beautiful song,' he said when it was finished. 'What is your opinion of Cuban music, Jose? Don't you find it beautiful?'

I laughed.

'The Cuban is impassioned and romantic, there is no denying that,' Sarmiento said, and took my arm to lead me over to the Administración. I told him I wanted to say good-bye, in case I did not see him the next day. 'Did you hear what Fidel said about you North Americans?' he said, referring to a speech Castro had made that week in which he paid tribute to the anti-war movement and the demonstrations held in New York and on the West Coast.

'I have had my impact on Cuba, there is no denying that,' I said, parodying Sarmiento. 'What is your opinion of us Americans now?'

'That you have not filled any polyethylene bags at the Administración,' he said. 'You have been wasting your favours elsewhere.' By which he meant that he had seen me filling small black plastic bags with fertilized earth in the driveway behind the kitchen at the Bitirí, with the girls there.

Now that the Playa Girón fortnight was over, a whole new set of voluntary tasks had been undertaken by the mass organizations. This year coffee planting was being expanded even more than in previous years and the mountains of the second front, a coffee area, required millions of new seedlings. Just starting the nurseries required an enormous labour force to fill the plastic bags for the seedlings, so the Party had suggested that the work be brought to the towns. Truck drivers brought loads of fertilized earth to the towns and dumped them at work centres that had asked for them; they also left the small plastic bags into which the earth was to be packed. All week you saw people, in spare moments, crouched over mounds of rich earth filling the bags by hand; three or four hours later the pile of earth had disappeared and the trucks had taken the rows of plastic bags to the nurseries in the mountains.

During Playa Girón it had rained so much that the cane cutting had slowed down, and many of the volunteer cane-cutters had stayed for another month. Besides that work, there were the May Day projects for civic improvement – the region had been promised enough paint for five hundred houses, bulldozers were lent the Administración to level some of the muddy lanes of the town (already the impassable streets around the Reforma Urbana had had their ruts smoothed and a layer of gravel imbedded in their clayey surface), shrubs were being planted along the sidewalks. And there was the problem of the aqueduct, on which work had stopped since the beginning of the harvest. The party had suggested to the CDRs that they take on this task, and though I had not seen it, some blocks had already dug trenches and laid the pipes for their stretch, under the direction of a technician from Micons.

On the sidewalk in front of the Administración there were hundreds of filled plastic bags, and an old man who lived on that block was sweeping the bits of earth left into the gutter. 'We are going to get two more truck-loads soon,' Sarmiento said, 'you cannot get out of it.' So I promised to return as soon as I had dinner. When I did, the bags were gone and a pyramid of dark, moist earth sat on the sidewalk. I made a place next to the old man and the lawyer who lived across the street. It was still daylight, and as people on the street finished their dinner the mound became crowded like an anthill. It was night-time when I had filled five hundred bags; I got up, stretched, and saw Sarmiento, who had come and gone, return to the Administración. 'Ahaa!' I said reproachfully.

'Look at my hands!' he said; they were black with dirt. 'I have to show up at a couple of other places. Why don't you come with me?'

We got into his jeep. First we went to pick up Pepe, an Administración man in charge of *areas verdes* – literally 'green areas' – who wanted to go with us to El Cocal at the other end of town where the people of the neighbourhood were beginning to build a park. 'Everyone is out doing something tonight,' said Sarmiento; he was joyous about taking me along. 'And it will be like that for many nights. You know when Fidel was in New York in 1960 and they were throwing him out of his hotel? Well, there was no room in the town park for the people who came to sleep there because Fidel had said he would sleep in your Central Park if necessary. You should have seen the numbers of people sleeping out in the street to show Fidel they were with him!'

On a side street near the Palace of Justice, they were working on the aqueduct. A huge Soviet crane had dug a rough trench down the length of the block, and it was now filled with men with picks and shovels, deepening it, smoothing it, levelling it. 'First gravel, then soft sand, then the pipes!' said Sarmiento. Strings of lights hung over the trenches; I recognized a taxi driver, the accountant from the Bitirí, an electrician, all men who lived on the block. One threw an empty rum bottle to Sarmiento. 'You finished it!' Sarmiento exclaimed.

Back in the jeep, Sarmiento said, 'We have a problem – every block wants to be working on their aqueduct right away, but you have to finish one first, have the pipes ready to be connected to the next one to be laid. You know what a thirst there is for water in Mayarí!'

El Cocal is the neighbourhood furthest east, and from it you begin climbing up to Los Pinares. The streets are all dirt, the main one of gravel, so bumpy sometimes that I called it the Tooth Loosener. At an intersection, the Cocal people had selected a site for a park. It was not in the budget but the Administración had relented and promised the materials if they did the work. An engineer from Physical Planning had made the design; lines of whitewash indicated where the kerb was to be laid and men and boys were working with picks – it was the first night of work on the park – to dig a foot-deep trench for the granite kerb. I took a pick and in ten minutes was gasping for breath; the ground was hard and resistant.

A fat man next to me laughed. 'Take it easy,' he said, and a boy with a large can of water dipped a small can into it and passed it to me.

I said to the fat man, 'You are not an Oriental?'

Samiento heard me and announced that Romá, the fat

man, was the delegate from El Cocal to the municipality. He was in his fifties and had a regular job during the day.

'But it is true that I am not an Oriental,' Román said. 'I came here from Camagüey. In 1933, because I was in the revolutionary strike and the police here did not know me. After a while I started a grocery in El Cocal and I led la dulce vida.' He pointed up and down the street. 'All this was bars and cock-fights. Women, the easy life. Then Fidel woke me up again. Now you see me here . . . our lives are an open book.'

Over his head I could see a big sign about Los Pinares. It listed how many acres would be devoted to growing tomatoes, lettuce, alfalfa, strawberries, melons. I thought of copying down the statistics but decided against it; it was my last night and there was no time for all the statistics I had not taken. Sarmiento saw me stare at the sign, and called, 'Jose, when you come back to Mayarí, it will be all parks and gardens – a valley of paradise!'

Soní and El Moro came by in their jeep to take a look, and I got in with them to go back. When we passed the bank, I told them I had been there talking to the twenty-four-year-old manager, and he had told me that his ambition was to be released from his job for one in production. 'Soní, what would you leave your job for?' I asked.

'Remember I told you one must not fall in love with one's job?' he said. 'I do not know what I would leave it for. It is not a personal decision. I would discuss it with the Party and the compañeros.'

'I see,' I said, remembering the minister and his personal decision. I knew why I did not like him and why my sympathy for the injustice done him was purely formal: whether he would leave his country and his congregation was a personal matter. Back home in the States the minister's attitude would seem quite natural – even a sacred right – for the right to privacy, the inviolability of the individual, the cult and curse of personal anguish are all based on what seems an indisputable fact: man dies alone.

Maybe man neither lives nor dies alone; maybe it is all a cultural attitude. I laughed, and Soní looked at me to see what had amused me. He had just drawn up at the Bitirí and it was too late to tell him that I was having an exalted night thought, one which I would not dare to say aloud back home but which I could see the possibility of expressing in Mayarí without self-consciousness. The workers and campesinos in the C D RS had taken the first steps toward a new cultural attitude – inadvertently, it seemed to me, for it had been forced upon them by misery in the past. They brought a wonderful sanity and healthiness to their organization's pushiness about people's lives: an insistence that the open life – open to the view of one's neighbours – is the natural life of man. I decided that this might well be what would make Mayarí a valley of paradise.

I was sweated and dirty, and there was no water in my room. I came out again and saw Amelia standing at the reception desk gossiping. I did not hesitate to call for help. 'Amelia, Amelia! Bring me a bucket of water!' I yelled. 'Do you want me to go to Havana with all the dirt of Mayarí?'

More about Penguins and Pelicans

Penguinews, which appears every month, contains details of all the new books issued by Penguins as they are published. From time to time it is supplemented by *Penguins in Print*, which is a complete list of all books published by Penguins which are in print. (There are well over three thousand of these.)

A specimen copy of *Penguinews* will be sent to you free on request, and you can become a subscriber for the price of the postage – 4s. for a year's issues (including the complete lists). Just write to Dept EP, Penguin Books Ltd, Harmondsworth, Middlesex, enclosing a cheque or postal order, and your name will be added to the mailing list.

Some other books published by Penguins are described on the following pages.

Note : *Penguinews* and *Penguins in Print* are not available in the U.S.A. or Canada

Report from a Chinese Village

Jan Myrdal

The enormous changes in contemporary China are
revealed in microcosm in this unique account of one tiny
village. Jan Myrdal lived for a month in Liu Ling in the
northern province of Shensi observing the daily activities
of the villagers and recording their comments and ideas.
In their own words he has documented their attitudes
towards the revolution and the parts they played in it, the
changes in their day-to-day life and attitudes over the last
fifty years, and the difficulties of adjusting to the new
regime.

Report From a Chinese Village is one of those few timely
books that perfectly translates a new and complicated
society.

Not for sale in the U.S.A.

Division Street: America

Studs Terkel

'I was out to swallow the world. My world was my city. What with the scattering of the species, it had to be in the nature of guerrilla journalism.'

Studs Terkel's city is Chicago. In over sixty interviews he captures the here and now of a city that might be Everycity. An interviewer of genius, he moves behind the fashionable responses to discover the pragmatic philosophies, the uncelebrated problems and grievances of ordinary living.

'A city speaks uninhibitedly through this book. Reading it, one learns the night-thoughts of urban man' – Nadine Gordimer

'It reports not only multitudes divided, but the division in ourselves, and does this so compassionately that the general reader will find it as exciting as a good novel' – Nelson Algren

Not for sale in the U.S.A. or Canada